T0214846

Communications in Computer and Information Science 804

Commenced Publication in 2007
Founding and Former Series Editors:
Alfredo Cuzzocrea, Xiaoyong Du, Orhun Kara, Ting Liu, Dominik Ślęzak,
and Xiaokang Yang

More information about this series at http://www.springer.com/series/7899

Shriram R · Mak Sharma (Eds.)

Data Science Analytics and Applications

First International Conference, DaSAA 2017
Chennai, India, January 4–6, 2017
Revised Selected Papers

 Springer

Editors
Shriram R
Crescent University
Chennai
India

Mak Sharma
Birmingham City University
Birmingham
UK

ISSN 1865-0929   ISSN 1865-0937 (electronic)
Communications in Computer and Information Science
ISBN 978-981-10-8602-1   ISBN 978-981-10-8603-8 (eBook)
https://doi.org/10.1007/978-981-10-8603-8

Library of Congress Control Number: 2018934353

Printed on acid-free paper

This Springer imprint is published by the registered company Springer Nature Singapore Pte Ltd.
part of Springer Nature
The registered company address is: 152 Beach Road, #21-01/04 Gateway East, Singapore 189721, Singapore

Patron's Message

Dr. S. Ganesan
Registrar, Anna University

"I believe in innovation and that the way you get innovation is you fund research and you learn the basic facts," said Bill Gates, CEO, Microsoft Corporation. We believed in this principle and used it to equip the university with the finest and latest infrastructure, state-of-the-art libraries and laboratories, a formal and ideal learning environment with committed faculty and supportive administrative staff. The committed and dedicated faculty members of the university are also well knowledgeable to render consultancy services to government institutions, NGOs, public sector undertakings and private corporate sector on very competitive terms and conditions.

I am happy to see that the Department of Computer Science and Engineering, Anna University, Chennai, organized an international conference for the second time to quench their thirst for knowledge in the areas of data analytics and applications. I am also glad to learn that many academics and research scholars especially from Asia participated in this conference.

International conferences such as these provide an environment for academics to interact, collaborate, and share knowledge derived from their research in the field of data science analytics and applications. I hope this conference results in active coordination among researchers working in similar areas, which would lead to creative and innovative technologies yielding new research ideas for the benefit of society.

As a member of the university family since its inception and being the registrar, it gave me great pride to welcome the conference participants to be a part of this enthusiastic and enchanting environment.

S. Ganesan

Co-patron's Message

Dr. P. Narayanasamy
Dean, CEG Campus

"Research is what I'm doing when I don't know what I'm doing," said Wernher von Braun, developer of the rocket technology of Nazi Germany. In addition, I reinstate research and innovation are necessary and essential components of a knowledgeable and growing society. Research ideas leading to innovative products to serve society are primary inputs for achieving excellence in education. The products that are off-spring of the research input work as catalysts in the socioeconomic progress of the university and in turn of the country.

With this as a primary concept, Anna University, a leading educational institution in India, imparts quality education on par with national and international standards. The aim of the College of Engineering (CEG) is to create world-class facilities to support research and innovation. To facilitate this support, with great pleasure and enthusiasm we hosted the First International Conference on Data Science Analytics and Applications (DaSAA 2017), held at Anna University (CEG Campus), during January 4–6, 2017, in Chennai, India.

The theme of the conference was "Data Science Analytics and Applications" with the focus on thrust areas of computer science. This innovative educational forum enabled attendees to advance their knowledge and connect with their peers, creating new professional contacts among the national and international experts in this field. DaSAA 2017 was designed to be an academic feast, with a structured program in a manner where participants had ample time to interact after the sessions, which were enriched by the presence of distinguished international and national participants.

With the right vision, the right people, and programs in the right place, we at the CEG make an attempt to create the right set of contributions for different disciplines of research. The aim of education at Anna University is to assist the students in developing their intellectual, esthetic, emotional, moral, and spiritual being. We, at CEG, impart futuristic, stress-free education and instill a high degree of discipline among them, thereby setting global standards and making our students think logically and analytically.

I believe DaSAA helps to achieve these goals.

P. Narayanasamy

Convenor's Message

Dr. D. Manjula
Head, DCSE

"Understand well as I may, my comprehension can only be an infinitesimal fraction of all I want to understand," said English mathematician and first computer programmer Ada Lovelace. These words struck me to the core and I believe that we need to gather researchers and students with plenty of ideas and knowledge so that they would get a share of it with the fullest understanding. We at the Department of Computer Science and Engineering started conducting international and national conferences to share and impart knowledge to researchers and students.

It gave me much pleasure to witness another major milestone for the department, in organizing and holding the First International Conference on Data Science Analytics and Applications (DaSAA 2017), during January 4–6, 2017. The success realized in organizing and hosting the conference goes a long way to not only showcase DaSAA as a major hub of academic research, but also inculcate the Department of Computer Science and Engineering as a rich reservoir for research activity.

I wish, on behalf of DaSAA, to take this opportunity to thank all those who contributed in one way or another toward the success of the conference. I particularly appreciate the various presenters who submitted well-researched and highly relevant presentations, and the DaSAA Organizing Committee for the long hours spent to ensure the success of the conference.

My heartfelt thanks to Springer, to have conditionally agreed to publish the conference proceedings. My sincere thanks also goes to the conference sponsors, for the very generous assistance toward the organization of the conference. Continued consultations and the cooperation of all parties mentioned above ensure that the second international conference in the Department of Computer Science and Engineering will indeed be a remarkable success. Thank you once again and I encourage you to maintain this working spirit.

The conference program has been designed to provide ample opportunities for researchers to network and to share ideas and information about data science analytics. I hope all attendees found DaSAA 2017 to be enjoyable, memorable, and productive and I look forward to the technological innovations that result from their networking and discussions.

D. Manjula

Preface

DaSAA 2017

The First International Conference on Data Science Analytics and Applications (DaSAA 2017) was held during January 4–6, 2017, with a preconference tutorial on January 3, by the Department of Computer Science and Engineering, CEG, Anna University, Chennai. Some of the major research areas of the department include networks, database, theoretical computer science, machine learning, cloud computing, text mining, natural language processing, information retrieval, multimedia, image processing, software engineering, data mining, big data analytics, grid computing, and fog computing.

DaSAA 2017 aimed to provide a techno forum with market trend topics to help researchers, engineers, scientists, and academics as well as industrial professionals from all over the globe to present their innovative research ideas and developmental activities in data science analytics and applications. DaSAA 2017 was unique because of its focus on the recent developments in data science analytics and applications, and papers were invited from a wide range of topics including data modeling and analytics, data storage and access, data privacy and security, data mining, cloud computing, machine learning, text classification and analysis, information retrieval, information retrieval query processing, specialized information retrieval, image and video processing.

A total of 77 papers were received from India and the USA, of which 16 were selected for presentation at the conference after a thorough double-blind review process by a Technical Program Committee consisting of distinguished researchers. All accepted papers are published in this *Communications in Computer and Information Science* series by Springer. CCIS is abstracted/ indexed in DBLP, Google Scholar, EI-Compendex, Mathematical Reviews, SCImago, and Scopus. Selected papers after being extended will be considered for publication in one of the following journals: *International Journal of Grid and High-Performance Computing* (IJGHPC; Scopus indexed) or *International Journal of Big Data Intelligence* (IJBDI; Google scholar indexed).

The conference also had a one-day preconference tutorial session consisting of three tutorials by a mix of eminent researchers both from industry and academia in the areas of cloud computing, deep learning and network security. The conference hosted five keynote talks by invited speakers from India, the USA, and UK on varied topics including symbolic and numeric learning, big data in biology and medicine, Internet of Things and big data modeling.

We hope DaSAA 2017 has set a stage for continuous and sustained research in this trending field.

January 2017

S. Chitrakala
Rajeswari Sridhar
Angelin Gladston

Organization

Advisory Committee

Vijayan Sugumaran	Oakland University, USA
Rafael Stubs Parpinelli	State University of Santa Catarina, Brazil
Rajkumar Buyya	The University of Melbourne, Australia
Ales Zamuda	University of Maribor, Slovenia
Patrick Siarry	Université Paris-Est Creteil (UPEC), LiSSi, France
Andrey V. Savchenko	National Research University Higher School of Economics, Russia
Ankit Chaudhary	Truman State University, USA
Xiaolong Wu	California State University, USA
Khaled A. Kamel	Texas Southern University, Houston, USA
Akbar Sheikh Akbari	Leeds Beckett University, UK
Athanasios V. Vasilakos	Lulea University of Technology, Sweden
Valentina Emilia Balas	Aurel Vlaicu University of Arad, Romania
S. G. Ponnambalam	Monash University, Malaysia
Reyer Zwiggelaar	Aberystwyth University, UK
Ashraf Elnagar	University of Sharjah, Sharjah, UAE
Sohail S. Chaudhry	Villanova School of Business, Villanova University, USA
Sourav S. Bhowmick	Nanyang Technology University, Singapore
Palaniappan Ramaswamy	University of Kent, UK

Technical Program Committee

Cham Athwal	Birmingham City University, UK
Mak Sharma	Birmingham City University, UK
Jagdev Bhogal	Birmingham City University, UK
William Campbell	Birmingham City University, UK
An Hai Doan	University of Wisconsin, Madison, USA
Jude Shavlik	University of Wisconsin, Madison, USA
Kasi Periyasamy	University of Wisconsin-La Crosse, USA
Slobodan Vucetic	Temple University, USA
Jie Wu	Temple University, USA
Sanjiv Kapoor	Illinois Institute of Technology, USA
John Korah	Illinois Institute of Technology, USA
Randal Westrick	Oakland University, USA
Vijay Varadharajan	Macquarie University, Australia
Rajib Mall	IIT Kharagpur, India
Asif Ekbal	IIT Patna, India
Sudip Roy	IIT Roorkee, India

Sudarshan Iyengar	IIT Ropar, India
K. K. Shukla	Indian Institute of Technology (BHU), Varanasi, India
Shanmuganathan Raman	Indian Institute of Technology Gandhinagar, Palaj, India
Shyam Kumar Gupta	Indian Institute of Technology Delhi, India
R. B. Mishra	Indian Institute of Technology (BHU), Varanasi, India
Tushar Jain	Indian Institute of Technology (IIT) Mandi, India
K. Chandrasekaran	National Institute of Technology Karnataka, Surathkal, India
Annappa	National Institute of Technology Karnataka Surathkal, India
Shashidhar G. Koolagudi	National Institute of Technology, Karnataka, Surathkal, India
Raju Nayak Bhuyka	NIT Warangal, India
Naveen Chauhan	NIT, Hamirpur (H.P.), India
Siddhartha Chauhan	NIT, Hamirpur (H.P.), India
Geetha V.	NITK Surathkal, India
M. P. Singh	National Institute of Technology Patna, India
Durga Prasad Mohapatra	CSE, National Institute of Technology, Rourkela, India
Pravati Swain	NIT Goa, India
S. Mini	National Institute of Technology Goa, India
Tanmay De	National Institute of Technology Durgapur, India
D. V. L. N. Somayajulu	National Institute of Technology, Warangal, India
Anurag Singh	NIT Delhi, India
Arun B. Samaddar	NIT Sikkim, India
Narendran Rajagopalan	NIT Puducherry, Karaikal, India
Ruchira Naskar	National Institute of Technology, Rourkela, India
Virender Ranga	National Institute of Technology Kurukshetra, Haryana, India
B. Surendiran	NIT Puducherry, India
M. M. Dhabu	Visvesvaraya National Institute of Technology, Nagpur, India
Korra Sathya Babu	National Institute of Technology Rourkela, India
Santosh Kumar Vipparthi	Malaviya National Institute of Technology, Jaipur, India
R. Mohan	National Institute of Technology, Tiruchirapalli, India
S. Selvakumar	NIT Tiruchirapalli, India
Leela Veluchamy	NIT Tiruchirapalli, India
Binod Kumar Singh	NIT Jamshedpur, India
Dipti P. Rana	Sardar Vallabhbhai National Institute of Technology (SVNIT), Surat, India
Pinki Roy	National Institute of Technology Silchar, India
Rekh Ram Janghel	National Institution of Technology (NIT) Raipur, India
Md. Tanwir Uddin Haider	NIT Patna, India
Mushtaq Ahmed	Malaviya National Institute of Technology Jaipur, India
R. Padmavathy	NIT Warangal, India

Govind P. Gupta	NIT Raipur, India
Sanjoy Pratihar	NIT Meghalaya, India
Mantosh Biswas	National Institute of Technology-Kurukshetra, India
N. Ramasubramanian	NIT Trichy, India
Sangram Ray	National Institute of Technology Sikkim, India
B. N. Keshavamurthy	National Institute of Technology Goa, India
Saroj Kumar Biswas	National Institute of Technology, Silchar, India
Mamata Dalui	NIT Durgapur, India
Pradeep Singh	National Institute of Technology, Raipur, India
P. S. Deshpande	Visvesvaraya National Institute of Technology, Nagpur, India
Madhu Kumari	National Institute of Technology Hamirpur, India
Manish Kumar	IIIT, Jhalwa, Allahabad, India
B. SivaSelvan	Indian Institute of Information Technology, Design and Manufacturing, IIITDM, Kancheepuram, India
Vrijendra Singh	Indian Institute of Information Technology Allahabad, India
W. Wilfred Godfrey	ABV – IIITM Gwalior, MP, Autonomous Institute of MHRD, Govt. of India
G. Ramakrishna	IIIT Chittoor, Sri City, India
Viswanath Pulabaigari	IIIT Chittoor, Sri City, India
Anupam Agrawal	Indian Institute of Information Technology Allahabad (IIIT-A), India
Krishna Pratap Singh	Indian Institute of Information Technology Allahabad, India
Thoudam Doren Singh	IIIT Manipur, India
Meenakshi D'Souza	IIIT Bangalore, India
Vinay Kumar Mittal	IIIT Chittoor, Sri City, India
S. Venkatesan	IIIT Allahabad, India
Kabita Thaoroijam	Indian Institute of Information Technology Manipur, India
Rakesh Kumar Lenka	IIIT Bhubaneswar, India
O. P. Vyas	Indian Institute of Information Technology, Allahabad, India
Manish Kumar Bajpai	PDPM Indian Institute of Information Technology, Design and Manufacturing, Jabalpur, India
B. Vijayakumar	BITS Pilani, Dubai Campus, UAE
Chittaranjan Hota	Birla Institute of Technology and Science-Pilani, Hyderabad Campus, India
Vadivel S.	BITS Pilani, Dubai Campus, UAE
Neena Goveas	ARC, Birla Institute of Technology and Science, Pilani, Goa, India
Madiajagan M.	BITS Pilani, Dubai Campus, UAE
Sujala D. Shetty	DRC Convenor, Birla Institute of Technology and Science, Pilani, Dubai Campus
Siddhaling Urolagin	Birla Institute of Technology and Science, Pilani, Dubai
K. Sridhar Patnaik	Birla Institute of Technology, Mesra, Ranchi

Partha Paul	BIT, Mesra, Ranchi
Sanjay K. Sahay	Birla Institute of Technology and Science, Pilani, Goa, India
Amritanjali	BIT Mesra Ranchi, India
Sujan Kumar Saha	Birla Institute of Technology, Mesra, Ranchi, India
Sudip Kumar Sahana	Birla Institute of Technology, Mesra, India
Aruna Jain	Birla Institute of Technology, Mesra, India
K. K. Senapati	Birla Institute of Technology, Mesra, India
Renuka A.	Manipal Institute of Technology, Manipal, India
Dinesh Acharya U.	Manipal Institute of Technology, Manipal, India
Smitha N. Pai	Manipal Institute of Technology, Manipal, India
N. V. Subba Reddy	Manipal Institute of Technology, Manipal, India
Krishanamoorthi Makkithaya	Manipal Institute of Technology, Manipal, India
Poornalatha G.	Manipal Institute of Technology, Manipal, India
Vivekananda Bhat K.	Manipal Institute of Technology, Manipal, India
Geetha M.	Manipal Institute of Technology, Manipal, India
Radhika M. Pai	Manipal Institute of Technology, Manipal, India
R. Balasubramanian	Manonmanian Sundaranar University, Tirunelveli, India
K. M. Mehata	B. S. Abdur Rahman University, India
V. Ganapathy	SRM University, India
S. Kupuswami	Kongu Engineering College, India
Chandrasekaran R. M.	Annamalai University, Chidambaram, India
Devaraj D.	Kalasalingam University, India
Dhavachelvan P.	Pondicherry University, India
Jitendra Kumar	Central University of Rajasthan, India
Parameshwar P. Iyer	Indian Institute of Science, Bangalore, India
Rajesh Kannan V.	Bharathidasan University, India
Ramadoss B.	NIT Trichy, India
Ramamohan Reddy	Sri Venkateswara University, Tirupati, India
Ramalingam V.	Annamalai University, India
Ramar K.	Einstein College of Engineering, India
Ramaraj E.	Alagappa University, India
Rangarajan R.	University of Madras, India
Sahoo P. K.	Chang Gung University, Taiwan
Satheesh Kumar	University of Kerala, India
Surya Durbha	IIT, Bombay, India
Thambidurai P.	Perunthalaivar Kamarajar Institute of Engineering and Technology (PKIET), Karaikal, India
Venkatesan S.	IIIT Allahabad, India
Vivekanandhan K.	Pondicherry Engineering College, Pondicherry, India
Chitra Babu	SSN College of Engineering, Chennai, India
Milton	SSN College of Engineering, Chennai, India
K. Suresh Joseph	Pondicherry University, India
S. Saraswathi	Pondicherry Engineering College, Pondicherry, India
S. Lakshmana Pandian	Pondicherry Engineering College, India

K. Sathiyamurthy	Pondicherry Engineering College, India
R. Parthasarathi	Pondicherry Engineering College, India
A. Jaya	B. S. Abdur Rahman University, India
Angelina Geetha	B. S. Abdur Rahman University, India
R. Shriram	B. S. Abdur Rahman University, India
Shital Raut	VNIT, India
J. Jagadeesan	SRM University, Ramapuram Campus, Chennai, India
P. Bhargavi	Sri Padmavathi Mahila Visvavidyalayam (Women's University), Tirupati, Andhra Pradesh, India

Conference Committee

Patron

S. Ganesan	Anna University, Chennai, India

Co-patron

P. Narayanasamy	Anna University, Chennai, India

Convenor

D. Manjula	CEG, Anna University, Chennai, India

Organizing Chairs

S. Chitrakala	CEG, Anna University, Chennai, India
Rajeswari Sridhar	CEG, Anna University, Chennai, India
Angelin Gladston	CEG, Anna University, Chennai, India

Organizing Committee

T. V. Geetha	CEG, Anna University, Chennai, India
K. S. Easwarakumar	CEG, Anna University, Chennai, India
T. V. Gopal	CEG, Anna University, Chennai, India
Arul Siromoney	CEG, Anna University, Chennai, India
S. Valli	CEG, Anna University, Chennai, India
A. P. Shanthi	CEG, Anna University, Chennai, India
V. Mary Anita Rajam	CEG, Anna University, Chennai, India
V. Vetriselvi	CEG, Anna University, Chennai, India
S. Bose	CEG, Anna University, Chennai, India
R. Baskaran	CEG, Anna University, Chennai, India
P. Geetha	CEG, Anna University, Chennai, India
P. Uma Maheswari	CEG, Anna University, Chennai, India
S. Sudha	CEG, Anna University, Chennai, India
G. S. Mahalakshmi	CEG, Anna University, Chennai, India

T. Raghuveera	CEG, Anna University, Chennai, India
R. Arockia Xavier Annie	CEG, Anna University, Chennai, India
S. Renugadevi	CEG, Anna University, Chennai, India
K. Selvamani	CEG, Anna University, Chennai, India
B. L. Velammal	CEG, Anna University, Chennai, India
M. Shanmugapriya	CEG, Anna University, Chennai, India
D. Shiloah Elizabeth	CEG, Anna University, Chennai, India
P. Velvizhy	CEG, Anna University, Chennai, India
M. S. Karthika Devi	CEG, Anna University, Chennai, India
J. Senthil Kumar	CEG, Anna University, Chennai, India
V. Suganya	CEG, Anna University, Chennai, India
K. Geetha	CEG, Anna University, Chennai, India
J. Angel Arul Jothi	CEG, Anna University, Chennai, India
K. Lalitha Devi	CEG, Anna University, Chennai, India
T. Munirathinam	CEG, Anna University, Chennai, India
P. Elumalaivasan	CEG, Anna University, Chennai, India
J. Vijayarani	CEG, Anna University, Chennai, India
U. Kanimozhi	CEG, Anna University, Chennai, India
A. R. Arunarani	CEG, Anna University, Chennai, India
Deepika Roselind	CEG, Anna University, Chennai, India
R. Bhuvaneshwari	CEG, Anna University, Chennai, India
K. Thangaramya	CEG, Anna University, Chennai, India
G. Sudhakaran	CEG, Anna University, Chennai, India
G. Logeswari	CEG, Anna University, Chennai, India
D. Swathigavaisnave	CEG, Anna University, Chennai, India
A. Menaka Pushpa	CEG, Anna University, Chennai, India
T. M. Thiyagu	CEG, Anna University, Chennai, India
G. David Raj	CEG, Anna University, Chennai, India
N. Kalaichelvi	CEG, Anna University, Chennai, India
R. Thamizhamuthu	CEG, Anna University, Chennai, India
G. Manikandan	CEG, Anna University, Chennai, India
T. Anitha	CEG, Anna University, Chennai, India
K. R. Raghi	CEG, Anna University, Chennai, India

Panellists

T. V. Geetha	CEG, Anna University, Chennai
K. S. Easwarakumar	CEG, Anna University, Chennai
T. V. Gopal	CEG, Anna University, Chennai
Arul Siromoney	CEG, Anna University, Chennai
S. Valli	CEG, Anna University, Chennai
A. P. Shanthi	CEG, Anna University, Chennai
Kannan A.	IST, CEG, Anna University, Chennai
Ranjani Parthasarathi	IST, CEG, Anna University, Chennai
Uma G. V.	IST, CEG, Anna University, Chennai

Saswati Mukherjee   IST, CEG, Anna University, Chennai
S. Thamarai Selvi   CT, MIT, Anna University, Chennai
P. AnandhaKumar   CT, MIT, Anna University, Chennai
V. Rhymend Uthariaraj   IT, MIT, Anna University, Chennai

Contents

A Comparative Study of Task and Fault Tolerance Clustering Techniques for Scientific Workflow Applications in Cloud Platform

Soma Prathiba[1]($\boxtimes$), S. Sowvarnica[1], B. Latha[1], and G. Sumathi[2]

[1] Sri Sairam Engineering College, Chennai, India
somaprathi25@gmail.com
[2] Sri Venkateshwara College of Engineering, Chennai, India

Abstract. Scientific workflows are characterized by the existence of complex tasks, which involve multifaceted mathematical and scientific calculations and multiple dependencies. These dependencies can be modeled as Directed Acyclic Graphs (DAG). System overheads that are present in these workflows result in the longer execution time of the task that has otherwise a very short runtime. Hence clustering of the tasks is performed where smaller tasks are combined to form a job, thereby reducing the system overhead and increasing the runtime performance of the tasks. This survey paper discusses the clustering mechanisms that are suitable for the scientific workflow along with the fault tolerance mechanisms that help to make the system robust. The analysis of the performance of various clustering algorithms is also discussed in this paper.

Keywords: Scientific workflow · Clustering · Fault tolerance

1 Introduction

Scientific workflows are composed of multiple tasks that have diverse data types and complex dependencies between them. The dependencies in the tasks can be modeled as DAG where the nodes represent the tasks and the edges are present between the tasks when there is a dependency relation between them. These workflows can be optimally scheduled in a distributed environment like cloud due to the features of cloud such as the provision of resources and services, dynamic allocation of resources and pay-as-you-go on-demand services. Though the individual execution times of these tasks are less, the system overhead that are present in the heterogeneous distributed environment such as queue delays, network communication delays increase the runtime of these tasks. Therefore an optimization technique, clustering is used which merges smaller tasks to form a job such that the overall runtime of the workflow is improved and the system overhead is reduced. It is also important to address the fault tolerance mechanisms for the workflows since distributed environment is more prone to errors.

The paper is organized as follows: Sect. 2 discusses a few of existing scientific workflow applications. Section 3 gives an overview of various clustering methods for the scientific workflows and fault tolerance clustering mechanisms are discussed

Shriram R and M. Sharma (Eds.): DaSAA 2017, CCIS 804, pp. 1–7, 2018.
https://doi.org/10.1007/978-981-10-8603-8_1

in Sect. 4 and the comparative performance of the clustering methods are analyzed in Sect. 5.

2 Examples of Scientific Workflows

There are many workflows that are available in the various fields. The following are few of these workflows in the fields of astronomy, biology, etc.

2.1 Montage

Montage is a NASA/IPAC Infrared Science Archive open toolkit [1] that generates custom mosaics of the sky using the input images in the Flexible Image Transport System (FITS) format. The input images are reprojected onto a sphere and an overlap, thus formed is calculated for each input image. By rectifying the images to a common flux scale and background level, the images are added and the reprojected image will result in the final mosaic which provides a deeper understanding of the portion of the sky under study.

2.2 CyberShake

CyberShake [2] is an application that is used in the field of seismology by the Southern California Earthquake Center (SCEC) to calculate Probabilistic Seismic Hazard curves for geographic sites located in the Southern Californian region. An MPI based finite difference simulation is performed in the given region to generate Strain Green Tensors (SGTs). Synthetic seismograms are calculated for each of the series of predicted ruptures from the SGT data and then spectral acceleration and probabilistic hazard curves are calculated from the seismograms to illustrate the seismic hazard.

2.3 Epigenomics

The Epigenomics [3] workflow is essentially a data parallel processing that makes use of the Pegasus workflow management system to automatically execute various genomes sequencing operations. The data required for the workflow is obtained from the Illumina-Solexa Genetic Analyzer in the form of DNA sequence lanes. These data are then converted into a form that is understandable to the sequence mapping software which then tries to construct the entire genome.

2.4 SIPHT

Untranslated RNAs (sRNAs) are used to regulate several processes such as secretion or virulence in bacteria [4]. The kingdom-wide prediction and annotation of sRNA encoding genes involve a variety of individual programs that are executed in the proper order using Pegasus.

2.5 LIGO Inspiral Analysis

The Laser Interferometer Gravitational Wave Observatory (LIGO) is used to detect gravitational waves produced by different events in the universe according Einstein's theory of general relativity [5]. The data obtained from the coalesce of compact binary systems are analyzed using LIGO. LIGO Inspiral workflow is an example of data – intensive workflow.

3 Clustering

Scientific workflows are characterized by the existence of a large number of tasks which should be scheduled optimally to produce a meaningful result. To avoid system over-heads which cause increase in the task's execution time, clustering is performed which combines a collection of individual tasks to form a job. While performing clustering it is important to consider the interdependence that exist between the tasks such as data dependency and runtime dependencies.

3.1 Types of Clustering

The following are the some of the clustering methods

Horizontal Clustering: Horizontal Clustering is implemented on the workflow tasks at the same horizontal level. The horizontal level of a task t is defined as the longest distance from the entry task to the task t under consideration [6]. Thus, all the tasks having the same horizontal level can be merged to form a cluster.

Vertical Clustering: Vertical Clustering is performed by merging the tasks that are in the same pipeline of the DAG. The tasks that are present in the same pipeline have a single-parent-single-child relationship [6].

Balanced Clustering: As improper task clustering may lead to load imbalance in a distributed environment, it is necessary to consider the dependencies that exist between the tasks before clustering them. Two common types of imbalances are Runtime imbalance and Dependency imbalance. Runtime imbalance occurs when a particular task having the longest runtime delays the execution of the other tasks. Runtime imbalance of a task can be determined by calculating the Horizontal Runtime Variance (HRV). HRV is defined as the ratio of the standard deviation of a task runtime to the average runtime of tasks/jobs at the same horizontal level of a workflow [6]. If R_t is the runtime a single task and n is the number of tasks in the same horizontal level then HRV can be expressed using the following formula

$$HRV = \frac{\sigma(R_t)}{\sum R_t/n} \qquad (1)$$

Dependency imbalance is one which occurs when a task at one level forces the tasks at the next level to experience data locality problems. Impact factor variance and the distance variance are the two variances to measure the dependency imbalance. Impact Factor Variance (IFV) which measures the importance of a task in the workflow is the standard deviation of the tasks' impact factors. Impact Factor (IF) of a task t_u is defined as follows

$$IF(t_u) = \sum_{t_v \in Child(t_u)} \frac{IF(t_v)}{\|Parent(t_v)\|} \tag{2}$$

Horizontal Impact Factor Variance (HIFV) calculates IFV among the tasks at the same horizontal level. Distance Variance (DV) which indicates the closeness between the tasks in a given job is defined as the sum of the distance to their closest common successor. The distance variance (DV) is the standard deviation of distances between a set of tasks. Horizontal Distance Variance (HDV) is the distance variance calculated among the tasks in the same horizontal level. HDV for a set of tasks with distance d being the distance between any two given tasks can be expressed as below

$$HDV = \sigma^2(d_{t_i}) \tag{3}$$

Based on the imbalance metrics discussed above, the following clustering algorithms have been proposed: Horizontal Runtime Balancing (HRB) which aims to cluster tasks by balancing the runtime variances of the tasks, Horizontal Impact Factor Balancing (HIFB) algorithm clusters tasks based on the impact factor variance and Horizontal Distance Balancing (HDB) performs clustering based on the horizontal distance variance (Table 1).

Table 1. Summary of clustering methods

S.No	Clustering method		Clustering criteria	Purpose	Time complexity
Clustering of tasks in scientific workflows					
1	Horizontal clustering		Tasks at the same level	To reduce System overhead	O(l.t) where l denotes the number of levels and t denotes the number of tasks in the level
2	Vertical clustering		Single-parent-single-child	To reduce system overhead	O(n.t) where t denotes the number of the tasks and n denotes the number of child tasks for a given task t
3	Balanced clustering	Runtime balancing	Runtime	Improve low performance of short running tasks	O(W.l) where W is the depth of the workflow and l is the number of tasks in a given depth
		Impact factor balancing	Impact factor (similarity of tasks)		O(W.l) where W is the depth of the workflow and l is the number of tasks in a given depth
		Distance vector balancing	Distance (closeness of the tasks)		O(W.l) where W is the depth of the workflow and l is the number of tasks in a given depth

4 Fault Tolerance in Clustering

Scientific workflows consist of tasks that are very critical. A fault in any one task can affect the entire workflow in the worst case scenario. Therefore implementing fault tolerance mechanisms will ensure that the occurrence of fault is minimal and even in case of fault the workflow can perform efficiently with minimum or no damage. In general, there are two types of failures which can affect any system. The first is the transient failure where the normal function of the system is briefly affected and it is possible to recover from the failure. The next kind of failure is the permanent failure where the system is affected permanently. The following are the different types of failures that can occur in scientific workflow model. One is task failure where the failure of a single task does not cause failure to other tasks and the other failure is a job failure where the job failure causes all the tasks within the job to fail. According to these failures two failure models have been proposed, Task Failure Model (TFM) where the failure of a task is a random event and Job Failure Model (JFM) where the failure of a job is a random event. Chen [7] proposes three techniques to handle failures in scientific workflows. The first method is the Dynamic Clustering (DC) which adjusts the clustering factor which is defined as the number of tasks in a cluster, according to the failure rate of already completed jobs. The second method proposed is Selective Reclustering (SR) where task retry is done only for the tasks that have failed. The last method proposed is Dynamic Reclustering (DR), where the failure information of the previous jobs is taken into account and clustering is performed only for the failed tasks by adjusting the clustering factor.

5 Results and Discussion

The makespan of various workflows based on different clustering mechanisms are compared in this section. WorkflowSim [8] is a tool which is used to simulate the workflow, clustering and fault tolerance mechanisms and the analysis in this section is the result of these simulations. Figure 1 shows the makespan variation for various workflows with respect to different clustering algorithms (Horizontal, Vertical, and Balanced Clustering). For this comparison, the number of Virtual Machines is taken as 20. The comparison of fault tolerant clustering methods is shown in Fig. 2 where NOOP stands for No Optimization which means that there is no fault tolerance clustering applied.

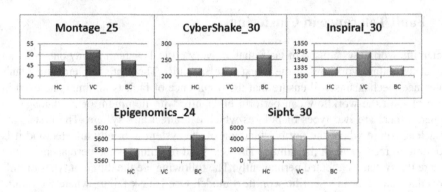

Fig. 1. Makespan comparison for workflows when VM = 20 for clustering methods

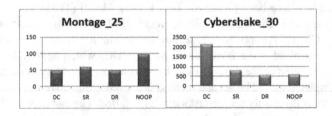

Fig. 2. Comparison of fault tolerance clustering methods with respect to makespan

6   Conclusion

This paper has highlighted the importance of clustering in the scientific workflows and a few methods to perform clustering for different scientific workflows. A single clustering method cannot provide an optimistic solution for all the workflows since each workflow has different characteristics therefore various workflows must be analyzed to choose the clustering method that is suitable. Integrating fault tolerance mechanism along with the clustering mechanisms will provide an optimistic and robust scheduling.

References

1. Berriman, G.B., Deelman, E., Good, J.C., Jacob, J.C., Katz, D.S., Kesselman, C., Laity, A.C., Prince, T.A., Singh, G., Su, M.: Montage: a grid-enabled engine for delivering custom science-grade mosaics on demand. In: SPIE Conference on Astronomical Telescopes and Instrumentation, vol. 5493, pp. 221–232 (2004)
2. Graves, R., Jordan, T., Callaghan, S., Deelman, E., Field, E., Juve, G., Kesselman, C., Maechling, P., Mehta, G., Milner, K., Okaya, D., Small, P., Vahi, K.: CyberShake: a physics-based seismic hazard model for Southern California. Pure. appl. Geophys. **168**(3–4), 367–381 (2011)
3. USC Epigenome Center. http://epigenome.usc.edu

4. Bharathi, S., Chervenak, A., Deelman, E., Mehta, G., Su, M.-H., Vahi, K.: Characterization of scientific workflows. In: 2008 Third Workshop on Workflows in Support of Large-Scale Science (2008)
5. Brown, D.A., Brady, P.R., Dietz, A., Cao, J., Johnson, B., McNabb, J.: A Case Study on the Use of Workflow Technologies for Scientific Analysis: Gravitational Wave Data Analysis. Springer, London (2007). https://doi.org/10.1007/978-1-84628-757-2_4
6. Chen, W., da Silva, R.F., Deelman, E., Sakellariou, R.: Using imbalance metrics to optimize task clustering in scientific workflow executions. Future Gener. Comput. Syst. **46**, 69–84 (2015)
7. Chen, W., Deelman, E.: Fault tolerant clustering in scientific workflows. In: 2012 IEEE Eighth World Congress on Services (2012)
8. Chen, W., Deelman, E.: WorkflowSim: A toolkit for simulating scientific workflows in distributed environments. IEEE (2012)

A Frequent and Rare Itemset Mining Approach to Transaction Clustering

Kuladeep Tummala, C. Oswald[(✉)], and B. Sivaselvan

Department of Computer Engineering, Indian Institute of Information Technology,
Design and Manufacturing Kancheepuram, Chennai, India
{coe11b026,coe13d003,sivaselvanb}@iiitdm.ac.in

Abstract. Data clustering is the unsupervised learning procedure of grouping related objects based on similarity measures. Intra cluster similarity is maximized and inter cluster similarity is minimized in the clustering technique. Distance based similarity measures are employed in k-means, k-mediods, etc. which are some of the clustering algorithms. This project explores the scope of guided clustering, wherein frequent and rare patterns shall be employed in the process of clustering. The work focuses on having a better centre of a cluster, employing variants of frequent and rare itemsets such as Maximal Frequent Itemset (MFI) and Minimal Rare Itemset (MRI). The literature supports several instance of association rule based classification and the effort is to have a MFI/MRI based clustering. The proposed model employs MFI and MRI in the process of choosing cluster centers. The proposed algorithm has been tested over benchmark datasets and compared with centroid based hierarchical clustering and large items based transaction clustering algorithms and the results indicate improvement in terms of cluster quality.

Keywords: Clustering · Jaccard similarity · k-means clustering
Maximum support · Minimal rare itemset

1 Introduction

The technique of discovering hidden patterns which may be of interest to the user and providing valuable information, constitute the Data Mining process. It is one of many techniques to analyze the data and has attracted a lot of attention in the past few years. The ease and efficiency with which the Data Mining techniques can process vast amounts of data makes it better than other existing data analyzing tools. With the growing demand and application space, Data Mining algorithms should be efficient, scalable and are required to deal with diverse data types. Data Mining is considered as a vital phase in the discovery of knowledge rather than the process itself [1]. There are many other important steps which come along the entire process. Cleaning of Data and integration, data selection come under the data pre-processing techniques. The selected data is mined and the discovered knowledge is evaluated and presented to the user. The user should be able to interpret the information discovered by the data mining techniques and this is why knowledge presentation is also of prime importance in the entire process.

© Springer Nature Singapore Pte Ltd. 2018
Shriram R and M. Sharma (Eds.): DaSAA 2017, CCIS 804, pp. 8–18, 2018.
https://doi.org/10.1007/978-981-10-8603-8_2

Clustering is an unsupervised learning approach where a set of objects are grouped in such a way that objects in the same group, called as cluster have similar characteristics than that of other clusters. There is no generic notion of a cluster defined in the literature which is why there are so many clustering algorithms and also means of clustering the given data and is highly dependent on the application domain [2]. Clustering is applied in many applications in the areas like Genetic Clustering, medical imaging, Market research, grouping of products in a store, social network analysis, image segmentation and weather prediction. This project deals with a specific area of clustering called transaction clustering.

Transaction clustering is where a database containing transactions is clustered. Consider a transaction database of a store containing a transaction for a single customer. Each transaction contains the set of items or products bought by the customer. These data is used to group customers where their buying patterns are similar, into one cluster and customers with different buying patterns into different clusters. These clusters provide the store with information to improve their sales by targeting a particular cluster of customers. For example, a cluster may contain customers who bought imported products very often indicating that the customer belong to a high income group and another cluster may contain customers who bought books and stationery more often who have school going children at home.

The market basket database is only an instance of data with categorical attributes which has boolean attributes indicating whether an item is present or not in the transaction. If an item is present in a transaction, it is denoted by '1' and its absence denoted by '0'. The analysis remains unaltered even when there are more values for an attribute other than true or false.

2   Related Work - Association Rule Mining and Frequent Itemsets

Association Rule Mining (ARM) was introduced by Aggarwal et al. which is the area of Data Mining, discovering interesting and hidden relationships in large datasets [3, 4]. Association Rule Mining (ARM) is a 2-step process which consists of itemset generation and rule generation. I is a nonempty set of 'n' items or attributes. The transaction data set consists of transactions in which every transaction contains a collection of itemsets. The number of transactions in which an itemset X occurs is defined as the support of X. The itemsets which occur more than a certain pre-fixed support threshold (*min_sup*) are called Frequent Itemsets (FI). An itemset X is a frequent itemset if, the following condition holds,

$$support(X) \geq min\_support$$

As the dataset size increases, the number of frequent itemsets also increases which makes it difficult to further process the data. The alternative representations of frequent itemsets like Closed Frequent Itemset and Maximal Frequent Itemset are also derived. A frequent itemset with none of its immediate supersets being frequent is referred as Maximal Frequent Itemset. They provide smallest and compact representation of FI which will prove useful when space is an issue. A frequent itemset is considered to be a *closed* frequent itemset if there is no other superset of the frequent itemset with the same support. The relationship between *FI*, *CFI* and *MFI* is given below.

$$MFI \subseteq CFI \subseteq FI$$

Maximal frequent itemset is the most compact representation of frequent itemsets. There may be a group of items which occur less number of times in the dataset but holds vital information. The itemsets whose support is less than a certain pre-fixed support threshold are called Rare Itemsets (RI). An itemset X is a rare itemset if,

$$0 < support(X) \le max\_support$$

2.1 Clustering

Clustering is a Data Mining technique where the data is grouped into different clusters which maximizes the intra cluster and minimizes the inter cluster similarity whereas classification is the task of assigning instances to pre-defined classes, like deciding whether a patient is associated with a specific disease. There is only a thin line between Clustering and Classification [1]. The latter is a supervised learning technique and needs training data for the classifier to learn. At times, the training data may not contain all the possible data instances and the classifier fails when such a data object occurs in the dataset being classified.

Clustering being an unsupervised technique, needs no such training and this makes clustering more robust than classification as it is adaptable to change. Apart from making room for adaptability, clustering algorithms should be scalable to deal with large data-sets, able to deal with various data types, discover clusters with arbitrary shape and also deal with high dimensional space. Clustering algorithms which are sensitive to noise or missing data may lead to poor quality clusters.

Using association rules for prediction has rapidly increased in recent times. There are certain classification algorithms based on association rules in the literature. This project aims at throwing some light on the concept of using the association between the attributes of the given data to cluster the dataset. We use frequent and rare itemsets to bring forward a novel approach to cluster the transactional datasets.

Clustering methods can be mainly classified into four categories as follows [5].

Partitioning Method: First and the foremost basic clustering method is partitioning method in which data is divided into '*k*' partitions and each partition represents a cluster. In this method, each cluster should have at least an object and each of that object must belong to only 1 group.

Hierarchical Methods: This method produces a hierarchical decomposition of the given dataset. Based on the type of decomposition, there are two methods of hierarchical clustering.

- **Agglomerative Approach:** This is a bottom-up approach which starts by considering each object as a cluster and merges the clusters which are close to each other until all the clusters are merged into one single cluster or the termination condition is met.

- **Divisive Approach:** In contrast to the previous approach, this is a top-down approach. It starts with 1 cluster containing all the objects and further splits into smaller clusters until each object is a cluster or the terminating condition is met.
- **Density-based Method:** The basic idea behind this method is to keep the cluster grow till the density in its neighbourhood satisfies some threshold. Every point in a cluster should have at least minimum number of points within its radius.
- **Grid-based Method:** This method is a space-driven approach where the previous approaches are data driven. The given space is partitioned into cells without considering the distribution of the objects in the dataset.

2.2 Clustering Algorithms

There are many clustering algorithms given the wide application space of the clustering technique. The prime focus of this work is to design a novel approach to transaction clustering and a few traditional data clustering algorithms are studied with respect to transaction data and the drawbacks of each are discussed in this section.

2.2.1 *k*-means Algorithm

A renowned unsupervised learning algorithm which is k-means, falls under partitioning methods for clustering [6]. The algorithm works on a easy and simple way to group a given dataset through a random number of clusters k, fixed in advance. k centers are defined, one for each cluster. The algorithm starts by assigning k points, each to a single cluster in a random manner, which represent the cluster as centers. Then it assigns each object to the cluster that has the center which is closest. Recalculation of the centers of each cluster are done, when all the objects are assigned. Now move the objects to the closest center after update. Repeat the last two steps until the centers no longer change.

By clustering the above transaction dataset in Table 1, by the method of k-means with $k = 2$, we get two clusters with their details tabulated below in Table 2 and the results are analyzed to highlight the drawbacks in using distance based methods for transactional datasets.

Table 1. Example transactional data set over items (1, 2, 3, 4, 5, 6, 7).

Transaction ID	Transaction item set	Boolean representation
T_1	1, 4, 6, 7	1 0 0 1 0 1 1
T_2	2, 3, 5, 6	0 1 1 0 1 1 0
T_3	1, 4, 5	1 0 0 1 1 0 0
T_4	1, 2, 3, 7	1 1 1 0 0 0 1
T_5	1, 3	1 0 1 0 0 0 0
T_6	3, 4, 5	0 0 1 1 1 0 0
T_7	1, 2, 3	1 1 1 0 0 0 0
T_8	2, 3, 4, 6, 7	0 1 1 1 0 1 1
T_9	1, 4, 5, 6	1 0 0 1 1 1 0
T_{10}	1, 2, 4, 5	1 1 0 1 1 0 0

Table 2. Results of clustering by k-means method.

Cluster	Transactions	Mean point (centre)
Cluster I	$T_1, T_2, T_3, T_6, T_8, T_9, T_{10}$	(4/7, 3/7, 3/7, 6/7, 5/7, 4/7, 1/7)
Cluster II	T_4, T_5, T_7	(1, 2/3, 1, 0, 0, 0, 1/3)

In the above clustering transactions, in T_1 and T_2 which are $\{1, 4, 6, 7\}$ and $\{2, 3, 5, 6\}$ there is only one item in common, but both the transactions are in the same cluster and T_2 share two items $\{2, 3\}$ in common with T_4 and T_7 but still they end up in different clusters. This explains the inefficiency of k-means or similar distance based algorithms in clustering transactions.

2.2.2 k-modes Algorithm

k-modes, one of the earliest clustering algorithms for categorical data is introduced, in which, extension of the k-means algorithm to categorical data is done [7]. Similar to k-means, the algorithm starts by selecting k initial modes, one for each cluster and allocates all the objects in the database to the cluster with the nearest mode. The mode of each cluster is updated after every addition. After allocating all the objects, the dissimilarity between each object and present modes of clusters is tested and objects are reallocated to nearest modes. Until there is no further change in the modes, this process is repeated.

2.3   Other Transaction Clustering Algorithms

Similar to k-means, there are centroid based approaches to hierarchical clustering. In this method, the distance between any 2 clusters is the distance between their centroids, which are the mean points of the cluster. At each level, the clusters with smallest centroid distance are merged. This provides the basis for discussing the ROCK algorithm. A hierarchical clustering ROCK, is based on the notion of links to arrive at a better solution to cluster transactions [8]. A pair of transactions in any cluster has very few items in common, but linked by a number of other transactions in the cluster. A link between a pair of transactions is defined as the number of common neighbours between them. It draws a random sample from the given dataset and applies a hierarchical clustering which employs links on the sampled data. The clusters generated through sampled data are used to assign the remaining transactions to the clusters. The number of clusters to be formed which is k, is specified by the user. An approach to cluster transactions using large items is presented in [9]. As a similarity measure of the clusters, the notion of large items is defined as the items which occur at least in a minimum user specified number of transactions within a cluster. Here the large items are local frequent items to cluster. The main drawback with this approach is that not every cluster may have frequent items, there can also be clusters where rare items dominate which we focus in our approach. And also selection of minimum support by the user which may be hard to define is a challenge in this approach.

Another clustering approach based on weighting maximal frequent itemsets is put forward by Huang et al. [10]. This method generates maximal frequent itemsets of the given dataset and assigns some weight to the numerical attributes also as opposed to other transaction clustering algorithms. Though few of the algorithms discussed above presented better approaches than the existing works, but none has addressed the issue of grouping relevant data together while effectively avoiding noise from impeding the quality of clusters. This work focuses on the same and proposes a novel and effective approach to cluster transactional datasets.

The similarity measure in most of the basic data clustering algorithms is the distance of a point from the center of the cluster which it belongs to. This approach can be efficient for numerical attributes, but a transactional dataset which consists of categorical attributes or boolean attributes cannot be efficiently clustered using the same approach.

A transaction dataset has very large number of attributes which are items here and in contrast, the size of each transaction is small. From the set of items, a transaction has only a subset of items that represents the cluster. In such a scenario, it will be more efficient to employ frequent patterns in the data set to arrive at a better clustering solution to clustering transactions. Also the transactions which fall apart from most other transactions should be taken care of by considering rare patterns in the data set. The paper focuses on using compact representations of the frequent and rare itemsets in the process of clustering and implementing the complete algorithm which can be efficiently scaled to cluster real time data sets. Transaction clustering has to be performed employing MFI and MRI in the process of fixing cluster representatives.

3 Proposed MFI and MRI Based Clustering

Any clustering algorithm has to cluster the given data into distinct groups such that objects inside a cluster are similar and objects of different clusters are dissimilar. A similarity measure is defined to cluster the data. And the other important aspect is selecting the center of the cluster. The focus is laid on the similarity measures and selecting center of the cluster in the following sections.

3.1 Similarity Measures

As discussed in the previous chapter, the distance similarity measure used in k-means algorithm does not fit for categorical attributes. A transaction is most likely a set of items, in which case, we need a measure which finds the similarity between two sets. Jaccard index or Jaccard similarity coefficient, a static measure used to compare similarity of sets is used in the algorithm [11]. The equation for Jaccard similarity coefficient is given below.

$$J(A, B) = \frac{|A \cap B|}{|A \cup B|}, 0 \leq J(A, B) \leq 1.$$

If both A and B has same objects, then J(A, B) is 1 and if there are no objects in common between A and B, J(A, B) will be 0.

3.2 Frequent and Rare Itemsets in Clustering

For a large data set, the number of FI's and RI's grows exponentially and in turn create issues with storage and analysis and it is for this purpose that an alternative representation has been derived that reduces the initial set but can generate all other itemsets using the reduced set. The paper aims to explore the scope of guided clustering by incorporating maximal frequent itemset and minimal rare itemset mining in the process of clustering of transactional data sets.

An itemset is a MFI [12] if it is frequent itemset for which none of its immediate supersets are frequent. An itemset X is a MFI if,

$$\text{support}(X) \geq \text{minsup} \ \& \ \forall Y \supset X, \text{support}(Y) < minsup$$

Example: Consider a transaction data set over 5 items 1, 2, 3, 4, 5 as T_1 {1, 3, 4}, T_2 {2, 5}, T_3 {1, 2, 3, 5}, T_4 {2, 3, 5} and T_5 {1, 2, 3, 5}. With a minimum support of 2 on the data set, we get the MFI {1, 2, 3, 5} with a support of 2. An itemset is minimally rare, i.e. an MRI if it is rare but all its proper subsets are frequent [13]. An itemset X is an MRI if,

$$\text{support}(X) < \text{minsup} \ \& \ \forall Y \subset X, \text{support}(Y) \geq minsup$$

Example: Consider a transaction data set over 5 items 1, 2, 3, 4, 5 as T_1 {1, 2, 4, 5}, T_2 {1, 3}, T_3 {1, 2, 3, 5}, T_4 {2, 3, 5} and T_5 {1, 2, 3, 5}. With a minimum support threshold of 3 on the dataset, we get the MRI's as {4}, {1, 3, 5}, {1, 2, 3} with the support of 1, 2, 2 respectively.

3.3 Algorithm

We use this MFI's and MRI's to represent a cluster and assign the transactions based on their similarity with the cluster center that may be one among the MFI's or MRI's.

Approach

- Generate MFI's and MRI's taking a minimum support threshold as an input from the user.
- Use the MFI's and MRI's as centers to different clusters and merge any two clusters together if they are similar.
- Assign each transaction in the data set to the cluster whose center is most similar to. Similarity criterion is the number of common items in the transaction and cluster center.

To generate the MFI's in the first step, CHARM-MFI [12] algorithm is used and to generate MRI's Apriori-Rare [13] algorithm is used. After generating the MFI's and MRI's by specifying the minimum and maximum support respectively, we select a group of MFI's and MRI's as centers of the cluster. Now, each transaction in the dataset is compared individually with each of the cluster center and using Jaccard similarity index mentioned above, assign them to the clusters with the maximum Jaccard index. The working of our algorithm over a sample dataset from Table 1 is presented below to draw a comparison between our algorithm and the centroid based k-means algorithm.

3.4 Illustration

Clustering the example data set in Table 1 using our approach of considering MFI's and MRI's as the center of the clusters will give the following clusters. The clustering of the example data set with a minimum support and maximum support of 3, generates 3 clusters with MFI's as centers of two clusters and MRI as center of third cluster. Clustering does not have a unique solution, here we consider a single instance of the solution. Transaction T_1 and T_8 contain the itemset $\{4, 6, 7\}$ which is rare in the given example data set. If the MRI is not considered as a center, then the transaction T_1 would have been ended up in Cluster I as it has two items $\{1, 4\}$ in common with the center of the first cluster and also T_8 would have been in Cluster II as it has two items $\{2, 3\}$ in common with its center. But T_1 and T_8 has $\{4, 6, 7\}$ in common and that itemset is rare in the dataset which is given in Table 3.

Table 3. Results of clustering based on the proposed approach.

Clusters	Center of the cluster	Transactions
Cluster I	$\{1, 4, 5\}$	T_3, T_6, T_9, T_{10}
Cluster II	$\{1, 2, 3\}$	T_2, T_4, T_5, T_7
Cluster III	$\{4, 6, 7\}$	T_1, T_8

This example gives a glimpse of the superiority of our approach over the traditional distance based or centroid based approaches. The results of the experimentation with benchmark datasets like Mushroom will further strengthen our arguments that our algorithm is better than centroid based approaches.

4 Simulation Results and Discussion

The algorithm designed is implemented and tested in R version 3.2.0 (2015-04-16) [14]. R is free, open source and most comprehensive package for statistical analysis. It has all the standard statistical tests, analyses and models inbuilt. It is also portable and runs on any platform. RStudio [15], an IDE for R language is also used. The MFI's and mRI's in the first step of the process are generated using an open source java software SPMF [16]. All the software packages mentioned above and implementations are run on Windows 7 64-bit Operating System upon the hardware of HP Pavilion dv4 notebook pc with Intel CORE i3, 2.2 GHz processor and 4 GB RAM and 600 GB HDD. The algorithm is experimented with Mushroom dataset obtained from UCI Machine Learning Repository [17]. Physical properties of a mushroom are contained in the attributes. Among all the real-life benchmark datasets, this is the largest with 8124 records and 22 attributes. All the attributes are of categorical type, for example, the odour attribute takes one value from spicy, foul, pungent, etc. There are few missing values in the original dataset which are ignored in this implementation. Also the class information about the records is also presented. There are 4208 Edible mushrooms and 3916 Poisonous mushrooms in the dataset.

To generate the MFI's, the minimum support is specified to be 40% of the transaction dataset. In Mushroom dataset, there are 8124 records in total and 40% of them would be 3250. And to generate MRI's, the maximum support is specified as 5% which is 406 records. The following figures describe the results of our algorithm and other algorithms we are comparing with. Table 4 shows the results of clustering the mushroom dataset with the traditional centroid based hierarchical clustering [5]. As the table indicates, the clusters formed through this algorithm contain mushrooms from both edible and poisonous mushrooms in equal number in each cluster. The quality of the clusters formed is not effective.

Table 4. Results of centroid based hierarchical clustering

Cluster no.	No. of edible	No. of poisonous	Cluster no.	No. of edible	No. of poisonous
1	666	478	11	120	144
2	283	318	12	128	140
3	201	188	13	144	163
4	164	227	14	198	163
5	194	125	15	131	211
6	207	150	16	201	156
7	233	238	17	151	140
8	181	139	18	190	122
9	135	78	19	175	150
10	172	217	20	168	206

Table 5 below presents the results of the transaction clustering algorithm based on large items [9]. Some of the clusters formed using this algorithm are pure, but many clusters still contain transactions from both groups. Table 6 describes the results of the proposed MFI and MRI based algorithm for transaction clustering. The first eight clusters i.e. Cluster 1 to Cluster 8 are represented by MFI's and the rest of the clusters are represented by the MRI's. The results clearly indicate that most of the clusters are pure which means that mushrooms in each cluster were either all edible or all poisonous. About 75% of the clusters formed through the proposed method are pure against 50% of clusters through the approach based on the large items. The results obtained using the traditional centroid based hierarchical clustering algorithm does not contain at least one pure cluster. The sizes of the cluster formed are also highly varied. The largest cluster contains 972 mushrooms and the smallest cluster having only 16 mushrooms in them.

Table 5. Results of large items based clustering

Cluster no.	No. of edible	No. of poisonous	Cluster no.	No. of edible	No. of poisonous
1	94	0	8	0	287
2	13	0	9	61	3388
3	6	0	10	372	77
4	682	26	11	9	0
5	2631	30	12	19	10
6	121	37	13	21	0
7	69	61	14	110	0

Table 6. Results of MFI/mRI based transaction clustering.

Cluster no.	No. of edible	No. of poisonous	Cluster no.	No. of edible	No. of poisonous
1	0	16	15	0	120
2	0	72	16	36	16
3	0	228	17	36	0
4	680	0	18	36	0
5	684	0	19	56	96
6	692	0	20	0	216
7	0	40	21	72	0
8	324	12	22	180	0
9	0	972	23	108	0
10	0	200	24	48	0
11	268	328	25	72	4
12	0	924	26	72	0
13	0	200	27	268	140
14	140	624	28	144	0

5   Conclusions and Future Work

This paper focused on an efficient approach to clustering and proposed a frequent and rare itemset based clustering strategy. This work was done with the help of a scan efficient rare itemset mining algorithm already implemented by us. As a part of this work, we explored the scope of association rules in the context of clustering, along the lines of association rule based classification. This research work has culminated in an efficient clustering approach that employs Maximal Frequent Itemset mining and Minimal Rare Itemset mining in the process of fixing cluster centers. Results indicate better clustering compared to centroid based hierarchical clustering and large items based clustering. Future work may explore the domain of outlier analysis to use it in the clustering approach. Efficient data structures for improving time efficiency is an another challenging direction to work with.

References

1. Han, J., Kamber, M.: Data Mining: Concepts and Techniques, 3rd edn. Morgan Kaufmann Publishers, Burlington (2010). ISBN 1-55860-901-6
2. Jain, A.K., Murty, M.N., Flynn, P.J.: Data clustering: a review. ACM Comput. Surv. **31**, 264–323 (1999)
3. Agrawal, R., Imielinski, T., Swami, A.N.: Mining association rules between sets of items in large databases. In: ACM SIGMOD International Conference on Management of Data, Washington, D.C. (1993)
4. Agrawal, R., Mannila, H., Srikant, R., Toivonen, H., Inkeri Verkamo, A.: Fast discovery of association rules. In: Advances in Knowledge Discovery and Data Mining, pp. 307–328. AAAIPress, Menlo Park (1996)
5. Jain, A.K., Dubes, R.C.: Algorithms for Clustering Data. Prentice Hall, Upper Saddle River (1988). ISBN 0-13-022278-X
6. Hartingan, J.A., Wong, M.A.: A k-means clustering algorithm. J. Roy. Stat. Soc. **28**(1), 100–108 (1979)
7. Guha, S., Rastogi, R., Shim, K.: A clustering algorithm for categorical attributes. Technical report, Bell Laboratories, Murray Hill (1997)
8. Guha, S., Rastogi, R., Shim, K.: ROCK: a robust clustering algorithm for categorical attributes. Inf. Sys. **25**(5), 345–366 (2000)
9. Wang, K., Xu, C., Liu, B.: Clustering transactions using large items. In: ACM CIKM International Conference on Information and Knowledge Management, pp. 483–490, November 1999
10. Huang, F., Xie, G., Yao, Z., Cai, S.: Clustering transactions based on weighting maximal frequent itemsets. In: International Conference on Intelligent System and Knowledge Engineering (2008)
11. Tan, P.-N., Steinbach, M., Kumar, V.: Introduction to Data Mining. Addison Wesley, Boston (2005). ISBN 0-321-32136-7
12. Szathmary, L.: Symbolic Data Mining Methods with the Coron Platform, Universit´e Henri Poincar´e - Nancy I (2006)
13. Szathmary, L., Napoli, A., Valtchev, P.: Towards rare itemset mining. In: Proceedings of the 19th IEEE International Conference on Tools with Artificial Intelligence (ICTAI 2007), Patras, Greece, vol. 1, pp. 305–312, October 2007
14. The Comprehensive R Archive Network. http://cran.r-project.org/
15. RStudio. http://www.rstudio.com/
16. An Open-Source Data Mining Library. http://www.philippe-fournier-viger.com/spmf/index.php?link=documentation.php
17. UCI Machine Learning Repository. http://archive.ics.uci.edu/ml/

A Systematic Review on Biomedical Named Entity Recognition

U. Kanimozhi[(⊠)] and D. Manjula

Department of Computer Science and Engineering, College of Engineering,
Guindy, Anna University, Chennai, India
kanimozhiu.03@gmail.com, manju@annauniv.edu

Abstract. The amount of biomedical textual information available in the web
becomes more and more. It is very difficult to extract the right information that
users are interested in considering the size of documents in the biomedical
literatures and databases. It is nearly impossible for human to process all these
data and it is even difficult for computers to extract the information since it is not
stored in structured format. Identifying the named entities and classifying them
can help in extracting the useful information in the unstructured text documents.
This paper describes various approaches and techniques used for Named Entity
Recognition in biomedical domain.

Keywords: Biomedical named entity recognition · Classification
Machine learning

1 Introduction

Named entity recognition (NER) is one of the most important tasks in information
extraction of text mining. A Named Entity (NE) is a noun or nominal phrase that
belongs to a specific semantic type. Person, organization, place are some of the Named
Entity. NER is a task of identifying proper nouns in the natural language text and
classifying them according to a specific named entity class. NER is a basic tool that
plays an important role in various research areas of Natural Language Processing
(NLP) like Question Answering and Summarization Systems, Information Retrieval,
Information Extraction, Machine Translation, Video Annotation, Semantic Web
Search, Text Mining, Genetics Bioinformatics etc.

Medical data have valuable knowledge for medical applications, like drug-drug
interactions, protein interactions adverse drug effects and structuring electronic health
records. Biomedical literature grows exponentially each and every day, it reached a
point where the information cannot be extracted manually. New techniques for
extracting useful knowledge from text in a more accurate and efficient manner is
needed. Biomedical named entity recognition (Bio-NER) is a task of identifying the
biomedical terms in unstructured biomedical documents. Gene, protein, drug, DNA,
RNA, disease are some common named entity classes considered in biomedical
domain.

The entity may not contain single word, it may have multiword. It is very difficult
to identify the exact boundary of multiword entity, for example e.g. Diabetes mellitus

© Springer Nature Singapore Pte Ltd. 2018
Shriram R and M. Sharma (Eds.): DaSAA 2017, CCIS 804, pp. 19–37, 2018.
https://doi.org/10.1007/978-981-10-8603-8_3

type 1. In medical domain new diseases and drugs are continuously evolving and new terms are used in the literatures will make the recognition of entities more difficult. A term may have different meaning. Words with homonyms can be incorrectly recognized as Named entity. The term with spelling mistakes is difficult to identify. The biomedical literature does not follow strict naming conventions. Entity can contain symbol, digits, and Roman letters. The biomedical entity does not have any formats and is very highly unstructured. Abbreviation is used in biomedical literature creates more problem in recognizing the entity and they often leads to homonyms. Different name can be used to refer the same Bio-medical entity where the type depends on the context where they exist.

2   Approaches in Named Entity Recognition

Different types of approaches are used to identify Named Entities from unstructured text. These methods are Rule-based NER, Dictionary based NER, Machine Learning-based NER and Hybrid NER.

2.1   Rule-Based NER

Rule-based NER is based on the formulating set of hand-crafted rules by the experts and dictionary mapping to identify and extract the named entities. The output of this approach is done by checking the rules and dictionary mapping. For each type of classification different rules are used. Whenever the system gets the text it first searches for the named entity and then compares it with the rules. Once the rule is matched, the system gives the classified output. The performance of this system is highly based on the coverage of rules. The Rule-based system is often domain specific and cannot be applied to a new domain. It will produce better results for restricted domains. This approach will be able to detect named entities with spelling mistakes. There are some disadvantages of this approach (i) Cost for developing and maintaining rules and dictionaries is high. (ii) The performance is not too good on larger datasets. (iii) Since the rules have to be developed manually it will be more difficult to extend to other domains and adapting new entity classes.

2.2   Dictionary-Based Approach

Dictionary-based approach tries to find all Named entity in the text by looking up the dictionary. This approach solely depends on dictionary which contains list of protein or gene names, semantically classified words for comparison and identification. This approach nearly resolves the boundary detection problem because multi-word terms are already stored in the dictionary. It cannot detect any named entity with a spelling mistake. As medical terms are continuously increasing, it is hard to maintain a complete and up-to-date dictionary. It also detects homonymy word that does not represent an actual NE. Relying solely on dictionaries is often insufficient, as they tend to lack in coverage, and string-matching methods typically do not perform well with noisy data.

2.3   Machine Learning Approach

Machine learning approach uses different algorithms in identifying biomedical entities from the unstructured text. It is more popular than the above two approaches because it does not need to use dictionary nor will it need any manually framed rules. They are also more portable than both of them. There are many advantages using this approach. They are not domain dependent; therefore they do not require domain experts like rule-based techniques.

They do not require a high level of maintenance, as required by dictionary based techniques. They can also identify new named entities which are not included in dictionaries. ML techniques are less sensitive to spelling mistakes, and are capable of handling ambiguity in text. Machine learning approaches are based on statistical models to make predictions about named entities in a given text. These models have their own mathematical approaches and techniques for training the corpus, determining the probabilistic values and have their own methodologies of working to get the desired result. In this type of approach a corpus is initially studied and based on the corpus a training module is made where the system is trained to identify the named entities. Based on the occurrences of named entity in the corpus with particular context and class, a probability value is counted. Every time when text is processed the result is based on the probability value. Machine learning techniques can be supervised, semi-supervised or unsupervised (Fig. 1).

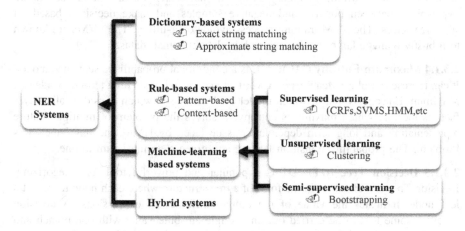

Fig. 1.   Types of approaches for NER systems

2.3.1   Supervised Learning Approach

Supervised techniques require annotated data during training phase. Annotated data are expensive because they require time for data preparation and annotation. Supervised methods learn a model by looking at annotated training example data. This method produces very good result and is most frequently used in Named Entity Recognition. Large amounts of annotated training data are required for these models to be effective, which makes this method costly. Some of the supervised machine learning techniques are Hidden Markov Model (HMM), Decision Trees (DT), Maximum Entropy Models (ME), Support Vector Machine (SVM) and Conditional Random Field (CRF).

2.3.1.1 Hidden Markov Model (HMM): HMM is a generative model which is very successful in classifying entity. The HMM introduces the concept of a hidden state which is not part of the input sequence. Hidden means the states are unobserved. When labelling, future observations are taken into account. The advantage of this model is that it is easy to understand. It assigns joint probability to observation state and labelling sequence. The main drawback of this approach is that it is not possible to represent multiple overlapping features and the model makes assumptions about the data.

2.3.1.2 Conditional Random Fields (CRF): CRF is also known as discriminative undirected probabilistic graphical model which is a high performance method for sequence labeling problem. CRFs calculate the conditional probability of values on assigned output nodes. CRF has been successfully used in many natural processing tasks such as sequence segmentation and labeling tasks. The conditional probability of output nodes can be calculated based on other designated input nodes. It deals with sequences problem, and utilizes many correlated features. It avoid label bias problem and is capable of handling arbitrary features.

2.3.1.3 Support Vector Machines (SVM): SVM is a popular machine learning approach. SVM is a kind of binary classifiers that search for an optimal separating hyper-plane between positive and negative samples and make decisions based on support vectors. The SVM training process avoids over-fitting. The SVMs are known to robustly manage large feature sets and a relatively small dataset.

2.3.1.4 Maximum Entropy (ME): ME is a conditional probabilistic sequence model. It can represent multiple features of a word and can also handle long term dependency. Maximum Entropy is that in which model for least biased which considers all known facts is the one which maximizes entropy. It solves the problem of multiple feature representation and long term dependency issue faced by HMM and has Label Bias Problem. The probability transition leaving any given state must sum to one.

2.3.1.5 Decision Tree (DT): DT is a popular and powerful tool for categorizing. Decision Tree is a classifier in the form of a tree structure where each node represent a leaf node, indicates the value of the output attributes of expressions. A decision specifies some text to be carried out on a single attribute value with one branch and sub-tree for each possible outcome of the text. It is an inductive approach to acquire knowledge on classification.

2.3.2 Semi-supervised Approach

In semi-supervised approach, a model is initially trained on small set of annotated data, then predictions are made on a separate set of unannotated data. Based on the predictions of previously developed models, the model is improved. With each iteration, more annotations are generated and stored until a certain threshold occurs then it will stop the iterations. Semi supervised learning algorithms use both labeled and unlabeled corpus to create their own predictions. The semi-supervised algorithm is used to overcome the problem of lack of annotated corpus and data sparsity. However, they still cannot able to produce similar results as from supervised techniques. Bootstrap is one of the semi supervised algorithm.

2.3.2.1 Bootstrap Approach: Bootstrapping algorithm is an iterative algorithm which is used in many applications, because it only requires a small amount of training samples. Initially small examples are given by the user. The system searches for these examples in the text and look for other examples with identical context of given examples. The learning process is then applied to the newly found examples to discover new relevant contexts. By repeating this process, a large number of entities are then identified in the biomedical text.

2.3.3 Unsupervised Approach

A major problem with supervised method is the requirement of specifying large number of features. For learning a good model, a robust set of features and large annotated corpus is needed. Since, annotated corpus is not available for every domain. Unsupervised algorithms are used in NER to deal with lack of annotated text in domains. Unsupervised techniques do not require annotated data. The main technique behind unsupervised learning is clustering. Entities belong to similar context grouped together and the system will learn this cluster. Whenever this method is used it will cluster the similar entities in a single cluster. This approach can be easily ported to different domains or languages. While machine learning techniques such as HMM, SVM and CRF have proven to be quite effective in recognizing named entities, their performance depends heavily on the quality and quantity of the selected features and the training set. Building a large training set requires considerable manual effort and any discrepancy in annotation may adversely affect the training and evaluation of these classifiers.

2.3.4 Hybrid NER

Hybrid approach uses the advantages of both the above mention techniques and come out as the strongest technique of all. Hybrid NER is popular and successful technique than the other techniques since it achieves more performance than the individual techniques. The idea behind hybrid NER is to integrate two or more of the above mentioned techniques. The idea behind hybrid NER is to integrate two or more of the above mentioned techniques. The combined techniques can be of the same or of different categories. Combining more than one machine learning technique is a popular and useful hybrid technique. Other hybrid techniques combine dictionary with rule based or rule based technique with machine learning techniques. These techniques are used to improve the performance of NER.

3   Related Works on Biomedical NER Systems

Leaman and Lu (2016) proposed a machine learning model for NER and normalization. This model consists of a semi-Markov structured linear classifier and supervised semantic indexing for normalization. TaggerOne is not specific to any entity type. It requires only annotated training data and a lexicon. Here, two corpus namely NCBI Disease corpus and BioCreative V Chemical Disease Relation task corpus were used. The NCBI Disease corpus is annotated with disease mentions, using concept identifiers from either MeSH or OMIM. Their system had an average throughput of 8.5 abstracts per second for disease. Also, false positives and negatives remained a significant source of error. It can handle multiple entity type but the gene names are frequently confused with both diseases and chemicals. TaggerOne achieved high performance on diseases whose f-score is 0.829 in NCBI Disease corpus and on chemicals whose f-score is 0.914 in BioCreative 5 CDR corpus. Munkhdalai et al. (2015) presented a semi-supervised learning method to exploits unlabeled data. They used the extended BANNER and obtained an F-Score of 87.04% on the Bio Creative II Gene Mention (BC2GM) dataset. This system includes extraction of features for word representation feature sets. For word representation features, Brown clustering models and Word Vector (WV) models were used. However, Word Vector Class used here sometimes degraded the system performance by adding some level of complexity to this model.

Tang et al. (2015) developed a machine learning-based system based on conditional random fields (CRFs) and structured support vector machines (SSVM) for chemical entity recognition in biomedical domain. This system uses rule-based module for sentence boundary detection and tokenization, and then machine learning classification algorithm, conditional random fields (CRF) and structured support vector machines (SSVM) for NER. Three types of word representations (WR) features Brown clustering-based, random indexing-based and skip-gram-based WR are used in this system. Obtained an F-Score of 85.20% on the PubMed abstracts dataset. The SSVM-based CEM systems outperformed the CRF-based CEM systems when using the same features. The performance on chemical entities was lower and is more challenging and requires additional improvement. Li et al. (2015) proposed an approach for Protein-Named Entity Recognition and Protein-Protein Interaction Extraction. The developed protein-protein interaction extraction system uses Support Vector Machine (SVM) and parse tree. The proposed PPI extraction system consists of three parts, the natural language processing (NLP), protein-named entity recognition, and protein interaction discovery. Three datasets extracted from the GENIA for Protein-NER evaluation and five corpora were used as experimental dataset provided by AIMed, BioInfer, HpDR50, IEPA, and LLL were used for PPI Extraction evaluation. This system obtained F-score of 90.97%. Here dictionary-based and machine learning based method are used to construct the protein name recognition model. The performance will be improved if the discovered patterns and features are merged.

Li et al. (2015) presented an Extended Recurrent Neural Networks to recognize biomedical entities. The Elman-type RNN model is extended by adding recurrent connections at the output layer captures probability information. Distributed representations of words are trained by Word2Vec tool is utilized for word embeddings.

They used BioCreative II GM corpus of 15,000 training sentences and 5,000 testing sentences. This system achieves f-measure of 81.87%. Recurrent Neural Network (RNN) which considers the predicted information from the prior node and external context information. Extracting complex hand-designed features is skipped and replaced with word embeddings. This extended RNN models performs better than CRF model, original RNN model and deep neural networks. Keretna et al. (2015) proposed new graph-based technique for representing unstructured medical text. This system uses the i2b2 medication challenge data set. The treatment entities are extracted from unstructured text. New representation is used to extract features that are able to enhance the NER performance. Six different classifiers, CRF, KNN, Naive Bayes, Random Tree, Random Forest, and C4.5 were used. Enhanced results have been achieved from five out of six classifiers, with CRF showing the same performance. The F-measure results improvement of up to 26% in performance. In the graph, each word represents a unique node with connections to all other words that directly precede or follow the designated word in the text. New features are then extracted from the constructed graph, and are used in the classification process.

Lim et al. (2014) proposed a technique to extract drug named entities from unstructured medical text using a hybrid model of dictionary-based and rule-based techniques. A dictionary is first used to detect drug named entities, rules are then applied to extract undetected drug names. The designed rules use part of speech tags and morphological features for drug name detection. The dataset utilized is i2b2 2009 medication challenge, and achieved an f-score of 66.97%. The dataset consisted of 1243 discharge summary reports in which 268 manually annotated reports were used for training the hybrid model, while the remaining reports were used for testing. This technique improved the recall rate but it also increased the false positive rates, which lead to lower precision. This is because some NEs extracted from the postfix or prefix rules are actually not drug names, but some words with same stem as the one being checked. The WordNet lexical database is used for Part of Speech (POS) tagging through the JAWS Java API library. The f-score achieved was 66.97%. Some of the features that can be used in the designed rules are not valid because of using unstructured and informal text as the input. Informal text used in the dataset poses challenges for the designed rules.

Keretna et al. (2014) presented an approach combining the CRF and ME classifiers using ensemble voting method to recognize named entities. Input features in each data set need to be extended to provide more coverage, in order to increase the detection accuracy rates. This system achieved F-Score of 81.8% which is much better than individual classifiers with i2b2 2010 medication challenge dataset. Verma et al. (2013) presented a system based on an ensemble approach, where Decision Tree C4.5 and Memory-based Learner are used and the outputs of these two methods are combined together using a weighted voting approach. The overall F-measure value achieved with threshold 0.2 is 73.71%. This system proposed an active learning technique to select the informative samples from the unlabeled data and which will be helpful for many applications where there is a scarcity in the amount of available labeled data. Huang et al. (2013) presented a new method of utilizing biomedical knowledge by both exact matching of disease using disease dictionary and adding semantic concept feature through UMLS semantic type. This system shows improvement in the performance of entity recognition. This system obtained F-score of 56.67 on the Biotext corpus, which contained 3655 annotated sentence. Campos et al. (2013) provided models for recognition of biomedical entities from scientific text. Gimli achieved an F-measure of 87.17% on GENETAG and 72.23% on JNLPBA corpus, significantly out performing existing open-source solutions. They used many tools like MALLET for implementation of Conditional Random Field, GDep is used for tokenization and for linguistic processing, Bio Thesaurus and Bio Lexicon used as the lexical resource for identifying the biomedical domain terms used in the text. It presented a significant improvement of F-measure in comparison with GENIA Tagger.

Rocktaschel et al. (2012) presented ChemSpot, an NER tool for identifying chemicals in texts, including drugs, abbreviations, molecular formulas. ChemSpot uses a hybrid approach combining a Conditional Random Field with a dictionary. ChemSpot achieved a precision of 67.3%, a recall of 68.9% and an F1 measure of 68.1% on the SCAI corpus. ChemIDplus dictionary has been used to extract drugs, abbreviations, trivial names, molecular formulas. ChemSpot missed some entity present in the text due to the absence of these entity names in the dictionary or that they were not recognized by the CRF (72%). Munkhdalai et al. (2012a, 2012b) proposed an Active Co-Training (ACT) algorithm for biomedical named-entity recognition. ACT is a semi-supervised learning method in which two classifiers based on two different feature sets iteratively learn from informative samples that have been queried from the unlabeled data. This method efficiently exploits a large amount of unlabeled data by selecting a small number of samples. However, a parameter-tuning step is still needed in active co-training. This system obtained F-score of 89.28% on GENIA v3.02 corpus. Zhu et al. (2012) used a hybrid method by combining SVM and CRF for recognizing biomedical entity. SVM is used to separate terms from non-biological terms and CRF is used to determine the types of biological terms. Here both the algorithms are completely utilized in which SVM as a binary-class classifier and the data-labeling capacity of CRF. GENIA corpus and JNLPBA 04 data are used as dataset and achieved F1-measure 91.67% with the GENIA corpus and 84.04% with the JNLPBA 04 data. Although this method has high F1-score when the number of feature dimensions is much higher than the size of training set, over-fitting is very likely to happen. SVM had higher precision but it tended to miss terms and unstable when trained with a small-sized data set.

Munkhdalai et al. (2012a, 2012b) modified the original Co-training algorithm which extracts the Bio-NER feature from a number of unlabeled data. This system obtained an F-Score of 83.6% on the GENIA v3.02 corpus and achieved significant learning from unlabeled data. The number of samples to be picked is too small, so the improvement of classifier F-score is also small. When large number of samples to be used it will degrades the improvement in system. Liao et al. (2012) presented a skip-chain conditional random fields (CRFs) model. Their system obtained an F-score of 73.2%, on the GENIA version 3.02. The training dataset consisted of 2000 MEDLINE abstracts of the GENIA corpus with named entities in IOB2 format. The testing dataset consists of 404 abstracts. This system used GRMM Java package. Performance is high in this system but needs improvement in the accuracy of named entities boundaries.

Zhenfei et al. (2011) presented a SVM based approach to recognize the names of genes, proteins, cell types and cell lines. Support vector machine (SVM) is an effective and efficient tool to analyze data, recognize patterns and biomedical named entities. Their system obtained a Precision of 84.24% and Recall 80.76% on the 1999 text format files from GENIA corpus. Yang and Zhou (2010) presented a two phase semi-CRF based approach to recognize Bio-NEs. The training data of the shared task is GENIA corpus v3.02, which consisted of 2000 abstracts. Their system obtained an F-Score of 73.20% on the JNLPBA 2004 dataset. Deep domain knowledge is not needed and the computational cost is high for two phase semi- CRF. Cai and Cheng (2009) presented a Co-training style learning algorithm for Bio-NER. This algorithm used three different classifiers (CRF, SVM and MEMM) to exploit unlabeled data. The tri-training learning approach can more effectively and stably exploit unlabeled data. In each iterations, a new sample is selected by considering the agreements of the three classifiers. The labeled data is from GENIA 3.02 corpus, which contains 2,000 abstracts, annotated with semantic information. 800 abstracts were used as the original labeled set, and the remaining 1200 abstracts were used as testing set and 487,458 abstracts of unlabeled data downloaded from MEDLINE. More noises due to misclassifications generated during the Tri-training process. The major issue to be concerned in the tri-learning method is to effectively identify the wrongly labeled samples and filter noise.

Gong et al. (2009) presented a hybrid approach to recognize biomedical entity. This system uses POS (Part-of-Speech) tagging, rules-based and dictionary-based approach using biomedical ontology for identifying entity names like disease, gene in biomedical texts. This method utilizes natural language processing tools for POS tagging and heuristics rules for finding noun phrase, and applies dictionary based biomedical ontology to find entity's concepts. GENIA 3.02 corpus is used and this system obtains the F-score 71.5%. Rules based approach needs experts to write rules to classify entity. Wang et al. (2008) used conditional Random Field as underlying classifier model and the relativity between classifiers is exploited by using co-decision matrix to exchange decision information among classifiers. The experiments are carried on GENIA corpus with the result of 77.88% F-sore. The multi-agent classifier fusion strategy proposed here is superior to the individual classifier based method and more effective than the classifiers fusion approach of boosting and bagging. There is much room to improve the BNER performances and accuracy. GENIA Version 3.02 corpus is used as dataset. GENIA corpus is divided into three parts, 1520 abstracts were used as bootstrap samples into multiple training subsets, and 400 abstracts were used as fusion training corpus, and the remaining 80 abstracts were used as fusion testing corpus (Table 1).

Gu et al. (2007) proposed an approach for recognizing named entities in biological text in the absence of any human annotated corpus. The idea is to use a dictionary lookup to label the training sentences. The positive words are labelled by the dictionary and the negative words from unlabeled text are identified by an SVM-based self-training algorithm. This method does not give the performance up to the level achieved by traditional supervised learning. BioNLP-2004 Shared Task is used as dataset. Even after using the 100% dictionary to selecting the most reliable predictions to label the corpus, the performance of the system is still about 0.1 f-score less than the other method's performance. This system achieves the F-measure 46.15%. Wang et al. (2006) presented a classifiers ensemble approach for Bio-NER. Generalized Winnow, Conditional Random Fields, Support Vector Machine, and Maximum Entropy are combined through three different methods. JNLPBA 2004 dataset was used and the system achieved an

Table 1. Summary of the related works on Bio-NER

Author	Method	Dataset	F-Measure	Pros	Cons
Leaman et al. (2016)	Semi-Markov, Supervised semantic indexing	NCBI Disease, BioCreative V	0.829 in NCBI 0.914 in BioCreative 5	Improves performance	False positives and negatives remain a significant source of error
Munkhdalai et al. (2015)	Semi-supervised learning	Bio Creative II Gene Mention (BC2GM)	87.04%	Efficiently exploits unlabeled data	Word Vector Class degraded system performance
Tang et al. (2015)	CRF, SSVM	PubMed abstracts	85.20%	Outperformed the CRF-based systems	More patterns and features need to be identified
Li et al. (2015)	SVM and parse tree.	GENIA, AIMed, BioInfer, HpDR50, IEPA, LLL	90.97%	Protein-Protein Interaction Extraction	Target entity name and trigger words
Li et al. (2015)	Recurrent Neural Network	BioCreative II GM	81.87%	Extract complex hand-designed features	Time complexity
Keretna et al. (2015)	CRF, KNN, Naïve Bayes, Random Tree, Random Forest, and C4.5	i2b2 medication challenge	Improvement up to 26% in performance	Achieved highest accuracy	More features needs to be extracted from the graph
Lim et al. (2014)	Dictionary-based and Rule-based techniques	i2b2 2009	66.97%	Improvement of recall rate	Some of the features used are not valid
Keretna et al. (2014)	Ensemble voting, CRF	i2b2 2010	81.8%	Achieves an f-score better than individual classifiers	Input features need to be extended to provide more coverage
Verma et al. (2013)	Decision Tree C4.5 and Memory-based Learner	GENIA version 3.02	73.71%	Selection of informative samples from the unlabeled data	More features are needed
Huang and Hu (2013)	String Matching and Semantic concept feature	Biotext	56.67%	Disease NER is High	Overall accuracy is poor
Campos and Matos (2013)	CRF	GENETAG JNLPBA corpus	87.17%	Improvement of F-measure	Lexicons need to improve for better precision
Rocktaschel et al. (2012)	CRF	SCAI corpus	68.1%	Outperforming available chemical NER tool	Missed some entity present in the text
Munkhdalai et al. (2012a, 2012b)	Active Co-training	GENIA v3.02	89.28%	Exploits a large amount of unlabeled data	Parameter-tuning step is still needed

(continued)

Table 1. (*continued*)

Author	Method	Dataset	F-Measure	Pros	Cons
Zhu and Shen (2012)	SVM and CRF	GENIA corpus and JNLPBA 04	91.67%	Improved performance	Overfitting occurs
Munkhdalai et al. (2012a, 2012b)	Co-training algorithm	GENIA v3.02	83.6%	Learn from unlabeled data	Small examples gives small improvement
Liao and Wu (2012)	CRF	GENIA 3.02	73.2%	Good Performance	Need improvement in setting NE boundaries
Zhenfei et al. (2011)	SVM	GENIA	82.46%	Efficient way to detect entities	Size of the data is too small
Yang and Zhou (2010)	Semi-CRF	JNLPBA 2004, GENIA	73.20%	Deep domain knowledge not needed	Computational cost is high
Cai and Cheng (2009)	Tri-Learning Approach	GENIA 3.02	Significant Improvement	Effective and stable for unlabeled data	More noises due to misclassification
Gong et al. (2009)	Rules and Dictionary based approach	GENIA 3.02	71.5%	Can find untagged entity	Need experts to write rules
Wang et al. (2008)	CRF (co-decision matrix)	GENIA 3.02	77.88%	Effective than Boosting and Bagging	Need improvement in performance and accuracy
Gu et al. (2007)	SVM-based self-training	BioNLP-2004	46.15%	Annotated corpus is not needed	Performance is very low
Wang et al. (2006)	CRF, SVM and ME	JNLPBA 2004	77.57%	Improves recognition accuracy	Need improvement in efficiency

F-score of 77.57%. Classifiers ensemble can improve the classification performance of individual classifiers. Here, three distinct strategies are tested to combine multiple predictions from separate base classifiers and the strategies are arbitration rules, stacked generalization including class-stacking and class-attribute-stacking, cascade generalization. However class-attribute stacking method of classifiers ensemble strategy outperformed the other strategies in this approach.

4 Biomedical Named Entity Recognition and Classification

A typical Named Entity Recognition and Classification system consist of the following process. In which, the input documents are the collection of texts related with the target domain.

4.1 Pre-processing

In this step, the unstructured input document is processed so they can be used for entity recognition. To remove noisy data, reduce the size of data and to identify the root word of actual word in text.

4.1.1 Abbreviation Resolution

Many biomedical terms consists of abbreviation, it may not be recognized as entity if it not expanded properly. So the abbreviation resolution is done before identification of entity to avoid true negative values.

4.1.2 Tokenization

Tokenization is a process of breaking the sentence of unstructured text into tokens of word. It is done to explore the word in the sentence. Tokenization is an important task for Named Entity Recognition. Many tools are available for tokenization such tools are GENIA Tagger, JTBD.

4.1.3 Lemmatization

Lemmatization is similar to stemming but it removes the suffix of word and return the word in dictionary form. Lemmatization is a process in which full morphological analysis is done to accurately identify the lemma for each word.

4.1.4 POS Tagging

Part of Speech (POS) Tagging is the process of classifying words present in the text into their parts of speech and labeling them according to their parts of speech. Tokens are grouped into a class with same syntactic behavior. Examples: Nouns, Verbs, Adjectives, Adverbs, Determiners.

4.1.5 Normalization

Normalization is used to reduce the string variation of similar words. In this process, the special characters are removed and uppercase is changed to lowercase. Normalization is used in preprocessing because it makes the training faster (Fig. 2).

4.2 Entity Recognition

In the entity recognition module the following steps are followed.

4.2.1 N-gram Matching

In N-gram matching combinations of tokens are considered as a single token. N-gram is used to recognize the multiword and to detect the boundary of the entity. The number of tokens is configurable and based on the consideration of average length of entity names and the speed of entity extraction (Table 2).

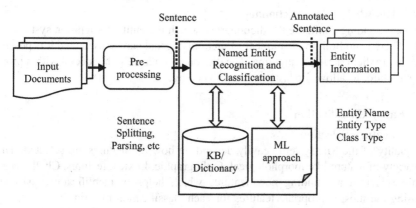

Fig. 2. Work flow of named entity recognition and classification

Table 2. Features used in typical NER systems

Features categories	Description	Examples
Linguistic	This feature finds the root term, assign each token to a grammatical category	Chucking, lemmatization, stemming and Part-of-speech (POS) tagging
Orthographic	This feature is used to capture the knowledge about word formation	Capitalization, Counting, symbols, punctuation, and word length
Morphological	This feature is used to identify the common structures or sub-sequences of characters, thus finding similarities between distinct tokens	Prefix, suffix, singular version, stem, char n-grams and word shape patterns
Lexicons	Dictionary terms are used to match the entity and the resulting tags are used as features	Target entity name and trigger words
Context	Context features are used to establish relationship between the tokens	Conjunctions

4.2.2 Candidate Entity Filtering
This step is to filter the candidate entities which are mentioned in the unstructured documents. To filter candidate entities POS filtering and stop word removal are used. During POS filtering, the tokens like determiner, adverbs are removed.

4.2.3 Semantic Tagging
Semantic tagging is a process of recognizing all entity types present in the biomedical documents and automatically tag the entities with ontology.

4.2.4   Knowledge Base/Dictionary

Dictionary loading configure the dictionaries, which the entity-recognition system then loads. There is no limit to the number of dictionaries that can be used, and it is possible to add more dictionaries at any time. The dictionary data are to be loaded with a proper data structure, to allow for faster n-gram matching.

4.3   Entity Classification

4.3.1   Feature Selection

The quality of the ML system heavily depend on how the features are selected. They are variety of feature like morphological, Orthographic, Lexical features. Challenges in feature selection are finding new features which helps in identification tasks and choosing the most appropriate features for each classification method.

4.3.1.1 Orthographic Features: Many biomedical entities contain numbers, upper case characters. The purpose of Orthographic features is to capture capitalization, digitalization spelling, hyphenation, capitalization, word breaks, emphasis, and punctuation and other word formation information. These features helps in performance enhancement of NER system.

4.3.1.2 Morphological Features: Morphological Features such as words, prefix, and suffix of the word are used in identifying named identities. Prefixes and suffixes can give us good clues for classifying Named entities. It has been widely used in the biomedical domain.

4.3.1.3 Linguistic Features: Linguistic features like the Part of Speech tags considered as important feature for identifying entity boundaries of multi word biomedical named entities. Part of speech features can help in improving performance of the system.

4.3.1.4 Lexicon Features: Lexicon feature uses dictionary terms to match the entity present in the biomedical text. Domain knowledge from dictionary is added to the set of features for optimizing the NER system.

4.3.1.5 Context Features: Context features are used to establish relationship between the words present in the biomedical text.

4.3.2   Classification Algorithm

In entity classification, the entities are classified into specified class like gene, disease. For classification machine learning algorithms like Hidden Markov Model (HMM), Decision Trees, Maximum Entropy Models (ME), Support Vector Machine (SVM) and Conditional Random Field (CRF) are used to classify the entities in the biomedical documents.

5   Corpora for Bio-NER

A corpus is a set of text documents that usually contain annotations of one or various entity types. Such annotations are used to train ML models, inferring characteristics and patterns of the annotated entity names. Thus, the trained model is highly dependent on the quality of the annotations present on those corpora. There are two types of annotated corpora, varying with the source of the annotations, Gold Standard Corpora (GSC): annotations are performed manually by expert annotators, following specific and detailed guidelines and Silver Standard Corpora (SSC): annotations are automatically generated by computerized systems. Table 3 presents a list of relevant GSC available for the various biomedical entity types. As we can see, most of the research efforts have been on the recognition of gene and protein names, with various corpora containing several thousands of annotated sentences.

Such effort is a consequence of two different factors: the importance of genes and proteins on the biomedical domain, and the high variability and no standardization of names. As we can see on Table 3, only small sets of documents have been annotated, due to the complexity of generating GSC. The CALBC [24] (Collaborative Annotation of a Large Bio-medical Corpus) project aimed to minimize this problem, providing a large-scale biomedical SSC automatically annotated through the harmonization of several NER systems. This large corpus contains one million abstracts with annotations of several biological semantic groups, such as diseases, species, chemicals and genes/proteins.

Table 3. Some resources for Bio-NER systems

Corpus	Entity	Type Size (Sentences)
PennBioIE	Gene and Protein	18,148 annotations, 1,414 abstracts
JNLPBA	Gene, Protein, DNA, RNA	6,142 annotations, 401 abstracts
FSUPRGE	Gene and Protein	59,483 annotations, 3,236 abstracts
BioCreative II Gene Mention Test	Gene and Protein	5,144 annotations, 4,171 sentences
GENIA	Gene and Protein	100,000 annotations, 2000 abstracts
GENETAG	Gene and Protein	2000 sentences
SCAI-Test	Disease	1,206 annotations, 100 abstracts
Arizona Disease (AZDC)	Disease	3,206 annotations, 2,775 sentences
NCBI Disease corpus	Disease	793 abstracts, 6651 sentences
DDI corpus	Drug	792 texts, 232 abstracts
NaCTeM Metabolite and Enzyme corpus	Metabolite, Enzyme	296 abstracts
AnEM corpus	Anatomical concepts	500 documents

6 Evaluation

It is important to evaluate the performance of the system. Evaluation is done to analyze the behavior of the system in terms of measuring the accuracy of the generated annotations. Three performance evaluation metrics are used in almost all of the NER systems. They are Precision, Recall, F-measure. Those measures assume values between 0 (worst) and 1 (best). This can be performed by annotating a corpus and then compare the automatic annotations with the ones provided by expert curators. Thus, each automatic annotation must be classified as being a True Positive (TP): the system provides an annotation that exists in the curated corpus; True Negative (TN): the non-existence of an annotation is correct according to the curated corpus; False Positive (FP): the system provides an annotation that does not exist in the curated corpus; False Negative (FN): the system does not provide an annotation that is present in the curated corpus. Exact and approximate matching can be used to obtain performance results and to better understand the behavior of the system. With approximate matching we can find the performance when minor and non-informative mistakes are discarded. Such evaluation is important since various post-NER tasks, such as relation extraction and topic modeling, can be performed with imprecise annotations.

Precision measures the ability of a system to present only relevant names, and it is formulated as:

$$Precision = \frac{relevant\,names\,recognized}{total\,names\,recognized} = \frac{TP}{TP+FP}$$

On the other hand, recall measures the ability of a system to present all relevant names, and is formulated as:

$$Recall = \frac{relevant\,names\,recognized}{relevant\,names\,on\,corpus} = \frac{TP}{TP+FN}$$

Finally, F-measure is the harmonic mean of precision and recall. The balanced F-measure is most commonly used, and is formulated as:

$$F - measure = 2\frac{Precision \times Recall}{Precision + Recall}$$

7 NER Tools

Since dozens of tools are available for the recognition of a specific entity type (e.g. gene and protein), we decided to study the systems that better reflect the overall progress of the domain. On the other hand, some entity types do not have any relevant ML based systems. Many tools are available for biomedical Named Entity Recognition. Some tools are openly available. Table 4 presents Named Entity Recognition tools available over biomedical domain. Recognition and classification of named entities in

Table 4. Tools available for Bio-NER

NER tools	Tool link
Stanford CoreNLP	http://nlp.stanford.edu/software/CRF-NER.shtml
GATE	https://gate.ac.uk/
BioCreAtIvE Meta-server	http://www.biocreative.org/resources/metaserver/
HPE Haven OnDemand Entity Extraction API	https://dev.havenondemand.com/apis/extractentities
Wikifier	http://wikifier.org/
Textpresso	http://www.textpresso.org/
LingPipe	https://lingpipe-blog.com/
Mallet	http://mallet.cs.umass.edu/
NERD	http://nerd.eurecom.fr/
OpenCalais	http://www.opencalais.com/
Reflect	http://reflect.ws/
Sanchay	http://sanchay.co.in/
Yamcha	http://chasen.org/ ~ taku/software/yamcha/
ABNER	http://pages.cs.wisc.edu/ ~ bsettles/abner/

the biomedical domain is a much more complicated task than the other domains. Machine learning techniques are quite effective biomedical NER systems but their performance heavily depends on the quality and quantity of the selected features and the training set. Building a large training set requires manual effort and takes more time. Each approaches needs different requirements and some have many advantages over others.

Dictionary-based systems are more suitable when the entity names are correctly written in the documents. Rule-based NER approaches are not portable and it needs rule for every entity type. The ML approaches deals with spelling variation in the text and is cheaper than the other systems. Using a hybrid NER approach enables us to take advantage of two or more approaches. Performance of the hybrid system is high.

8 Conclusion

Many approaches from dictionary to hybrid are used to detect the biomedical entity in the biomedical literature. Each type of approaches has some advantages over others. Dictionary based approach needs up to date dictionaries to detect the new terms used in text and is time consuming. Rule based approach need experts to write rules to recognize the entity. These two techniques will not be very much useful in identifying new entity and are not portable. Machine learning approaches are popular in biomedical entity recognition as they perform much better. The supervised machine learning based approaches have made biomedical NER systems practical by far outperforming the rule or dictionary based methods but creating large training sets for them remains a problem. The semi supervised algorithm can be used to avoid training of annotated data required for supervised learning.

References

Leaman, R., Lu, Z.: TaggerOne: joint named entity recognition and normalization with semi-markov models. Bioinform. Adv. Access **32**, 2839–2846 (2016)

Munkhdalai, T., Li, M., Batsuren, K., Park, H.A., Choi, N.H., Ryu, K.H.: Incorporating domain knowledge in chemical and biomedical named entity recognition with word representations. J. Cheminformatics 7(Suppl. 1), S8 (2015)

Tang, B., Feng, Y., Wang, X., Wu, Y., Zhang, Y., Jiang, M., Wang, J., Xu, H.: A comparison of conditional random fields and structured support vector machines for chemical entity recognition in biomedical literature. J. Cheminformatics 7(Suppl. 1), S9 (2015)

Li, M., Munkhdalai, T., Yu, X., Ryu, K.H.: A novel approach for protein-named entity recognition and protein-protein interaction extraction. Math. Probl. Eng. **2015**, 10 (2015). Article ID 942435

Li, L., Jin, L., Jiang, Z., Song, D., Huang, D.: Biomedical named entity recognition based on extended recurrent neural networks. In: IEEE International Conference on Bioinformatics and Biomedicine (2015)

Keretna, S., Lim, C.P., Creighton, D.: Enhancement of medical named entity recognition using graph-based features. In: IEEE International Conference on Systems, Man, and Cybernetics (2015)

Keretna, S., Lim, C.P., Creighton, D.: A hybrid model for named entity recognition using unstructured medical text. IEEE (2014)

Khaled, S.K., Shaban, B.: Classification ensemble to improve medical named entity recognition. In: IEEE International Conference on Systems, Man, and Cybernetics, 5–8 October 2014

Verma, M., Sikdar, U., Saha, S., Ekbal, A.: Ensemble based active annotation for biomedical named entity recognition. IEEE (2013)

Huang, Z., Hu, X.: Disease named entity recognition by machine learning using semantic type of metathesaurus. Int. J. Mach. Learn. Comput. **3**(6), 494 (2013)

Campos, D., Matos, S.: JoseLu is Oliveira: Gimli: open source and high-performance bio medical name recognition. BMC BioInform. **14**, 54 (2013)

Rocktaschel, T., Weidlich, M., Leser, U.: ChemSpot: a hybrid system for chemical named entity recognition. Bioinformatics **28**(12), 1633–1640 (2012)

Munkhdalai, T., Li, M., Yun, U., Namsrai, O.-E., Ryu, K.H.: An active co-training algorithm for biomedical named-entity recognition. J. Inf. Process. Syst. **8**(4), 575–588 (2012a)

Zhu, F., Shen, B.: Combined SVM-CRFs for biological named entity recognition with maximal bidirectional squeezing. PLoS ONE **7**(6), e39230 (2012)

Munkhdalai, T., Li, M., Kim, T., Namsrai, O.-E., Jeong, S.-P., Shin, J., Ryu, K.H.: Bio named entity recognition based on co-training algorithm. In: 26th International Conference on Advanced Information Networking and Applications Workshops (2012b)

Liao, Z., Wu, H.G.: Biomedical named entity recognition based on skip-chain Crfs. In: International Conference on Industrial Control and Electronics Engineering. IEEE (2012)

Ju, Z., Wang, J., Zhu, F.: Named entity recognition from biomedical text using SVM. IEEE (2011)

Yang, L., Zhou, Y.: Two-phase biomedical named entity recognition based on Semi-CRFs. IEEE (2010)

Cai, Y.H., Cheng, X.Y.: Biomedical Named Entity Recognition with Tri-training learning. IEEE (2009)

Gong, L.-J., Yuan, Y., Wei, Y.-B., Sun, X.: A hybrid approach for biomedical entity name recognition. IEEE (2009)

Wang, H., Zhao, T., Li, J.: Multi-agent classifiers fusion strategy for biomedical named entity recognition. In: International Conference on BioMedical Engineering and Informatics (2008)

Gu, B., Dahl, V., Popowich, F.: Recognizing biomedical named entities in the absence of human annotated corpora. IEEE (2007)

Wang, H., Zhao, T., Tan, H., Zhang, S.: Biomedical named entity recognition based on classifiers ensemble. Int. J. Comput. Sci. Appl. 5(2), 1–11 (2006)

Rebholz-Schuhmann, D., Yepes, A.J., Van Mulligen, E.M., Kang, N., Kors, J., Mil-ward, D., Corbett, P., Buyko, E., Beisswanger, E., Hahn, U.: CALBC silver standard corpus. J. Bioinform. Comput. Biol. 8, 163–179 (2010)

Data Augmentation Techniques for Classifying Vertebral Bodies from MR Images

Jiyo S. Athertya and G. Saravana Kumar[✉]

Department of Engineering Design, Indian Institute of Technology Madras, Chennai, India
ed12d014@smail.iitm.ac.in, gsaravana@iitm.ac.in

Abstract. The article describes the effect of data augmentation on classification systems that are used to differentiate abnormalities in medical images. The imbalance in data leads to bias in classifying the various states. Medical images, in general, are deficit of data and thus augmentation will provide an enriched dataset for the learning systems to identify and differentiate between deformities. We have explored additional data generation by applying affine transformations and the instance based transformation that could result in improving the classification accuracy. We perform experiments on the segmented dataset of vertebral bodies from MR images, by augmenting and classified the same, using Naive Bayes, Radial Basis Function and Random Forest methods. The performance of classifiers was evaluated using the True Positive Rate (TPR) obtained at various thresholds from the ROC curve and the area under ROC curve. For the said application, Random Forest method is found to provide a stable TPR with the augmented dataset compared to the raw dataset.

Keywords: Data augmentation · MR imaging · Feature extraction · GLCM
Vertebral body

1 Introduction

Data augmentation is the process of developing and generating data by means of transforming the training data aimed at improving the accuracy and robustness of classification systems. By data augmentation in the context of image classification, one refers to perturbing an image by transformations (both rigid and non-rigid) that would leave the underlying class unaltered in terms of information. In other words, these are label-preserving operations. This method is popularly used for generating additional samples of a class.

Medical datasets, owing to their difficulty in availability, are often rendered imbalanced. A dataset is potentially identified as imbalanced if the classification categories are not approximately represented at part or equally. It is a common phenomenon where the abnormal or degenerative classes are fewer in number in contrast to the normal dataset. Hence, it becomes a potential threat for the classifier to identify or misclassify an abnormality as a normal case. This would lead to a delay in diagnosis that can become life threatening for a patient. In order to reduce bias [1] and to enhance the performance of classification systems, researches on data augmentation is proposed. For a deep

© Springer Nature Singapore Pte Ltd. 2018
Shriram R and M. Sharma (Eds.): DaSAA 2017, CCIS 804, pp. 38–45, 2018.
https://doi.org/10.1007/978-981-10-8603-8_4

learning network that demands larger dataset, augmentation techniques come handy [2]. For extracting anatomical organs from CT images, [3] propose a method using deep learning. They augment the data using random affine transformations and non-rigid transformations and have reported an increase in classification accuracy. In yet another application [4], data augmentation of random crop and horizontal flip increased validation accuracy by 10%.

Inappropriate choices of data augmentation schemes are likely to result in augmented samples that are not informative enough, which leads to no effect or detrimental effect on the accuracy and robustness of classifiers. The choice of the data augmentation strategy is therefore quite important to reach good accuracy and robustness properties. The current work explores the affine transformations (rotation, translation and scaling) as well as instance based augmentation, Synthetic minority over-sampling technique (SMOTE) [5] in classifying vertebral degeneracy from MR images.

2   Methodology

2.1   Data Set Description

The MR T1 images were collected from Apollo specialty hospitals, Chennai from 25 patients. From the T1 sagittal slices, 100 vertebral bodies were selected of which 94 were classified as normal and 6 were detected as degenerate cases by the physician. Figure 1 shows few of the cases that contains degenerate vertebra in the lumbar region. The T1 images are obtained from sagittal plane which provides maximum information in terms of degenerations and deformations.

 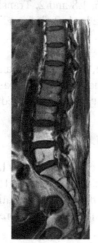 

Fig. 1.   Spine sagittal slices of T1 weighted MR images with degenerations

2.2 Segmentation

Vertebral body (VB) is prominently seen in T1 weighted images compared to T2 and other modes of MR acquisition. The segmentation approach involves fuzzy clustering and certain morphological processes which are obtained from our previous work [6]. Each VB is extracted separately as shown in Fig. 2 and features are extracted from the independent VB's.

Fig. 2. Palette of segmented VB's

2.3 Data Augmentation

i. *Rigid transformation - Rotation, Scaling, Translation*

The imbalanced dataset is augmented using 3 separate transformations and a combination as well to achieve affine transform. In the rotation based transformation, the entire dataset was rotated by angles 20, 40, 60, 80 and 100° and augmented. Then, the dataset was scaled by factor of 1.2, 1.4, 1.6, 1.8 and 2. Translation was carried out in both X and Y directions with a pixel change by 1, 2, 3, 4, and 5 pixels.

ii. *Smote*

Using the SMOTE [5] technique, the class imbalance problem is addressed. This is an instance based augmentation rather than feature based. The number of samples that are identified as belonging to minority class is sampled and doubled the previous count.

2.4 Feature Extraction Using GLCM

Since the dataset is obtained from a cancer speciality hospital, the abnormalities are an effect of radiations and subsequent degenerations. Hence, gray level co-occurrence matrix (GLCM) that characterize the texture variations, are employed. GLCM as described in [7] is employed for computing the features.

2.5 Classification

The classification task is performed and analyzed using 3 different classifiers namely Naive Bayes [8], Radial Basis Function [9] and Random Forest [10]. These are the most commonly used classifiers for differentiating the abnormalities from normal structures in images from literature [11, 12].

3   Results and Discussion

3.1   Evaluation Metrics

The augmentation effect is best reflected in terms of receiver operating characteristics curve (ROC) and the area under the same. These curves are cost-sensitive measures to evaluate classifier performance. The robustness to various threshold of separation between the classes is estimated from the ROC. Higher the area under the curve, more stable the classifier is, while providing the classification result. A 10 fold cross validation is used on all the dataset during classification. Apart from AUROC (area under ROC), the mean and standard deviation are also tabulated for estimating the spread of true positive rate (TPR). For each classifier, raw data, data augmented by SMOTE, translation, scaling, rotation and augmented with SMOTE were compared.

3.2   Bayes Classifier

Using the Naive Bayes classifier, an average ROC area of 0.9335 is obtained while classifying the degenerate vertebrae from the normal bodies. Figure 3 provides the box plot of TPR statistics for different combinations of augmentation performed on the dataset. A comparison with the raw data and instance-based sampling of data is provided to elicit the effects of data augmentation on the classifier. True positive rate is maintained as the feature to visualize the spread of data. From Table 1, it is seen that the mean TPR increases with the increase in number of samples using all affine transformation based augmentation. SMOTE augmentation reduces the TPR by 10% but the area under ROC is improved. Thus it could be inferred that the classifier tries to adapt and learn more eliminating the bias towards true positives with augmentation.

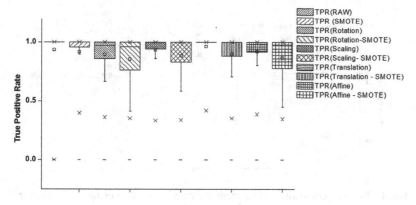

Fig. 3. Box plot comparison of augmented data with raw data using Bayes classifier

Table 1. Statistical analysis over ROC for Bayes classifier

Data	TPR mean	TPR standard deviation	AUROC
Raw	0.9135	0.163	0.945
SMOTE	0.8167	0.301	0.982
Rotation	0.9236	0.179	0.900
Rotation (SMOTE)	0.8201	0.293	0.916
Scaling	0.9435	0.161	0.945
Scaling (SMOTE)	0.8252	0.291	0.956
Translation	0.9551	0.152	0.962
Translation (SMOTE)	0.8289	0.290	0.972

3.3 RBF Classifier

The radial basis function provides relatively higher AUROC measure than Bayes classifier. However, the box plot in Fig. 4, which depicts the TPR statistics shows higher variation around mean value with SMOTE augmentation. The augmented data using translation and scaling gives better TPR than with raw data except in case of rotation. SMOTE augmentation reduces the TPR by 10% while marginally affecting the AUROC. Thus, it could be inferred that RBF classifies the data better than Bayes, though with data augmentation Bayes performs equally better (Table 2).

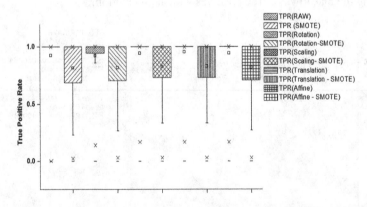

Fig. 4. Box plot comparison of augmented data with raw data using RBF classifier

Table 2. Statistical analysis over ROC for RBF classifier

Data	TPR mean	TPR standard deviation	AUROC
Raw	0.9257	0.209	0.957
SMOTE	0.8167	0.302	0.982
Rotation	0.9236	0.179	0.951
Rotation (SMOTE)	0.8201	0.293	0.984
Scaling	0.9435	0.161	0.973
Scaling (SMOTE)	0.8282	0.291	0.996
Translation	0.9551	0.152	0.985
Translation (SMOTE)	0.8289	0.290	0.997

3.4 Random Forest Classifier

Amongst the 3 classifiers, namely Bayes, RBF and Random Forest, the mean classification accuracy improves significantly due to SMOTE augmentation (as can be seen in Table 3) for Random Forest classifier. The area under the ROC curve also is better for Random Forest classifier as compared to other classifier. Performance of the classifier is poor in terms of TPR mean for the raw data while upon augmenting, the ROC is ~1 using SMOTE on the transformations. In the Fig. 5, it can be seen that the spread in TPR is more for this classifier as compared to other classifier with data augmentation involving only the geometric transformations. However, this is minimized when the instances are increased by SMOTE and thus stabilizing the performance. Since very high area under ROC is obtained for this classifier, it could be inferred to have a robust performance.

Table 3. Statistical analysis over ROC for Random Forest classifier

Data	TPR mean	TPR standard deviation	AUROC
Raw	0.6667	0.364	0.955
SMOTE	0.8106	0.273	0.996
Rotation	0.6310	0.315	0.981
Rotation (SMOTE)	0.883	0.201	0.998
Scaling	0.7156	0.319	0.996
Scaling(SMOTE)	0.9307	0.163	1.000
Translation	0.7368	0.285	0.995
Translation (SMOTE)	0.9386	0.150	1

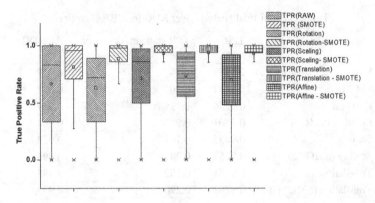

Fig. 5. Box plot comparison of augmented data with raw data using Random Forest classifier

4 Conclusion

Effect of data augmentation on different classifiers and their performance with respect to raw data is presented using a case study on classification of degenerate VB from MR images. Class preserving transformations addresses the critical issue of data imbalance. The main advantage in increasing the data count is to retaliate the bias on abnormal data over the dominating normal samples. This indirectly enhances the accuracy and robustness of classifiers and also boosts the confidence of the diagnosis. Amongst the classifiers studied, Random Forest performance was greatly improved by the data augmentation and provided best classification efficiency. As an extension to this approach, the authors intend to explore the classification method to other degenerations prevalent in MR of spine. Also future work would lie in exploring the classification using deep learning networks.

Acknowledgments. The first author would like to thank the Department of Science and Technology, India, for supporting the research through INSPIRE fellowship. The authors would like to thank Apollo Speciality Hospitals for providing images and Dr. G. Jayaraj, Senior Consultant, Dept of Radiology and Imaging Sciences, Apollo Speciality Hospitals, Chennai, for his valuable inputs.

References

1. McLaughlin, N., Del Rincon, J.M., Miller, P.: Data-augmentation for reducing dataset bias in person re-identification. In: 12th IEEE International Conference Advanced Video and Signal Based Surveillance, AVSS 2015, pp. 1–6 (2015)
2. Hauberg, S., Freifeld, O., Larsen, A.B.L., Fisher, J.W., Hansen, L.K.: Dreaming more data: class-dependent distributions over diffeomorphisms for learned data augmentation, vol. 41 (2015)

3. Roth, H.R., Lee, C.T., Shin, H.-C., Seff, A., Kim, L., Yao, J., Lu, L., Summers, R.M.: Anatomy-specific classification of medical images using deep convolutional nets. In: 2015 IEEE 12th International Symposium on Biomedical Imaging (ISBI), pp. 101–104 (2015)
4. Wang, K.K.: Image Classification with Pyramid Representation and Rotated Data Augmentation on Torch 7 (2015)
5. Chawla, N.V., Bowyer, K.W., Hall, L.O., Kegelmeyer, W.P.: SMOTE: Synthetic minority over-sampling technique. J. Artif. Intell. Res. **16**, 321–357 (2002)
6. Athertya, J.S., Kumar, G.S.: Segmentation and labelling of human spine mr images using fuzzy clustering. In: CS & IT-CSCP 2016, pp. 99–108 (2016)
7. Ghosh, S., Raja' S, A., Chaudhary, V.: Computer aided diagnosis for lumbar MRI using heterogenous classifiers. In: ISBI, pp. 1179–1182 (2011)
8. Unal, Y., Polat, K., Kocer, H.E.: Pairwise FCM based feature weighting for improved classification of vertebral column disorders. Comput. Biol. Med. **46**, 61–70 (2014)
9. Unal, Y., Polat, K., Kocer, H.E.: Classification of vertebral column disorders and lumbar discs disease using attribute weighting algorithm with mean shift clustering. Meas. J. Int. Meas. Confed. **77**, 278–291 (2016)
10. Ghosh, S., Chaudhary, V.: Supervised methods for detection and segmentation of tissues in clinical lumbar MRI. Comput. Med. Imaging Graph. **38**, 639–642 (2014)
11. Frighetto-Pereira, L., Menezes-Reis, R., Metzner, G.A., Rangayyan, R.M., Azevedo-Marques, P.M., Nogueira-Barbosa, M.H.: Shape, texture and statistical features for classification of benign and malignant vertebral compression fractures in magnetic resonance images. Comput. Biol. Med. **73**, 147–156 (2016)
12. Oktay, A.B., Albayrak, N.B., Akgul, Y.S.: Computer aided diagnosis of degenerative intervertebral disc diseases from lumbar MR images. Comput. Med. Imaging Graph. **38**, 9–613 (2014)

Face Tracking Using Modified Forward-Backward Mean-Shift Algorithm

V. Varadarajan[1], S. V. Lokesh[1], A. Ramesh[1], A. Vanitha[1(✉)], and V. Vaidehi[2(✉)]

[1] Department of Electronics Engineering, Madras Institute of Technology,
Anna University, Chennai 600044, India
vvaradu@gmail.com, lokeshsuganthan@gmail.com,
rameshsixface@gmail.com, anbu.vanitha17@gmail.com
[2] School of Computing Science and Engineering, VIT Chennai, Chennai, India
vaidehi.vijayakumar@vit.ac.in

Abstract. This paper addresses the problem of face tracking in video sequences in the presence of occlusions and target appearance variations. Existing method of Forward-Backward Mean-Shift (FBMS) has the problem in face tracking when the target moves fast and during long term occlusions of the target. Hence, this paper proposes Modified Forward-Backward Mean-Shift algorithm (MFBMS) method for face tracking. The tracker is initialized by Viola-Jones based face detection algorithm automatically without the need for any manual intervention. The proposed method chooses two dominant channels in the RGB domain for tracking. Bhattacharya distance based tracking failure detection along with forward-backward error evaluation scheme is used to detect long and short-term occlusions. When the tracking error exceeds the predefined threshold value, the tracker is reinitialized. The proposed MFBMS method is tested with standard databases such as YouTube Celebrity, manually created database and NRC-IIT face video databases. The results show that the proposed method gives accuracy of 96% on YouTube celebrity database and 98% on NRC-IIT face video database.

Keywords: MFBMS · Mean-Shift · Bhattacharya distance
Forward-Backward

1 Introduction

Visual tracking is an important task within the field of computer vision. Many computer vision applications require accurate tracking of human faces in real-time. This includes gaming, teleconferencing, surveillance, facial recognition, emotional analysis etc. The growth of high-end computers, easily accessible high quality video cameras, and the demand for automated video analysis makes visual tracking algorithms interesting. Visual tracking is challenging due to the loss of information caused by the projecting the 3D world on a 2D image, cluttered-background, noise in images, partial or full occlusions, complex object motion, illumination changes

© Springer Nature Singapore Pte Ltd. 2018
Shriram R and M. Sharma (Eds.): DaSAA 2017, CCIS 804, pp. 46–59, 2018.
https://doi.org/10.1007/978-981-10-8603-8_5

as well as real-time processing requirements, etc. The use of visual tracking is pertinent in the tasks of movement-based recognition, video surveillance, human–computer interaction and vehicle navigation, etc.

In order for a tracker to efficiently track an object, it must be able to clearly distinguish the target from the background. Another major problem in tracking is occlusion. In case of occlusion the target may be hidden partially or fully by some other object. A good tracking system must be able to track the target, by overcoming such difficulties. Therefore to overcome existing issues, this paper proposes a method of Modified Forward-Backward Mean-Shift (MFBMS) based face tracking system. Wang et al. [17] proposed Forward-Backward Mean-Shift (FBMS) algorithm which handles short term occlusions well and produces smooth tracking results.

Existing FBMS fails when the target moves faster and when the object is occluded for long time. In order to overcome the drawbacks of FBMS during this scenario, a Bhattacharya distance based occlusion detection and re-initialization scheme has been added. Also, in order to discriminate between the target and background, dynamic channel selection mechanism is introduced, which improves tracking accuracy. The proposed MFBMS is implemented in Visual Studio 12 with OpenCV C++ library and is found to perform better in terms of accuracy compared to FBMS.

A brief discussion of related work is carried out in Sect. 2. The proposed method is explained in detail in Sect. 3 and the results are discussed in Sect. 4. Section 5 followed by references concludes the paper.

2 Related Work

This section gives the review of recent approaches in tracking.

The template-based method [9] is a type of classical appearance-based methods, as it is robust to partial occlusion and non-rigidity. Tracking with fixed templates can be reliable over short duration, but the appearance changes over longer durations that accuracy affects most applications.

The probabilistic modelling, dynamical-model, and sampling modelling are employed to achieve efficient tracking. The dynamical model based method is often composed of two stages, a dynamic model is utilized to predict the next state in the first stage and the second stage prediction is refined by the image observations. The Kalman filter algorithm has been used to track objects via the randomness that is generated by a linear dynamic operator with the Gaussian noise [15]. However, it is hard to handle the nonlinear or non-Gaussian conditions. The particle-filter algorithm is to solve nonlinear problem, but the disadvantage of the this technique is its high computational cost [14].

Treating object tracking as an online selection problem has attracted much attention because it selects appropriate features to classify foreground pixels or background pixel. The first online-selection-based tracking algorithm was proposed by Collins et al. to select the features that can distinguish the background pixels and target (foreground) by switching the mean-shift tracking algorithm in different linear combinations of three colour channels [3]. But the above method affects accuracy in illumination changes. Liang et al. solved this issue by using the Bayesian error rate instead of variance ratio [13].

Similarly, Kwolek et al. presents multiple color histograms instead of the linear combination of the three color channels [2]. Background weighted methods [8] idea is to weaken inner-background features or make target features prominent for better tracking performance in different lighting conditions.

A family of online-learning-based tracking approaches optimally separates the target from the background in each frame [5]. However, the main difference between the two groups is the target representation i.e classification problem. For example, Grabner et al. designed an online boosting classifier that discriminate the background from the candidate by feature selection, these method is fast [4]. However, when the object is occluded, these methods may fail because it is hard to be detected.

Bradski et al. proposed the modified version of meanshift namely CAMshift (Continuously Adaptive Mean shift). CAMshift uses a dynamical search window which changes according to the size of the object [6]. CAMshift depends more on color distribution alone. This method is simple and produces reliable and robust results when the background and target is distinct.

In addition to CAMShift method Allan et al. introduced a 3D histogram for the target model so that they use all three colors of RGB color space [7]. This method improves the distinction between background and the target. CAMshift tracker fails to detect the target when the target shares the pixel with the background.

Stolkin et al. proposed a new tracking algorithm based on color channels called ABCshift (the Adaptive Background CAMSHIFT), works very well for small distance from a stationery camera [12]. ABCshift is robust to scene changes and camera motion by continuously relearning its background model for each frame, it fails when the background and target are similar.

Poornasingh et al. proposed PAMshift tracking algorithm, all points in the path towards the mode point are consider as final mode value. It is a fast tracking method [1]. However, this method may fail due to the improper selection of bandwidth and kernel.

Ming et al. proposed the fuzzy clustering mean shift method. In this method, a self-constructing cluster generates a fuzzy color histogram to reduce the interference from illumination changes [10]. This method is more robust and it requires less iterations than the conventional algorithm. This method is proposed only for RGB color model.

Wang et al. proposed a forward-backward mean-shift algorithm with local-background weighted histogram [17]. Local –background weighted histograms were introduced to make the target model more distinguishable from the background. Forward-backward algorithm was used to smoothen the tracking process by tracking in both forward and backward manner. The tracking result of this approach adaptively fuses two results i.e. the observation obtained from mean-shift and the prediction result of a median filter of historical trajectory.

Thus, several approaches exist for tracking, each having its own merits and demerits. This paper proposes MFBMS method to improve FBMS in terms of accuracy and make it immune to long term occlusions and fast target motion. Figure 1 shows the overall architecture of a face tracking system.

Fig. 1. Architecture of a face tracking system

3   Proposed Method

The basic concept behind Mean-Shift trackers followed by the Modified Forward-Backward Mean-shift algorithm is introduced below:

3.1   Overview of Mean-Shift Tracking

Mean-Shift is a non-parametric function to locate the local maxima of a density function (mode seeking algorithm). In this algorithm, the targets are usually characterized by their color histograms. Mean-shift tracking algorithm is an iterative scheme which compares the original object histogram in the current image frame and candidate region histogram in the next image frame. The main aim is to maximize the similarity between two histograms.

In Mean-Shift tracking, the target feature is the color PDF (Probability distribution function) of the target which is denoted as q in color space. The probable place of target with centre of y in next frame contains target candidate. To make candidate probability distribution function model, the probability distribution function of its locale shown by p(y) is used. Both probability distribution function (target and candidate), contains a good approximation of intrinsic feature of target. As one of the tracker's evaluation parameters is their processing time, normally to reduce that, quantized histograms are preferred. Equations (1) and (2) give the typical target and candidate representation.

$$\hat{q}_u = C \sum_{i=1}^{n} k(||x_i^*||^2)\delta\,[b(x_i^*) - u], \quad u = 1, \ldots m \text{ bins} \tag{1}$$

$$\hat{p}_u(y) = C_h \sum_{i=1}^{n_h} k\left(\left\|\frac{y - x_i}{h}\right\|^2\right)\delta\,[b(x_i^*) - u], \quad u = 1, \ldots m \text{ bins} \tag{2}$$

Where $\hat{q}_u$ is the target representation, $\hat{p}_u(y)$ is the candidate representation, y denotes location of the search window, x_i denotes the kernel center, k denotes Kernel function, h denotes bandwidth of the kernel, C and C_h are normalization coefficients and δ is the kronecker delta function.

Bhattacharya coefficient ρ given in Eq. (3) is used to compute the similarity between the target and the candidate. The aim of object tracking is to find a new location y so as to minimize the Bhattacharya coefficients between p(y) and q, given by $\rho(p(y), q)$ in Eq. (4). By expanding Eq. (2) with Taylor series expansion, it is found that this similarity is maximized when weights of the pixels in candidate region as given by Eq. (5).

$$d(y) = \sqrt{1 - \rho[\hat{p}(y), q]} \tag{3}$$

$$\rho[\hat{p}(y), q] = \sum_{u=1}^{m} \sqrt{\hat{p}_u(y)q_u} \tag{4}$$

Where d is the Bhattacharya distance
ρ is the Bhattacharya Coefficient

$$w_i = \sum_{i=1}^{m} \sqrt{\frac{\hat{q}_u}{\hat{p}_u(\hat{y}_0)}} \delta[b(x_i) - u] \tag{5}$$

Where w_i is the weight given to the pixel i.

3.2 Modified Forward-Backward Mean-Shift (MFBMS)

First step involved in face tracking is detection of the face. In this MFBMS system, face detection is performed by Viola-Jones detection algorithm. The co-ordinates obtained from the detection stage are taken as the input to the tracker. Histograms in MFBMS implementation are quantized to 16 bins.

Difficulty in tracking low resolution videos is the lack of quality features for tracking. Color is a primary feature available in all videos and so it can serve as good feature for tracking. So, the proposed MFMBS algorithm is based on the colour and statistical feature. Considering all the three channels in the RGB domain for Mean-Shift tracking increases the computational complexity. So, two of the three channels are generally taken for tracking.

Tracking will be efficient only when the tracking algorithm can discriminate between the target and the background. So, the two dominant colors among RGB in the target are chosen for tracking thus the MFBMS algorithm to efficiently distinguish the target from the background. The selection of dominant two channels is done by calculating their mean value over the target region and finding the top two values.

Occlusion is the case when the target being tracked is hidden by some other object or background. Forward-Backward Mean-Shift (FBMS) algorithm introduced by Wang et al. was able to smooth the tracking process as well as handle short term occlusions better than other mean-shift algorithms [17]. But, FBMS fails in situations where the target moves faster or when the object is occluded for longer durations. In order to rectify this, the target under such situations, the target and the candidate (detector output) are compared with each other in all the frames. The comparison is done in terms of Bhattacharya distance which is calculated from Eq. (1).

When the Bhattacharya distance exceeds a predefined threshold value (i.e 0.7), the detector is reinitialized to find the lost target or to find new targets in case if the target has left the region. Figure 2 shows the flowchart for the proposed MFBMS algorithm.

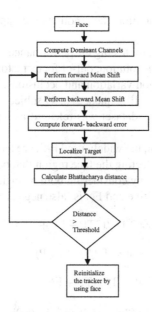

Fig. 2. MFBMS tracker

So, MFBMS algorithm can be summarized as follows.

MFBMS ALGORITHM
1. Search for a face in the frame using a face detector.
2. Initialize the MFBMS tracker with co-ordinates obtained from face detector.
3. Find the dominant two color channels
4. Perform forward mean-shift.
5. Repeat 4 till stopping criteria is met.
6. Perform backward mean-shift.
7. Compute the forward-backward error.
8. Predict the position in current frame based on historical trajectory.
9. Fuse the result with forward-backward error based on a weighted function.
10. Compute Bhattacharya distance between current target location and the actual target.
11. If the distance exceeds a threshold, reinitialize the detector and go to step 9. Else go to step 10.
12. Compare the found faces with original target. If the original target is found, reinitialize the tracker from the new location. Else end tracking.
13. Repeat from step 4 till stopping criteria is met.

4   Results and Discussions

OpenCV is an open source computer vision library. The library is written in C++ and runs under windows. MFBMS tracking with Viola-Jones detection was simulated in Visual Studio 2012 using OpenCV C++ library. The simulations were done on an Intel Pentium 2.10 Ghz processor with 2 GB Ram.

The proposed algorithm was tested on publicly available NRC-IIT Face Video, manually created database and YouTube celebrity video databases. NRC-IIT database contains short video clips of users showing their face with different types of emotions while sitting in front of the monitor, the emotions are captured by an Intel Webcam mounted on computer monitor.

This database is most suited for testing the performance with respect to such inherent to video-based factors as: low resolution, out-of focus factor, motion blur, facial orientation variation, facial expression variation and occlusions.

YouTube Dataset contains 1910 sequences of 47 subjects. All the videos are encoded in MPEG-4 at 25 fps rate. This dataset was released as a part of work done by Kim et al. [16].

For performance evaluation, the widely used F-Score has been adopted. The ground truth is created by manually selecting the face region that best covers the face. F-Score measures the tracking accuracy by considering both precision and recall i.e. Where TP is true positive, FP is false positive and FN is false negative.

$$F\text{-}Score = 2\,TP/(2TP + FP + FN) \tag{6}$$

$$Precision = TP/(TP + FP) \tag{7}$$

$$Recall = TP/(TP + FN) \tag{8}$$

Tables 1 and 4 show F-Score comparison results between original mean-shift and proposed MFBMS applied to some of the video sequences from YouTube celebrity and NRC-IIT face video databases.

Table 1. F-Score comparison of Original Mean-Shift and MFBMS using YouTube celebrity database

Video sequence	Original Mean-Shift	MFBMS
0016_01_016_adam_sandler.avi	0.9909	0.9955
0473_01_005_bill_gates.avi	0.7210	0.9264
0415_02_001_bill_clinton_avi	0.9520	0.9840
0487_03_004_bill_gates.avi	0.9440	0.9655
1058_02_008_jim_carrey.avi	0.9510	0.9642
0084_02_005_al_gore.avi	0.9950	0.9967
0125_01_006_al_pacino.avi	0.9780	0.9797

Table 2. Precision comparison of Original Mean-Shift and MFBMS using YouTube celebrity database

Video sequence	Original Mean-Shift	MFBMS
0016_01_016_adam_sandler.avi	0.9910	1
0473_01_005_bill_gates.avi	0.5	0.9264
0415_02_001_bill_clinton_avi	0.98	0.997
0487_03_004_bill_gates.avi	0.8364	0.927
1058_02_008_jim_carrey.avi	0.9264	1
0084_02_005_al_gore.avi	0.6691	0.9967
0125_01_006_al_pacino.avi	0.7835	1

Tables 2 and 5 show precision comparison results between original mean-shift and proposed MFBMS applied to some of the video sequences from YouTube celebrity and NRC-IIT face video databases.

Tables 3 and 6 show recall comparison results between original mean-shift and proposed MFBMS applied to some of the video sequences from YouTube celebrity and NRC-IIT face video databases.

Table 3. Recall comparison of Original Mean-Shift and MFBMS using YouTube celebrity database

Video sequence	Original Mean-Shift	MFBMS
0016_01_016_adam_sandler.avi	0.991	0.9934
0473_01_005_bill_gates.avi	0.9524	0.9664
0415_02_001_bill_clinton_avi	0.969	0.9703
0487_03_004_bill_gates.avi	0.6095	0.9859
1058_02_008_jim_carrey.avi	0.9264	0.9310
0084_02_005_al_gore.avi	0.9782	0.993
0125_01_006_al_pacino.avi	0.9563	0.9783

Fig. 3. MFBMS algorithm applied to the NRC-IIT face videos with random motion and occlusion

Figure 3 shows results from a video sequence from NRC-IIT database. Even in case of occlusion and jumping tracker is able to track the object. In frame 191, the face is occluded by the hand but the tracker continuously tracks accurately in the subsequent frames.

Figure 4 shows results from video sequences from YouTube celebrity database. Most of the videos are recorded at high compression and low resolution. This leads to low-quality image frames and noisy.

Fig. 4. MFBMS algorithm applied to video sequence of YouTube celebrity database.

Figure 5 shows results of video sequences which were recorded in laboratory environment. As can be observed from the figure, the tracker is able to track without any drift in cases of short as well as long term occlusions. The same MFBMS algorithm was extended to multiple targets and the results are shown in Fig. 6.

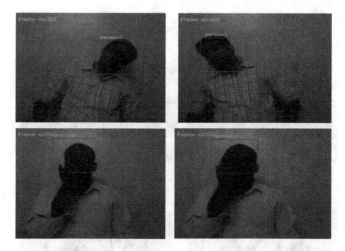

Fig. 5. Results for video sequences from manually created database with occlusion and different orientations.

Fig. 6. Multiple Objects Tracking

Results for video sequences from manually created database with scale variations as shown in Fig. 7. Figure 8 shows the results of face videos with bad illumination condition and different orientation recorded in the indoor environment with low resolution. The proposed MFBMS algorithm can able to track the object in different illumination condition and also different types of occlusion, motions and orientations.

Fig. 7. Results for video sequences from manually created database with scale variations.

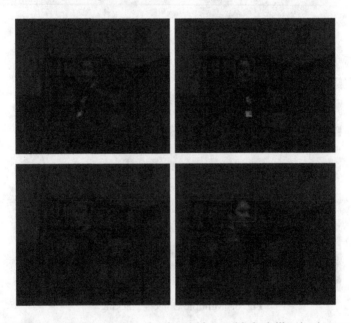

Fig. 8. MFBMS algorithm applied to the face videos with bad illumination and different orientation

Thus, the tracking algorithm is tested under conditions where the target undergoes random motions, partial and full occlusions. From the results, it can be inferred that the proposed system is able to track accurately overcoming these difficulties.

Tables 1, 2, 3, 4, 5 and 6 shows the value of F-Score, Precision and recall of different video databases. The table shows the proposed method gives better performance than the exiting method in different resolution videos. In Tables 5 and 6 the precision and recall performance value is same for both existing and proposed method because the video has less motion, orientation and occlusions. So, the performance value is same for both.

Table 4. F-Score comparison of Original Mean-Shift and MFBMS using NRC-IIT face video database

Video sequence	Original Mean-Shift	MFBMS
01-1.avi	0.9443	0.9856
02-2.avi	0.843	0.9856
01-1_2.avi	0.9443	0.9714
07-2.avi	0.9829	0.991
05 s-2.avi	0.9921	0.9926

Table 5. Precision comparison of Original Mean-Shift and MFBMS using NRC-IIT face video database

Video sequence	Original Mean-Shift	MFBMS
01-1.avi	0.9098	0.994
02-2.avi	0.7417	0.987
01-1_2.avi	0.9098	0.977
07-2.avi	0.9753	0.9877
05 s-2.avi	1	1

Table 6. Recall comparison of Original Mean-Shift and MFBMS using NRC-IIT face video database

Video sequence	Original Mean-Shift	MFBMS
01-1.avi	0.9814	0.9977
02-2.avi	0.9763	0.982
01-1_2.avi	0.9814	0.9966
07-2.avi	0.9753	0.9938
05 s-2.avi	0.9843	0.9843

5 Conclusion

Modified Forward-Backward Mean-Shift algorithm has been proposed in this paper. Selection of the dominant two among the three channels in RGB domain and the calculation of Bhattacharya distance between the candidate and the target aids in improving the performance of FBMS during occlusions. MFBMS algorithm was tested on YouTube celebrities and NRC-IIT face video databases. Experimental results show that tracker can effectively track faces of different scales and can avoid drift in case of occlusions.

6 Future Work

Asymmetric kernels which match the exact shape of the target can be used to improve the performance. Other features such as contour, gradients and motion features can be used to enhance target representation.

Acknowledgement. This work is supported by DAE-BRNS, Mumbai. The authors would like to extend their sincere thanks to DAE-BRNS for funding the project.

References

1. Pooransingh, A., Radix, C.-A., Kokaram, A.: The path assigned mean shift algorithm: a new fast mean shift implementation for color image segmentation. In: 15th IEEE International Conference on Image Processing ICIP (2008)
2. Kwolek, B.: Object tracking using discriminative feature selection. In: Blanc-Talon, J., Philips, W., Popescu, D., Scheunders, P. (eds.) ACIVS 2006. LNCS, vol. 4179, pp. 287–298. Springer, Heidelberg (2006). https://doi.org/10.1007/11864349_26
3. Collins, R., Liu, Y., Leordeanu, M.: Online election of discriminative tracking features. IEEE Trans. Patent Anal. Match. Intell. **27**, 1631–1643 (2005)
4. Grabner, H., Grabner, M., Bischof, H.: Real time tracking via online boosting. In: Proceedings of British Machine Vision Conference, pp. 47–56 (2006)
5. Gall, J., Lempitsky, V.: Class-specific hough forests for object detection. In: Criminisi, A., Shotton, J. (eds.) Decision Forests for Computer Vision and Medical Image Analysis, pp. 143–157. Springer, London (2009). https://doi.org/10.1007/978-1-4471-4929-3_11
6. Bradski, G.R.: Computer vision face tracking for use in a perceptual user interface. In: Proceedings of IEEE Workshop Applications of Computer Vision, pp. 214–219, October 1998
7. Allen, J.G., Xu, R.Y.D., Jin, J.S.: Object tracking using camshift algorithm and multiple quantized feature spaces. In: Proceedings of the Pan-Sydney Area Workshop on Visual Information Processing. International Conference Proceeding Series, vol. 100, pp. 3–7. Australian Computer Society, Darlinghurst. ACM (2004)
8. Manjunath, B., Ma, W.: Texture features for browsing and retrieval of image data. IEEE Trans. Pattern Anal. Mach. Intell. **18**(8), 837–842 (1996)
9. Mei, X., Ling, H.: Robust visual tracking using minimization. In: 2009 IEEE 12th International Conference on Computer Vision, pp. 1436–1443 (2009)
10. Ju, M.-Y., Ouyang, C.-S., Chang, H.-S.: Mean shift tracking using fuzzy color histogram. In: Proceedings of the Ninth International Conference on Machine Learning and Cybernetics, Qingdao, 11–14 July 2010. IEEE (2010)
11. Ning, J., Zhang, L., Zhang, D., Wu, C.: Scale and orientation adaptive mean shift tracking. IET Comput. Vis. **6**(1), 52–61 (2012)
12. Stolkin, R., Florescu, I., Baron, M., Harrier, C., Kocherov, B.: Efficient visual servoing with the ABCshift tracking algorithm. In: IEEE International Conference on Robotics and Automation Pasadena, CA, USA, 19–23 May 2008

13. Liang, D., Huang, Q., Gao, W., Yao, H.: Online selection of discriminative features using bayes error rate for visual tracking. In: Zhuang, Y., Yang, S.-Q., Rui, Y., He, Q. (eds.) PCM 2006. LNCS, vol. 4261, pp. 547–555. Springer, Heidelberg (2006). https://doi.org/10.1007/11922162_63

14. Wu, B., Nevatia, R.: Detection of multiple, partially occluded humans in a single image by bayesian combination of edgelet part detectors. In: ICCV (2005)

15. Yilmaz, A., Javed, O., Shah, M.: Object tracking: a survey. In: IPCV (2006)

16. Kim, M., Kumar, S., Pavlovic, V., Rowley, H.: Face tracking and recognition with visual constraints in real-world videos. In: IEEE Conference on Computer Vision and Pattern Recognition (2008)

17. Wang, L., Yan, H., Wu, H., Pan, C.: Forward-backward mean-shift for visual tracking with local-background-weighted-histogram. IEEE Trans. Intell. Veh. Transp. Syst. **14**(3), 1480–1489 (2013)

Frequent Pattern Mining Guided Tabu Search

Sandeep Avula, C. Oswald$^{(\boxtimes)}$, and B. Sivaselvan

Department of Computer Engineering,
Indian Institute of Information Technology,
Design and Manufacturing Kancheepuram, Chennai, India
{coe11b004, coe13d003, sivaselvanb}@iiitdm.ac.in

Abstract. The paper focuses on the search perspective of Data Mining. Genetic Algorithms, Tabu Search are a few of the evolutionary search strategies in the literature. As a part of this work, we relate Data mining in the context of Tabu Search to perform search for global optimum in a guided fashion. Sequence Pattern Mining (SPM) in generic and a variant of it, namely Maximal Sequence Pattern (MSP) is incorporated as a part of Tabu Search. The limitation of conventional Tabu Search is that the convergence rate is dependent on the initial population. The project proposes to arrive at an initial population employing SPM and hence result in improved convergence, in relation to conventional Tabu Search. The proposed algorithm has been tested for the N-Queens problem and empirical results indicate approximately 21% improved convergence.

Keywords: Candidate solutions · Maximal sequence pattern
N-Queens problem · Sequence pattern mining · Tabu search

1 Introduction

The word tabu in search means restricted move in search space. Tabu Search which is a Meta-Heuristic search method was initially introduced in 1986 by Dr. Fred Glover [1–9]. The basic idea of Tabu Search is to escape from local optimum by use of some additional memory called Tabu list. Tabu Search is able to reach optimum or near optimal solution. Tabu Search has important applications in the domain of VLSI testing, telecommunications, resource planning, scheduling and deadlock prevention [10–19]. Use of Memory structure in Tabu Search have four dimensions consisting of recency, frequency, quality and influence. Frequency based memory stores frequency count of all moves possible in search space. In general, these two memory structures complement each other. Quality based memory structure stores moves in good quality solution and discourage the moves in poor quality solutions. Influence based memory structure stores information about each move in search process. Recency based memory structures is having advantage over remaining memory structures because of specific bounds on finite convergence of Tabu Search [10]. Tabu Search is based on introducing memory structure along with restriction in search space and aspiration criteria. Tabu Search employs three strategies namely forbidden strategy, freeing strategy and short term strategy. Parameters of Tabu Search are Local search procedure, Neighborhood structure, Aspiration conditions, Tabu List and Stopping rule [1–9].

© Springer Nature Singapore Pte Ltd. 2018
Shriram R and M. Sharma (Eds.): DaSAA 2017, CCIS 804, pp. 60–71, 2018.
https://doi.org/10.1007/978-981-10-8603-8_6

The search space is the space of all possible solutions that can be visited during search process. Neighborhood structure is defined with respect to a problem. The most commonly used stopping conditions (terminating criteria) in tabu search are

- Fix the no of iterations Tabu search should run.
- When there is no improvement in the objective value after some consecutive number of iterations.
- When the objective function reaches a pre-specified threshold value.

Tabu search is an evolutionary search strategy that works on the basis of memory lists that help in avoiding counter-productive search paths. Various literatures and related work on Tabu Search and its associated algorithms can be found in [11–19]. To the best of our knowledge N-Queen's problem has not been dealt using Tabu Search by researchers in the past. Focusing on the search perspective of Data Mining, the project aims to relate data mining strategy of contiguous maximal sequence pattern mining in the domain of Tabu Search, with the specific case study of Tabu Search. A knowledge engineering guided tabu search will contribute in terms of efficiency and efficacy of the solution. The objective here is to find configuration (set of n cells where queens to be placed) that minimizes the total no of collisions [1–8]. Optimal solution is 0. For e.g. Consider a 4×4 chessboard and a possible solution is given as

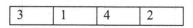

3	1	4	2

		Q	
Q			
			Q
	Q		

2 Introduction to Maximal Sequence Pattern Mining

For an ordered list of itemsets, a sequence S is denoted by $<S_1, S_2, S_3, ..., S_n>$, where S_j refers to an itemset [20–23]. The support of a sequence is the total no of transactions that support that sequence. Given a customer transaction database D, find all the sequence patterns which are satisfying a user specified minimum support count. A sequence having length k is called a k-sequence [20–23]. Let S be a frequent sequence pattern, if there exists no other sequence pattern which is a super sequence of S which is frequent, then S is called a maximal sequence pattern.

2.1 Procedure for Finding Maximal Sequence Patterns

Step 1: Find all sequence patterns level by using two step procedure of joining and pruning.

Joining phase: For two sequences S_1 and S_2 to be joined, if the subsequence obtained by dropping the first element of S_1 is same as subsequence obtained by dropping the last element of S_2. Joining is done by adding first and last elements to that subsequence.

Step 2: Once all frequent sequence patterns are found, the lower level frequent sequences which are subsequences of these upper level frequent sequences should be eliminated. Consider the following customer transaction database D. Minimum Support count is 2.

TID	Transaction Items
1	<2 3>
2	<1 2 3 4>
3	<3 4>
4	<1 2 3>

1-Sequence	Supp Count
(1)	2
(2)	3
(3)	4
(4)	2

L_1

2-Sequence	Support Count	2-Sequence	Support Count
(1 1)	0	(3 1)	0
(1 2)	2	(3 2)	0
(1 3)	2	(3 3)	0
(1 4)	1	(3 4)	2
(2 1)	0	(4 1)	0
(2 2)	0	(4 2)	0
(2 3)	3	(4 3)	0
(2 4)	1	(4 4)	0

C_2

2-Sequence	Support Count
(1 2)	2
(1 3)	2
(2 3)	3
(3 4)	2

L_2

3-Sequence	Support count
(1 2 3)	2
(1 3 4)	1
(2 3 4)	1

C_3

3-Sequence	Support count
(1 2 3)	2

L_3

The Maximal Sequence patterns are (1 2 3), (3 4). (1 2), (1 3) and (1 4) are not maximal sequences because they are subsequences of Frequent Sequence Pattern (1 2 3).

3 Case Study N-queens

N-queens is a classical combinatorial problem in literature. It is considered as a benchmark problem for Artificial Intelligence search problems.

3.1 Working of Tabu Search

Solving problem of 7 queens using basic Tabu Search method is given in Figs. 1, 2 and 3. Iteration no is 0. Collisions are 4.

Initial random solution is

4	5	3	6	7	1	2

1	7 *	-2
2	4	-2
2	6	-2
5	6	-2
1	5	-1

Fig. 1. Tabu memory before iteration 1

Iteration 1:

No of collisions are 2. Current solution is

2	5	3	6	7	1	4

2	4 *	-1
1	6	0
2	5	0
1	2	1
1	3	1

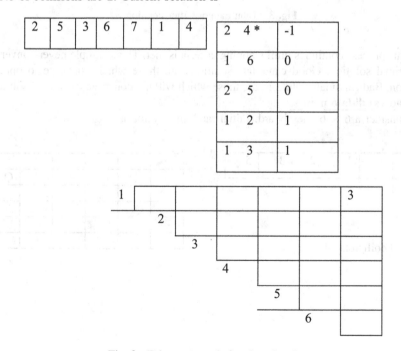

Fig. 2. Tabu memory before iteration 2

Iteration 2:

No of collisions are 1. Current best solution is

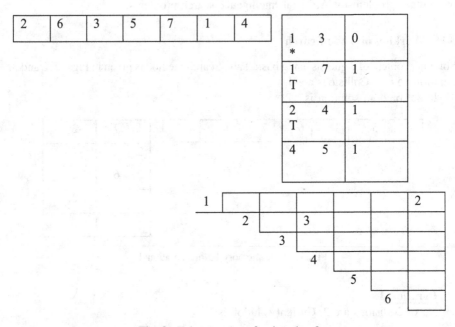

Fig. 3. Tabu memory after iteration 2

This process continues until stopping criteria is met. This example never converges to optimal solution. Good candidate solutions are those which converge to optimal solution. Bad candidate solutions are those which will not converge to optimal solution.

Bad candidate points:

Consider a 6 × 6 chessboard. Initial random solution is

4	6	1	2	3	5

No of collisions: 4

Iteration 1: Swap positions of queen 5 and queen 6.

4	6	1	2	5	3

			Q		
					Q
Q					
	Q				
				Q	
		Q			

No of collisions: 1

Iteration 2: Swap Q4 & Q6 positions.

4	6	1	3	5	2

			Q		
					Q
Q					
		Q			
				Q	
	Q				

No of collision: 1

Iteration 11970: Swap Q2 & Q3 positions.

3	6	4	1	5	2

		Q			
					Q
			Q		
Q					
				Q	
	Q				

Collision: 1

This process continues and never reaches optimal solution. Good Candidate points:

Initial random solution

2	3	4	1	6	5

	Q				
		Q			
			Q		
Q					
					Q
				Q	

No of collisions: 8

Iteration 1: Swap Q2 & Q5 positions.

2	6	4	1	3	5

Collisions: 2

	Q				
					Q
			Q		
Q					
		Q			
				Q	

Iteration 2: Swap Q2 & Q3 positions.

2	4	6	1	3	5

Collisions: 0

	Q				
			Q		
					Q
Q					
		Q			
				Q	

It reaches optimal solution. Bad candidate solutions are occurring because of initial random solution. Those bad candidate solutions can be avoided by reducing randomness in generation of initial solution.

4 Proposed MSP Based Tabu Search

In this section, we present the proposed version of Tabu Search which employs Data Mining to solve a problem of N-Queens. The basic idea of incorporating a Data Mining process is that the sequence patterns found in high quality solutions (frequently) will guide in improving search process.

4.1 Algorithm for Data Mining Guided Tabu Search

Step 1: Execute Tabu search with n different seed initial solutions. Good candidate solutions are called elite set. The d best solutions among the elite set are retained for mining.
Step 2: The mining of d best solutions is done by using maximal contiguous sequence pattern mining.
Step 3: Initial solution built is guided by a mined pattern selected from the set of mined patterns. Initially, all elements of the selected pattern are inserted into the partial solution.

Conventional Tabu Search is applied. Maximal sequence patterns are used in mining so that initial population generated avoids redundancy. Consider 6×6 chessboard.

Elite set of solutions:

2	3	4	1	6	5

Takes 2 iterations to converge

2	6	4	1	3	5

Takes 1 iteration to converge

2	4	6	1	3	5

Take 0 iteration to converge

3	1	5	4	6	2

Take 2 iterations to converge

3	1	5	2	6	4

Takes 1 iteration to converge

4	1	5	2	6	3

Takes 0 iterations to converge

1	6	2	5	3	4

Takes 1 iteration to converge

3	6	2	5	1	4

Takes 0 iteration to converge

Six best solutions among the elite set are taken for mining. Minimum support count is 2.

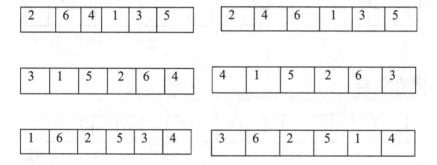

Maximal contiguous sequence patterns are:

Pattern	Support
(1,5,2,6)	2
(1,3,5)	2
(2,6,4)	2
(6,2,5)	2
(4,1)	2

Use the mined patterns in constructing Initial solution

Consider a 8 × 8 chessoard for which the illustration is given below.

Illustration 1

Initial Solution: Pattern selected: (1, 5, 2, 6)

Generated random number 2 positions

Iteration 1: swap Q4 & Q8

	1	5	2	6			

4	1	5	8	6	3	7	2

4	1	5	2	6	3	7	8

Collisions: 1

Collision: 0

Illustration 2

Pattern selected (1, 5, 2, 6). Generated random number 2.

	1	5	2	6			

8	1	5	2	6	7	3	4

Collisions: 2

Iteration 1: swap Q6& Q7.

8	1	5	2	6	3	7	4

Collisions: 1

Iteration 1: swap Q1 & Q5.

6	1	5	2	8	3	7	4

Collisions: 0

5 Analysis - Upper Bound on the Number of Iterations of Converging Tabu Search

Consider the worst case possibility of initial solution of placing all the queens on the diagonal of the chessboard. Initially number of collisions is $1 + 2 + 3 + ... + (n - 2) + (n - 1)$ is $((n - 1)(n)/2)$. During iteration 1 algorithm makes a best move. The number collisions after the iteration 1 are reduced to $n(n - 1)/2 - ((n - 2) + (n - 1)) + 1$. During iteration 2, algorithm makes a best move. The number of collisions after the iteration 2 are reduced to $n(n - 1)/2 - ((n - 2) + (n - 1) + (n - 3) + (n - 4)) + 1 + 1$. This process is iterated until number of collisions are $n/2$ and number of iterations of the algorithm are $n/2$. This process is iterated until no of collisions reach 1 and no of iterations at that point are $(n/2 + n/4 + ... + 1)$. Solving this series, the number of iterations allowed is n. Therefore the stopping criterion for Tabu Search are N iterations for an N-Queens problem.

6 Implementation

In this section, computational results obtained for conventional Tabu Search and Data mining guided Tabu Search are presented. N-queens for larger instances of N are presented: 60, 70, 100, 120, 150, 300, 400 and 500. Open source implementation of MSP is used. Conventional Tabu Search and proposed algorithm are implemented in C. The tests are performed on a 2.5 GHz Intel Core with 4 Gbytes of RAM, running on ubuntu 12.10. Both Tabu Search and Data Mining guided Tabu Search were run 100 times with different initial seeds. The size of elite set was 0.4% of size of N-queens. Maximal sequence pattern with a maximum gap of 1 is considered. Table 1 presents results related to execution time of both strategies. Second column indicates no. of initial seeds. Both algorithms were run. Fifth column indicates the training size of N used.

Table 1. Tabu search vs. Data mining bases Tabu search

N-queens	Conventional Tabu search			Data mining guided Tabu search		
	No. of initial solutions	No. of initial solution converges	Avg. No. of iterations converge	Mining of N-queens	No. of initial solution converges	Avg. no. of iterations converge
9	100	78	4.3	7	90	3.48
12	100	82	7.34	7	93	5.78
60	100	90	18.69	50	95	15.88
70	100	96	22.84	50	94	18.45
100	100	98	26.18	50	99	24.65
120	100	97	31.14	100	99	26.22
150	100	99	36.41	100	98	30.07
300	100	99	64.06	200	100	49.73
400	100	100	82.66	200	99	68.08
500	100	99	101.35	200	100	81.90

From the above results, it is observed that Data Mining guided Tabu search is 21.43% faster in converging to optimal solution than conventional Tabu Search.

7 Conclusions and Future Work

The paper focused the Search perspective of Data Mining, specifically in the context of Tabu Search. The case study of N-Queens problem has been considered to test the proposed Data Mining guided Tabu Search and results indicate improved convergence. SPM and MSP algorithms have been used to guide the Tabu Search. Relevance of Tabu Search and Data Mining guided Tabu Search in the domain of web search can be explored as a future work.

References

1. Glover, F., Laguna, M.: Tabu Search. Kluwer Academic Publishers, MA (1997)
2. Glover, F.: Tabu search-part I. ORSA J. Comput. **1**(3), 190–206 (1989)
3. Glover, F.: Tabu search—part II. ORSA J. Comput. **2**(1), 4–32 (1990)
4. Gendreau, M., Potvin, J.-Y.: Handbook of Metaheuristics, vol. 2. Springer, New York (2010). https://doi.org/10.1007/978-1-4419-1665-5
5. Hertz, A., de Werra, D.: The tabu search metaheuristic: how we used it. Ann. Math. Artif. Intell. **1**(1), 111–121 (1990)
6. Glover, F.: Tabu search fundamentals and uses. Graduate School of Business, University of Colorado, Boulder (1995)
7. Glover, F., Taillard, E.: A user's guide to tabu search. Ann. Oper. Res. **41**(1), 1–28 (1993)
8. Crainic, T.G., Gendreau, M., Rousseau, L.-M.: Special issue on recent advances in metaheuristics. J. Heuristics **16**(3), 235 (2010)
9. Glover, F., Kelly, J.P., Laguna, M.: Genetic algorithms and tabu search: hybrids for optimization. Comput. Oper. Res. **22**, 111–134 (1997)
10. Hanafi, S.: On the convergence of tabu search. J. Heuristics **7**, 47–58 (2001)
11. Glover, F., Laguna, M., Marti, R.: Fundamentals of scatter search and path relinking. Control Cybern. **29**, 653–684 (2000)
12. Gendreau, M., Hertz, A., Laporte, G.: A tabu search heuristic for the vehicle routing problem. Manage. Sci. **40**(10), 1276–1290 (1994)
13. Knox, J.E.: The application of tabu search to the symmetric traveling salesman problem (1989)
14. Nowicki, E., Smutnicki, C.: A fast tabu search algorithm for the permutation flow-shop problem. Eur. J. Oper. Res. **91**(1), 160–175 (1996)
15. Nowicki, E., Smutnicki, C.: A fast taboo search algorithm for the job shop problem. Manage. Sci. **42**(6), 797–813 (1996)
16. de Werra, D., Hertz, A.: Tabu search techniques: a tutorial and an application to neural networks. Oper. Res. Spektrum **11**(3), 131–141 (1989)
17. Chelouah, R., Siarry, P.: Tabu search applied to global optimization. Eur. J. Oper. Res. **123**(2), 256–270 (2000)
18. Resende, M.G.C., Werneck, R.F.: A hybrid heuristic for the p-median problem. J. Heuristics **10**, 59–88 (2004)

19. Resende, M.G.C., Werneck, R.F.: On the implementation of a swap-based local search procedure for the p-median problem. In: Proceedings of the Fifth Workshop on Algorithm Engineering and Experiments (2003)
20. Agrawal, R., Srikant, R.: Fast algorithms for mining association rules. In: Proceedings of the 20th International Conference on Very Large Data Bases (1994)
21. Han, J., Kamber, M.: Data Mining: Concepts and Techniques, 2nd edn. (2007)
22. Dietterich, T.G., Michalski, R.S.: Discovering patterns in sequences of events. Artif. Intell. **25**, 187–232 (1985)
23. Kang, T.H., Yoo, J.S., Kim, H.Y.: Mining frequent contiguous sequences patterns in biological sequences. IEEE (2007)

Multi-perspective and Domain Specific Tagging of Chemical Documents

S. S. Deepika[✉], T. V. Geetha, and Rajeswari Sridhar

Department of Computer Science and Engineering, College of Engineering,
Anna University, Chennai, India
deepu.deepika26@gmail.com, tv_g@hotmail.com,
rajisridhar@gmail.com

Abstract. Text document search typically retrieves documents by performing an exact match based on keywords. In all domains the exact match may not yield good performance as the morpheme or structure of the words has not been considered for the search. This problem becomes significant in the research field of chemistry, where the user could search using a keyword and the document could contain the keyword as a part of the chemical name. For example, the chemical name pentanone contains ketone functional group in it, which can be found by doing a morphemic analysis with the help of chemical nomenclature. Each of the chemical names contains a lot of information about the chemical compound for which it is being named. Hence, the chemical names in the document need to be tagged with all its possible meaningful morphemes to have efficient performance. A multi-perspective and domain specific tagging system was designed based on the available chemical nomenclature, considering the type of bond, number of carbon atoms and the functional group of the chemical entity. The tagging system begins with extraction of the chemical names in the document based on morphological and domain specific features. Based on these features and the contextual knowledge, models were created by designing a linear-chain conditional random field of order two, and they serve as a baseline for the chemical entity extraction process. A morphemic or structural analysis of the extracted named entity was done for the multi-perspective tagging system.

Keywords: Domain-specific tagging · Chemical entity tagging
Chemical entity recognition · Domain-specific search

1 Introduction

Scientific articles are being published in all disciplines and there is a huge volume of information which has to be extracted from these articles. Chemistry literature documents are rich source of information containing many chemical entities. As in any other field, these documents will be unstructured and contain domain-related information written using natural language. Hence it requires specialized knowledge of the subject domain and automation for information extraction [1]. Identifying chemical named entities from the text will be useful in many ways like mapping identified entities with the knowledge base, finding their properties, identifying similar chemical compounds

Shriram R and M. Sharma (Eds.): DaSAA 2017, CCIS 804, pp. 72–85, 2018.
https://doi.org/10.1007/978-981-10-8603-8_7

[2]. Chemical compound information from the research articles would also be helpful in the drug research area especially in the drug discovery process [2]. Newly developed drugs, their interaction with other drugs [3], their other properties would not be updated in the chemical database. So text mining would give an insight into these chemicals and their relationship with other chemicals.

Most of the research works in the field of bioinformatics have focused on recognition of protein and gene named entities [4, 7]. However, only few efforts have been made in recognition of chemical entities in the document [6]. This is due to the lack of annotated corpora, difficulty and high cost in its generation but it is an area which can benefit immensely from text mining. The ability to extract chemical entities from text documents automatically has great value to chemical research and development activities [8].

Chemical named entities are represented in different formats in these documents. So mining this information and tagging them based on domain specific features would be helpful for the chemistry research people, in finding documents related to their research. There exists a number of naming standards like IUPAC, SMILE for the chemical entities which makes the information extraction a difficult task [9].

Mining the chemical literature documents and identifying the chemical entities in the text can be done using different methodologies and it has the following challenges [8, 10].

- Infinite number of compounds present and new compounds being synthesized very frequently.
- High ambiguity in representing a chemical compound. A single chemical can be represented using trivial names, abbreviation, systematic names, chemical structures [11], registry numbers or formal descriptions like formulae [12].
- Very lengthy compounds, use of punctuation marks in between the chemical name for example 3-(4-(2-hydroxyethyl)-1-piperazinyl) propanesulfonic acid, 2-amino-2-ethyl-1,3,5-propanediol. Here Brackets, "-", "," should be identified as a part of the chemical entity.
- The prefix of the chemical words could align with the prefix of other non-chemical words which could impose a difficulty in tagging. For example, "meth" - root word, retrieves both "methyl" and "method".

Therefore, the creation and maintenance of chemical terminologies is a complex task.

In this paper, we have extracted one form of chemical entity representation, the IUPAC name which is the systemic way of representing the chemical compound. This is done using a supervised machine learning algorithm, conditional random fields [13] and available chemical ontology ChEBI [14]. We discuss the tags that we have created to tag the chemical entities based on the morphemic analysis of the IUPAC name. The tags used in other domains cannot be used in the chemistry domain as it makes the tagging more general. And also simple tags like chemical compound <CM> used in works like OSCAR [15] will not give much information about that chemical compound. So, tags specific to the chemistry domain were designed by analysing the chemical name using the IUPAC nomenclature [16], which will also be useful for the chemistry specific document search.

2   Related Work

The process of tagging starts with identifying the named entities. Named entity recognition (NER) system which is developed for one domain does not perform well on other domains. Therefore, developing a NER system is domain specific and needs a good understanding of the domain. Named entity recognition systems employ three main approaches [9]. Dictionary based [5], rule based and machine learning based approaches [10]. The dictionary based approach identifies the chemical entities in the text using the available chemical dictionaries like PubChem, which is a database of chemical molecules. This approach however depends on the availability and completeness of the dictionary, and is limited to the entities contained in them. Given the vast amount of possible chemical compounds, a dictionary covering all the chemical compounds till date is infeasible [9].

Rule based approaches use pattern-based rules and context-based rules to identify the chemical entities [17]. Rule-based approach for the chemical name recognition works well when we have an exhaustive set of rules. But when we have a slightly modified data, it will increase the maintenance cost. Machine learning based approach requires an annotated corpus which is used to learn a model and it can be applied for named entity recognition in new text [18]. Among the various methods like markovian models [15], conditional random field (CRF) [13] used to identify the chemical names, conditional random field gives better performance [9]. Conditional random fields can be used for handling words with multiple features and also it has the ability to relax the strong independence assumptions present in other models.

In the area of chemical text mining, many researchers have focused on named entity recognition [19]. After recognizing the chemical entities, giving them tags useful for the document search is also important. The GENIA Tagger includes Part of speech tags for biomedical text using maximum entropy modelling [20]. Peter et al. [21] have developed guidelines to annotate five types of named entities namely chemical compound, chemical reaction, chemical adjective, enzyme and chemical prefix and have evaluated their system using off-the shelf NER tool.

OSCAR tagger [15] is used to identify the chemical names, formulae, chemical prefixes and adjectives as well as dictionary lookup to identify a pre-determined set of ontology terms. Chemical tagger [22] focused on tagging the phrases related to chemistry and in role identification. Both the above mentioned taggers concentrated only on extracting the chemical entities and giving them a related tag like chemical name, enzyme and formula. But this alone will not be enough when a chemist does a search. We need a domain specific tagger which would be helpful in identifying all the tags related to each chemical entity. For example, the chemical name "2-hydroxy benzoic acid" contains alcohol in it, but it is not tagged using the normal tagger as alcohol. So, we mainly concentrate on tagging each chemical entity in different ways based on the chemical nomenclature, giving each chemical entity more than one tag which would be useful for the chemical document search. With the help of our proposed tagger, we can tag "2-hydroxy benzoic acid" as an alcohol. In the same manner, the proposed tagger gives the tags by tokenizing each chemical entity into meaningful terms and analyzing them to give the entity, multiple tags.

3   Methodology

The work mainly deals with information mining, getting information from the chemical names and tagging in a multi-perspective way to yield a better performance in the search. This system concentrates on the organic compounds as researches take place in these compounds and they contribute to more than 80% of the available chemical compounds, also millions and millions of organic compound are evolved every year. The architecture of the work is shown in Fig. 1.

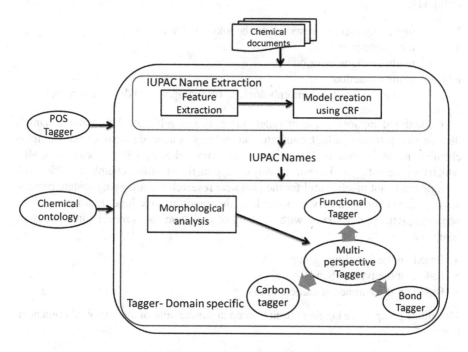

Fig. 1. System architecture

The two main tasks involved in this system are

- Feature Extraction and model creation using CRF of order two.
- Domain-specific and multi-perspective tagging of extracted chemical entities.

In this work we extract the IUPAC representation of the chemical name [23]. Before doing the morphemic analysis of the IUPAC name for the tagging system, they have to be extracted separately from the other non-chemical terms. For this many features were considered and the main one is the POS tag of the word. A chemical name may be a single word or it may be a very long one with brackets, numbers, and so many punctuations (orthographic features). So it is difficult to find where the chemical name starts and ends in the document [18].

Many Machine learning strategies are used in various fields for extracting the named entities in the document. For the chemical named entity recognition, as CRF works better handling the lengthy names, we have used this supervised algorithm for our named entity recognition [13]. A special case of CRF, linear-chain CRF of order 2 was used to extract the chemical name.

3.1 Linear-Chain CRF

$$P(y|x) = 1/Z(x).(\Sigma\ exp(\lambda j Fj(y, x))). \tag{1}$$

In Eq. (1),

X   input sequence, corresponds to the tokenized text
Y   label sequence
λ_j feature weight(on or off)
$F_j(y, x)$ feature function
        Features considered [morphological, orthographic and domain specific].

Conditional random fields of order one may not solve all the chemical name's demarcation problem, as high contextual knowledge is needed to extract many lengthy chemical names. Hence IUPAC names were extracted using CRF of order two, after which they were tagged. The normal way of tagging the identified chemical entities with a single tag is not much useful for the chemical researchers. A tagging system particularly designed for chemistry is needed. In this work, a three level multi-perspective tagging system was designed with the help of the chemical nomenclature. The three levels are

- Based on the functional groups
- Based on the type of bonds
- Based on the number of carbon atoms

This multi-perspective tagging requires deep understanding of the chemical nomenclature.

3.2 Feature Extraction and Model Reation

Chemical names in the document and the normal English words look alike. E.g. benzene is an English word, also a chemical compound. So the complexity lies in identifying chemical compound as a "chemical entity", differentiating from non-chemical terms in the document. As the IUPAC nomenclature is not followed strictly, IUPAC and partially IUPAC names were extracted from the document using "models" which were created from the features extracted from context of the chemical term in the document and also the nomenclature available.

Features that were considered for the model creation are:

- POS tag of the word
  - Adjective-Noun, Noun-Noun combination
    Example: ethyl methyl ketone – Adjective-Noun
    n-propyl ketone – Noun-Noun

- has braces
- has comma
- has dash
- has quote
- numbers – [0-9]
- key words related to chemistry like groups, derivatives, compounds, acid.
  Example: amino groups, ethyl groups, isopropyl derivatives,
  [4 - (2 – hydroxyethyl)-1-piperazinyl] propanesulfonic acid
- preposition list

Complex compound names like "2-amino-2-ethyl-2,3,5-propanediol", "4'-diaminomethane", and many acids include almost all the features. This model creation was done with the help of CRF++tool. Around eight models have been created using the above mentioned features. In the model, we have defined a new Chemical Separator (CS) Tag for each of the token in the chemical name like words, punctuations, braces and numbers. The CS tag differs for each model. The CS tag for the acid model is encoded as Label sequence consisting of eight entities and it is as follows.

$$L = \{I\text{-}B, I, A, BL, BR, SYM, CRD, O\}$$

A - The word acid
I-B - The word before acid
I - all the words before 'I-B'
BL - left parenthesis
BR - right parenthesis
, - SYM
" - SYM
Numbers - CRD
Hyphen - SYM
O - Outside

In the same manner, label sequences for all the models were created and with the help of CRF++ tool, these CS tags were assigned to the tokens present in the chemical name. The main difficulty here is to give the correct CS tag to the chemical entity. And it is mainly based on the POS tag of the word.

Example: Phrase I: "withdrawing group"
           Phrase II: "amino group"

Here POS tag of "withdrawing" is verb and that of "amino" is an adjective. Also, only the braces within the chemical entities should be considered as a part of chemical entity and other elements should be ignored. Along with the extracted chemical entities, some non-chemical terms were also identified as chemical entities. To resolve this, a suffix list based on the nomenclature, including primary and secondary suffixes was generated. This eliminates most of the non-chemical words and improves the precision but not 100%.

Example: Phrase1: "degrees of freedom in the host"
           Phrase2: "preferences of hexaethylbenzene by calculation".

With help of the suffix list created "freedom" was eliminated as it is a non- chemical term. In a similar manner, the false positives were eliminated using the created suffix list. (4-(hydroxyethyl)1-piperazinyl)hydrochloric acid is chemical entity and the CS tag assigned to it according to the acid model is shown in Fig. 2.

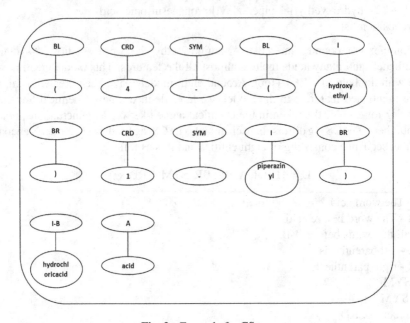

Fig. 2. Example for CS tag

3.3 Multi-perspective and Domain Specific Tagging

A tagging system was designed in this work which is specific to the chemistry domain. In organic chemistry, there are many ways in which a chemical compound can be viewed. A chemical compound may have many functional groups attached to them or it may differ in the way it is bonded, these could be the primary motive of the user who performs the search. These semantics of each chemical entity will not be specified explicitly in the document. Identifying the semantics within each chemical compound requires domain knowledge, for which the available chemical ontology [14] and nomenclature [16] were used and we do a morphemic analyzes of the chemical name. A new tagging system which is multi-perspective and domain specific was designed to tag the chemical entities. In each level a specific method was used to analyze and tag the chemical entity (CE). The peculiar part of this tagging system is that, the chemical compound gets different tag at each level and also it gets more than one tag in the same level.

Tagging Based on Functional Group. Each chemical compound has one or more functional groups in them and they are named based on these functional groups. Functional groups play an important role in the way that particular chemical compound reacts with other compounds. The functional group also determines the properties of the chemical compound. Hence, functional group tagging will be a very useful form of tagging. The important functional groups that were used to tag are

- Alcohol
- Amine
- Amide
- Acid
- Ketone
- Aldehyde
- Ether
- Ester
- Nitrile

For each functional group, their presence in the IUPAC name is identified through a set of prefix and suffix terms. Based on these morphemes of a IUPAC name, domain-specific tags were given to the chemical compound. For example considering the Alcohol group, if alcohol group is present in a compound, the possibilities are

– As a part of parent chain, it uses the suffix term "ol".
– If not, it uses the prefix "hydroxy".

If the user searches using the keyword 'alcohol', then the documents containing the 'alcohol' term explicitly in their text content will only be retrieved in normal search. But our system analyzes each chemical entity extracted from the document, finds whether it contains the alcohol functional group. So our system will retrieve documents which are related to the keyword, even if the keyword is not mentioned explicitly in it.

Tagging Based on Type of the Bond. The carbon atoms in the organic compound are bonded differently. The bond between different atoms in the chemical compound tells us about the attraction between the atoms. Different properties like reactivity, solubility are determined by these bond types. The three main types of bond that can be depicted using a chemical name are

- Single Bond
- Double Bond
- Triple Bond

Normally, all the carbon atoms will be bonded using single bond. So we don't explicitly tag the compound with the tag "Single Bond". If double or triple bond is used to bond the carbon atoms then it will be mentioned in their name. Hence, the unique suffixes and infixes used for double and triple bond were identified and it was used for tagging the chemical compound. In a typical document containing the chemical compound pent-1-en-4-yne can be tagged using DOUBLE and TRIPLE tags. In the chemical compound pent-1-en-4-yne,

- "-en-"corresponds to Double Bond
- "-yne-" corresponds to Triple Bond

The type of bond of the CE will not be usually mentioned separately in the document. By using this level of our tagging system, we can identify the type of bond of each CE which will be useful to retrieve more relevant documents during a search.

Tagging Based on the Number of Carbon Atoms. The number of carbon atom present in the chemical compound starts from one and it goes on. The number of carbon atoms in the parent chain or side chain can be identified using the root word which is unique for each number. In this level of tagging we don't find the total number of carbon atoms present in the compound. We tag the compound with the possible alkyl groups present in the side chain and number of carbon atoms present in the parent chain. The root word corresponding to alkyl group was identified and the tags were given to the CE. For example, the compound 4-methyl octane can be tagged using ONE CARBON and EIGHT CARBON tags.

Here,

- The root word "meth" correspond to ONE (single carbon atom)
- The root word "oct" corresponds to EIGHT (eight carbon atoms)

When the search is complex with key words like single bonded amino alcohol or double bonded ester acid, our system extracts the document containing the related tags which will not be done in the normal search.

4   Results

Chemical entity recognition and the domain specific, multi-perspective tagger were evaluated using the chemical documents from the "Beilstein journal of organic chemistry". For the IUPAC name recognition, different models created through CRF++, for the extraction process was considered for the evaluation. The non-chemical term removal module was evaluated using the same set of documents. The designed tagger was evaluated by considering only the extracted chemical entities. The chemical entities which were not extracted during the entity extraction process were excluded for the evaluation of the proposed tagger.

4.1   Chemical Entity Recognition

Evaluation of the identified entities is done with the help of precision, fraction of retrieved instances that are relevant. Figure 3 shows the average precision calculated for over 500 chemical documents using different models that were created. This analysis was done excluding the errors occurred during PDF format conversion. Noun-noun and adjective-noun model gives a low precision. This is due to high ambiguity in the model with non-chemical entities. But the overall precision with respect to each document was high.

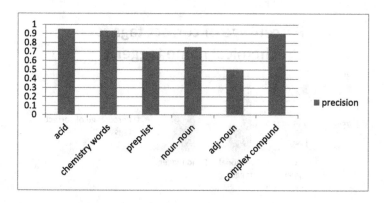

Fig. 3. Precision with respect to 'models'

To improve the precision of the chemical entity extraction, suffix list was created using the chemical ontology. Figure 4 shows considerable increase in the precision of the randomly chosen document after including the suffix list.

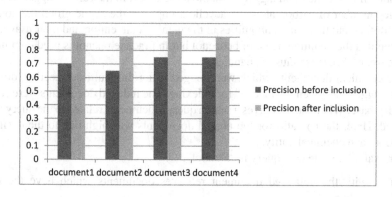

Fig. 4. Precision before and after inclusion of the suffix list

4.2 Multi-perspective Tagging

The percentage of correct tagging for each tagger namely functional tagger, carbon tagger, bond tagger is shown in Fig. 5. The functional tagger works well and shows a good performance as in most of the IUPAC names they mention the functional group through suffixes or prefixes. But we have handled only the most commonly used functional groups in organic chemistry. There are other functional groups which can be handled through additional rules.

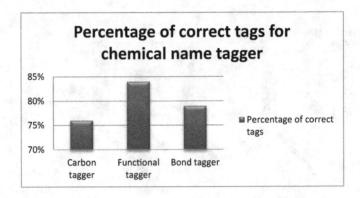

Fig. 5. Percentage of correct tags for chemical name tagger

The bond tagger gives a lesser performance than the functional tagger as the IUPAC names do not contain their bond information in them in all the cases. For e.g. Benzoic acid contains double bond in it but we can't find it through the suffixes or infixes. So, we should improve the bond tagger to handle these cases. In the carbon tagger we have identified number of carbon atoms in acyclic group. For the cyclic group the nomenclature differs and there are ambiguities in the naming convention and their usage. For e.g. Phenol is the common name of benzenol but in practice phenol is used commonly than benzenol. So, these must be handled.

The chemical documents which were tagged using the multi-perspective, domain specific tagger was given to "lucene" for indexing. The indexed documents were stored in the database. When the user gives a search query, documents related to the query were retrieved. Here, the hit ratio for the tagged documents was high due to the designed tagger for each chemical entity.

For example, if the user query is "alcohol",

- Search with the untagged document retrieves documents which have the term "alcohol", but
- Search with tagged document retrieves document which have the tag "<<alcohol>>", so even if the document contains "ethanol", or "3-hydroxybenzoic acid", the document will be retrieved.

Lucene was used to index both tagged and untagged documents. Figure 6 shows the precision measure between the untagged documents and documents tagged based on the chemical name tagger.

Precision = Retreived documents that are relevant ÷ Total number of documents relevant.   (2)

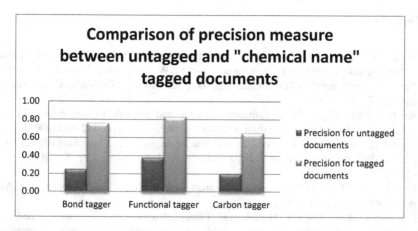

Fig. 6. Comparison of precision measure between untagged and "chemical name" tagged documents

Precision of the documents at all the levels of tagging using chemical name tagger was high compared to the untagged documents, since tagged documents have analyzed the chemical names in the document and were given domain specific tags. For example, a document containing the chemical name "propene-2-ol" will be having the tags <<alcohol>>, <<three>> <<double>>. So, this document will be retrieved for the queries; double bond, alcohol, three carbon.

5 Conclusion

The Multi-perspective tagging system designed especially for the chemical names will be very much useful for retrieving relevant chemical documents. Extraction of IUPAC names and partially IUPAC names was done using CRF and they were tagged using the proposed tagging system. By handling the drawbacks mentioned above and further morphemic analysis of the chemical names can improve the performance and yield additional levels in the three level tagging system. Compared to OSCAR tagger, which tagged the extracted chemical compounds with a single tag, our tagger analyzed the chemical compound in detail based on the chemical nomenclature and gave them specialized tags at each level with good accuracy. This tagging can be used for tagging all forms of the chemical representation like SMILES, Formula, and Chemical structure.

Along with text, images play an important role in the chemical literature as chemical structures are depicted in the form of images in the document. Existing entity extraction techniques focus on textual data and hence the important information conveyed by images is discarded and made inaccessible to users. So, we try to extract information from the chemical structures by analyzing the images and using it to tag the document. This could improve the domain specific search efficiency even better.

References

1. Kolárik, C., Klinger, R., Friedrich, C.M., Hofmann-Apitius, M., Fluck, J.: Chemical names: terminological resources and corpora annotation. In: Workshop on Building and Evaluating Resources for Biomedical Text Mining. Language Resources and Evaluation Conference, 6th edn., pp. 51–58 (2008)
2. Roberts, P.M., Hayes, W.S.: Information needs and the role of text mining in drug development. In: Pacific Symposium on Biocomputing, vol. 13, pp. 592–603 (2008)
3. Sonu, G.S., Harikumar, S.L., Navis, S.: A review on drug-drug and drug-food interactions in patients during the treatment of diabetes mellitus. Int. J. Pharmacol. Clin. Sci. 4(4), 98–105 (2015)
4. Cohen, A.M., Hersh, W.R.: A survey of current work in biomedical text mining. Briefings Bioinform. 6(1), 57–71 (2005)
5. Friedrich, C.M., Revillion, T., Hofmann, M., Fluck, J.: Biomedical and chemical named entity recognition with conditional random fields: the advantage of dictionary features. In: Proceedings of the Second International Symposium on Semantic Mining in Biomedicine, BMC Bioinformatics, vol. 7, pp. 85–89 (2006)
6. John Wilbur, W., Hazard, G.F., Divita, G., Mork, J.G., Aronson, A.R., Browne, A.C.: Analysis of biomedical text for chemical names: a comparison of three methods. In: Proceedings of the AMIA Symposium, pp. 176–180 (1999)
7. Zhou, G., Zhang, J., Su, J., Shen, D., Tan, C.: Recognizing names in biomedical texts: a machine learning approach. Bioinformatics 20(7), 1178–1190 (2004)
8. Grego, T., Pesquita, C., Bastos, H.P., Couto, F.M.: Chemical entity recognition and resolution to ChEBI. ISRN Bioinform. (2012). https://doi.org/10.5402/2012/619427. Article ID 619427, 9 pages
9. Eltyeb, S., Salim, N.: Chemical named entities recognition: a review on approaches and applications. J. Cheminform. 6, 1–17 (2014)
10. Umare, S.P., Deshpande, N.A.: A survey on machine learning techniques to extract chemical names from text documents. Int. J. Comput. Sci. Inf. Technol. 6(2), 1263–1266 (2015)
11. Algorri, M., Zimmermann, M., Friedrich C.M., Akle, S., Hofmann-Apitius, M.: Reconstruction of chemical molecules from images. In: Proceedings of the 29th Annual International Conference of the IEEE Engineering in Medicine and Biology Society, EMBC, pp. 4609–4612 (2007)
12. Sun, B., Tan, Q., Mitra, P., Giles, C.L.: Extraction and search of chemical formulae in text documents. In: Proceedings of the 16th International Conference on World Wide Web, pp. 251–260 (2007)
13. Lafferty, J., McCallum, A., Pereira, F.C.N.: Conditional random fields: Probabilistic models for segmenting and labeling sequence data. In: Proceedings of ICML (2001)
14. de Matos, P., Dekker, A., Ennis, M., Hastings, J., Haug, K., Turne, S., Steinbeck, C.: ChEBI: a chemistry ontology and database. J. Cheminform. 2, P6 (2010)
15. Jessop, D.M., Adams, S.E., Willighagen, E.L., Hawizy, L., Murray-Rust, P.: OSCAR4: a flexible architecture for chemical textmining. J. Cheminform. 3, 1–41 (2011)
16. IUPAC: Commission on the Nomenclature of Organic Chemistry. A Guide to IUPAC Nomenclature of Organic Compounds (Recommendations 1993). Blackwell Scientific Publications, Oxford (1993)
17. Lana-Serrano, S., Sanchez-Cisneros, D., Campillos, L., Segura-Bedmar, I.: Recognizing chemical compounds and drugs: a rule-based approach using semantic information. In: BioCreative Challenge Evaluation Workshop, vol. 2 (2013)

18. Corbett, P., Copestake, A.: Cascaded classifiers for confidence-based chemical named entity recognition. BMC Bioinform. **9**(Suppl. 11), 54–62 (2008)
19. Usié, A., Alves, R., Solsona, F., Vázquez, M., Valencia, A.: CheNER: chemical named entity recognizer. Bioinformatics **30**(7), 1039–1040 (2014)
20. Kim, J.D., Ohta, T., Tateisi, Y., Tsujii, J.: GENIA corpus - a semantically annotated corpus for bio-textmining. Bioinformatics **19**(1), i180–i182 (2003)
21. Corbett, P., Batchelor, C., Teufel, S.: Annotation of chemical named entities. In: Proceedings of the Workshop on BioNLP 2007: Biological, Translational, and Clinical Language Processing, pp. 57–64 (2007)
22. Hawizy, L., Jessop, D.M., Adams, N., Murray-Rust, P.: Chemical tagger: a tool for semantic text-mining in chemistry. J. Cheminform. **3**, 1–17 (2011)
23. Klinger, R., Kolárik, C., Fluck, J., Hofmann-Apitius, M., Friedrich, C.M.: Detection of IUPAC and IUPAC-like chemical names. Bioinformatics **24**, i268–i276 (2008)
24. Rocktäschel, T., Weidlich, M., Leser, U.: ChemSpot: a hybrid system for chemical named entity recognition. Bioinformatics **28**, 1633–1640 (2012)
25. Sun, B., Mitra, P., Giles, C.L.: Mining, indexing, and searching for textual chemical molecule information. In: Proceedings of the 17th International Conference on World Wide Web, pp. 735–744 (2008)
26. Wu, X., Zhang, L., Chen, Y., Rhodes, J., Griffin, T.D., Boyer, S.K., Alba, A., Cai, K.: ChemBrowser: a flexible framework for mining chemical documents. In: Arabnia, H. (ed.) Advances in Computational Biology, pp. 57–64. Springer, New York (2010). https://doi.org/10.1007/978-1-4419-5913-3_7
27. Lee, C., Hou, W.-J., Chen, H.-H.: Annotating multiple types of biomedical entities: a single word classification approach. In: International Joint Workshop on Natural Language Processing in Biomedicine and Its Applications (NLPBA/BioNLP) (2004)

Partition Aware Duplicate Records Detection (PADRD) Methodology in Big Data - Decision Support Systems

Anusuya Kirubakaran[1(✉)] [iD] and Aramudhan Murugaiyan[2]

[1] Mother Teresa Women's University, Kodaikanal, India
Anusuya.kirubakaran@outlook.com
[2] PKIET, Karaikal, Puducherry, India
Aranagai@yahoo.co.in

Abstract. As on today, the big data analytics and business intelligence (BI) decision support system (DSS) are the vital pillar of the leadership ability by translating raw data toward intelligence to make 'right decision on right time' and to share 'right decision to right people'. Often DSS challenged to process the massive volume of data (Terabyte, petabyte, Exabyte, Zettabyte etc.) and to overcome the issues like data quality, scalability, storage and query performance. The failure in DSS was one of the reasons highlighted clearly by United State Senate report regarding the 2008 American economy collapse. To keep these issues in mind, this work explores a preventive methodology for "Data Quality - Duplicates" dimension with optimized query performance in big data era. In detail, BI team extracts and loads the historical operational structured data (Data Feed) to its repository from multiple sources periodically such as daily, weekly, monthly, quarterly, half yearly for analytics and reporting. During this load unpremeditated duplicate data feed insertion occurs due to lack of expertise, lack of history, missing integrity constraints which impact the intelligence reporting error ratio & the leader ship ability. So the necessity of unintentional data quality issue injection prevention arises. Over all, this paper proposes a methodology to "Improve the Data Accuracy" through detection of duplicate records between big data repository vs data feed before the data load with "Optimized Query Performance" through partition aware search query generation and "Faster Data Block Address Search" through braided b+ tree indexing.

Keywords: Duplicate record detection · Braided tree indexing
Decision support system

1 Introduction

Today, most of the firms, governments & regulators across geographies understood and erudite from 2008 financial crisis that the necessity of quality of data to be in place for effective and wealthy macro-economic behaviors. Hence regulators are insisting the financial sectors to manage the quality of data which are useful for identification of risks across portfolios, proactive measure for business stabilization and challenges,

© Springer Nature Singapore Pte Ltd. 2018
Shriram R and M. Sharma (Eds.): DaSAA 2017, CCIS 804, pp. 86–98, 2018.
https://doi.org/10.1007/978-981-10-8603-8_8

stakeholders and customers relationship, and also for quick to market decisions to leverage business changes & opportunities, etc. So the organizations enforce the enterprise wide multisource, subject-oriented, time-variant, integrated big data repository to enable real time business intelligence process. The big data repository consist of many years of data accumulated periodically such as daily, weekly, monthly, quarterly, half yearly through ETL (extraction, transform, load) process may leads to inevitable and unintentional data quality issues through data consolidation, missing integrity constraints, redundant manual loading, process termination, manual restarting and lack of expertise etc.

In this paper, we are dealing with one of the key data quality dimension "duplicates" in big data repository. Duplicates have greater impacts on the business (E.g. Strategies, Profit and Loss Statements) which need to be prevented before the data ingestion for better quality eco system. To keep this scenario in mind, we have proposed a preventive methodology which locate the duplicate records in the data feeds versus big data repository. The proposed paper featured with amalgamation of B^+ Tree [1, 2], Braided Tree [3–5], horizontal range partitioning [6, 7], data dictionary [8, 9] to detect the duplicate records faster. Also this paper, proposes parallel dynamic partition aware subqueries generation for fastening the huge volume of data search. Let us describe the overview of chosen technique's suitability for proposed solution. B^+ trees are height balanced tree with multiple children per node consist of root, non-leaf nodes and leaf nodes which supports efficient access mechanism for disk, block oriented data retrieval shown in Fig. 1(a). The Braided B^+ Tree[3] shown in Fig. 1(b) is a doubly linked list denoted as (uk, R, prev, next) where uk is a unique key value, R is the block identifiers list attached to that node, and prev & next are predecessor and successor node's links. This braided B^+ tree facilitates tree traversal horizontally across multiples nodes irrespective of disjoint parents. This feature helps to extend the data blocks search across nodes without backtracking. Even for disjunction nodes, braided approach provides improvised data search time complexity by effortless finding of the neighborhood record path. Then the horizontal range partitioning technique splits the big data repositories' huge volume of records to predefined number of records partition based critical business element. This data partitioning approach helps to limit the data search area. Also using data dictionary,

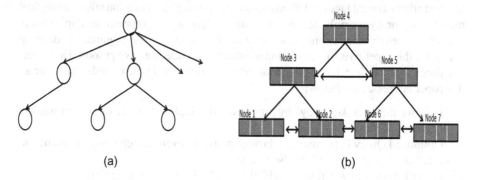

(a)   (b)

Fig. 1. (a) B^+ tree, (b) Braided B^+ tree

the data partition details are maintained which helps to generate the partition aware queries results optimized searching time.

2 Literature Survey

The existing duplicate detection methods deals with the perspective of duplicate records present in the data storage system after the data feed loaded to the repository based on tuple's (field) similarity estimation using Character-Based Similarity Metrics [10, 11], Token-Based Similarity Metrics [11, 12], Phonetic Similarity Metrics [13], Numeric Similarity Metrics, weight distribution [14]. Also the systems are trained to find the duplicate records using machine leaning algorithms such as naïve Bayes rule [15, 16], genetic algorithm [17], Support Vector Machine. To perform effective data comparison, the datasets were divided to fixed number records based on blocking [18, 19], windowing [19], indexing [19], clustering [19], and apply classification [20], nearest neighbor record finding [21], weight learning [22]. Also the duplicate records verification can be done though rule based [23] or iteratively [24] for structured and semi-structured data [25]. Since the proposed method focus on post data quality verification, we propose a method which prevents the duplicate records insertion to the repository.

3 Problem Definition

Now a day, the decision support system (DSS) turn out to be the vital pillar of intelligent management decision support, also to safe guard from reputational loss, revenue loss and regulatory actions. Also 'Time to Decision' is the key to business strategy planning and execution. Hence the ability of the DSS to gather raw data with high quality in terms of consistency, reliability, authenticity, timeliness, duplicates and asses the information from raw data are the step stone for 'right decision on right time'. To provide real time or near real time decisions, the BI team populate the transactional data (data feed) extracted from multiple heterogeneous production systems, cleansed, integrated, and loaded periodically to big data repository. During this ETL (Extract, transformation, Loading) processing, the single data feed being populated multiple times to business intelligence repository due to lack of knowledge, lack of training, partial thread execution and other external factors. This unintended duplicate feed injection affects analytical reporting accuracy for right decision-making on right time. To correct the duplicates in the big data environment, high cost, time & manual efforts are required. In order to overcome this repetitive, inevitable and unintentional issue, we have proposed a preventive duplicate records detection methodology with optimized time complexity. Over all this paper addresses the below:

- "Improve the Data Accuracy" by preventing the duplicate records insertion into the big data repository.
- "Optimized Query Performance" through partition aware search query generation to detect the duplicate records in the data feed.
- "Faster Data Block Address Search" through braided b$^+$ tree indexing.

4 Methodology

The historical data set stored in the big data repository for analytical processing W = {1, 2, 3, 4 .... n} and S = {1, 2, 3, 4 .... m} be the data feed extracted from the operational data source to temporary staging area for the periodic database dump loading. In traditional data processing, the data feed S being cleansed, integrated as part of transformation then the data feed S loaded into to the big data repository. Due to missing unique constraint, duplicate records inserted into the historical big data storage system which affects the analytics report quality error ratio proportionally. In order to overcome this issue, the proposed methodology aims to find the common records between big data repository versus data feed (S ∩ W) and remove the duplicate records from the data feed S before the data load to W. To implement the same, the proposed methodology introduced three phases between ETL's Transform and Loading phase shown in Fig. 2(a) for duplicate records insertion prevention.

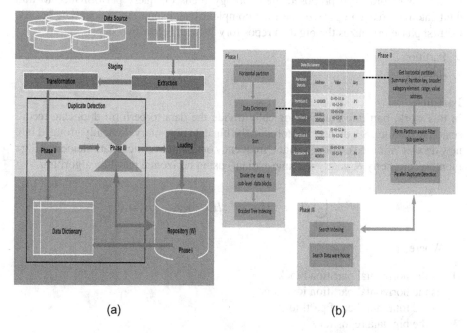

(a)   (b)

Fig. 2. (a) Proposed architecture, (b) Proposed architecture' steps

The outlines of the proposed methodologies' phases are described below and the detailed steps in each phase are shown in Fig. 2(b).

- Phase I - Organize the data:
  In this phase, organize the big data repository though dividing the massive volume of data to smaller data blocks for optimized query performance and to ignore the redundant & irrelevant data search. After data blocks partition, data blocks history being stored in Data Dictionary to generate partition aware queries. Also braided b^+

tree indexing created from data blocks partition to support faster data blocks address searching.

- Phase II - Partition Aware Filter Sub-Queries Generation:
  In this phase, using data dictionary's data block partition summary, partition aware filter sub-queries would be created to enable optimised query performance. Also partition aware sub-queries will be executed in parallel returns optimized turnaround time for duplicate records detection.
- Phase III – Search:
  This phase proposes the methodology to find the data block' address faster using braided b$^+$ tree indexing.

4.1   Phase I: Organize the Data

Since the big data repository W deals with Terabyte, petabyte, Exabyte, Zettabyte volume of records, the proposed methodology focus on query performance to find duplicate records. To optimize the time complexity and support efficient data access, the first phase organizes the big data repository W with below two steps:

- Partition
- Indexing

Partition

In this work, partition helps to logically divide the data to perform duplicate record search in parallel. So, dataset W stored in the big data repository, logically grouped into new dataset W' based on time-variant, frequency or business critical data elements (E.g.: monthly, quarterly & yearly for time-variant) using horizontal partition algorithm.

$$W' = \bigcup_{i=1}^{k} H_i \Rightarrow \forall H \in W' : H \subset W \wedge \bigcap_{i=1}^{k} H_i = \emptyset$$

Where

H   is the horizontal partition block
i   is the horizontal partition identifier
K   is the total number of partition
W   is the big data repository

After first level horizontal data partitioning, each and every partition address captured in the data dictionary to facilitate the partition aware queries generation feature. Since the data partitions divides the data based on broader category elements, the total number records belongs to each partitions will be huge in numbers. To exemplify, if the total number transactions captured for every month is 100 billion in online traders then the time complexity impacts during the duplicate record search. In order to optimize this scenario, the dataset belongs H will undergo second level horizontal partition based on the optimal size of the data records fit into each data block. Before the second level partition, data records needs to be sorted in

H to keep sequential data search rather than data search thread across multiple data blocks. And each data block b possesses f number of records.

$$H' = \bigcup_{x=1}^{n=\frac{|h|}{f}} b_x \Rightarrow \forall b \in H' : b \subset W' \wedge \bigcap_{x=1}^{n} b_x = \emptyset \, and \, b \rightarrow \{r_1, r_2, r_3, r_4 \ldots r_f\}$$

Where

H' is the second level partition
h   is the horizontal block
b   is the second level data block partition
x   is the second level data block identifier
n   is the total number second level data block partition
f   is the data block size

As discussed, partitioning has two levels to organize the big data to limited number of dataset as shown in Fig. 3. After data partition, for k number of horizontal partitions, k number of braided B^+ trees gets created to optimize the query performance. The detailed portrayal for indexing technique will be discussed in the following section.

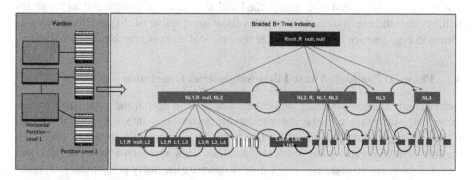

Fig. 3. Phase I – Data organization

Indexing

As part of organizing the data, braided B^+ tree indexing plays a dynamic role to optimize the duplicate record detection methodology. The proposed approach prefers B^+ Tree to index voluminous data through multiple child nodes. And the nodes are braided through predecessor and successor node reference linkages. The braided indexing needs to be performed in bottom-up approach i.e. leaf nodes get created first then the tree grows to non-leaf node and root node. So, the data blocks in H' grouped into m number of data blocks and the data block's reference added to the block identifier $R \rightarrow \{b_1, b_2, b_3, b_4 \ldots b_m\}$. The Leaf node L created as doubly link list (*uk, R, prev, next*) where uk is the leaf node key, R is block identifier, prev is the predecessor leaf node address and next is the successor leaf node address. For example *l1 = {l1, R null,*

L2) and R = {(*db1, 01-01-15, Toronto), (db2, 01-01-15, Los Angeles), (db3, 01-01-15, New York), ... (dbs, 01-01*-15, New York). The total number of leaf nodes in the braided indexing is calculated using,

$$Total\ Number\ of\ Leaf\ Nodes = \frac{Total\ Number\ of\ data\ blocks\ in\ H'}{Maximum\ no.of\ data\ blocks\ in\ Record\ Identifer\ (m)}$$

Once done with the leaf nodes creation, non-leaf (NL) nodes being created from the leaf nodes. The non-leaf nodes are denoted as doubly link list (*uk, R, prev, next*) as same as leaf nodes where uk is the non-leaf node key, R is block identifier stores the leaf-nodes references, prev is the predecessor non-leaf node' address and next is the successor non-leaf node' address. The total number of non-leaf nodes to be created is calculated as below:

$$Tot.\ no.\ of\ Non-Leaf\ Nodes\ T = \frac{Total\ Number\ of\ previous\ level'\ leaf\ nodes}{Max.\ no.\ of\ reference\ in\ one\ Non-leaf\ node}$$

Based in the above formula, T no. of non-leaf nodes being created at each level and each non-leaf nodes will contain m number of child nodes reference in block identifier R, predecessor and successor non-leaf references at single level. The bottom up for parent non-leaf node creation gets repeated till the total number of parent nodes become 1 as root node. At the end of indexing, the braided b$^+$ tree gets created and all the nodes will be have the previous and next nodes links irrespective of disjunction parents as shown in Fig. 3 which helps to optimize the physical address search time complexity.

4.2   Phase II: Partition Aware Filter Sub-queries Generation

Even though multiple indexing algorithms available to search the data, partition un-aware range-query searches the multiple data blocks for single thread. On the other hand, if the queries generated based on the data blocks' value range i.e. partition range then the filter can be created using same range values. This approach avoids the back and forth database search and saves lot of time & optimize the query performance. In order to detect the duplicate records between the data feed S Vs big data repository W, the list steps are given below

- Identify the Partition Range
- Organize the data feed
- Generate Partition aware sub-queries

Identify the Partition Range
To create the partition-aware subqueries, finding the horizontal partition which holds the data feeds becomes mandatory. Since the big data repository' partition summary being captured in data dictionary in phase I, for the data feed's time period or CDE (Critical Data Element used for W partition) fetch the first level horizontal H' partition details. During this data dictionary data retrieval, none of the data blocks in S' finds the relevant H' partition then the data feed is not yet loaded to big data repository. So the

next level steps can be ignored to find the duplicate records otherwise the proceedings steps needs to be executed to detect the duplicate records.

Organize the Data Feed

Since this approach deals with the big data and periodic data feed contains large volume data cannot be searched as a single thread to detect the duplicates. So based on the partition' details retrieved from the data dictionary, the data feed S sorted & divided into multiple data blocks S'. For example, {1, 2, 3 ... 10000} - partition 100, {100001, 100002, 100003 ... 20000} - partition 10 and {100001, 100002, 100003 ... 30000} - partition 11.

$$S' = \bigcup_{i=1}^{q} d_i \Rightarrow \forall d \in S' : d \subset S \land \bigcap_{i=1}^{q} d_i = \emptyset$$

Where

d   is the data feed' data block
i   is the identifier
q   is the total number of partition
S   is the data feed

Generate Partition aware sub-queries

Once the corresponding partition details are identified, the data feed will be divided into H' based data block. Since H' partitions is a first level partition which holds huge volume of the data, the S' will be divided into fixed of records q handled in parallel by the processors. The q value depends on the enterprise environment setup. After optimal sized data split, the filter sub-queries being generated with unique columns to be verified in W. Then execute the filter sub-queries parallel and detect the duplicate records faster. For Phase II, the list of steps are given in algorithm is given Algorithm I.

Algorithm I: Form Partition Aware Filter Sub-Queries

```
Input:
-Data feed S
-Big data Repository W
-Data dictionary dd

Output:
Duplicate records list

Find the data feed values range partition details in the data dictionary dd
    If ps==NULL then
        Exit    //Data feed is not loaded yet, further detection is not required.
    Else
        Group the Data feed' S to W' partition based dataset blocks S'.
        Divide the each data partition is S' to fixed number records R'
        Generate the Partition aware range-queries
        Execute the sub-queries in parallel to search the duplicates in big data
        repository W
        Return the duplicate records list
```

4.3   Phase III: Search

In this phase, the sub-query duplicate record search thread triggered in phase II, the data block's physical address in the data repository W needs to be identifier to eliminated non-relevant search. Since we have braided the indexing's, the data block's search can be traced between nodes without backtracking tree traversal. The detailed steps for the search are given in Algorithm II. Initially, the height of the indexing tree needs to be identified as specified in FindIndexingTreeHeight (BI). If the height of the tree is h then root node belongs to level 1, leaf nodes are present in h level and h-2 number of non-leaf nodes will be present. To trace the data block b, h-2 levels of non-leaf nodes to be compared for the tree traversal. So as shown in Fig. 4, the subquery thread starts the search from the root nodes. Using the root node's block identifier R list and the respective child nodes gets identified. To select the relevant child node, the range values of the R list will be compared. Same way, the non-leaf nodes get traced using the block identifier list. Finally, lead nodes provide the data block's physical address for the records search. The h-1 level of the tree traversal is shown in Fig. 4 with red dotted lines. During this relevant node selection, If the selected child nodes does not possess the expected data range then using childNode->Next, the next child node can be chosen for the traversal and childNode->prev to select the predecessor same level node irrespective of disjoint parents which is shown in the green lines in Fig. 4. This scenario often occurs for the leaf node, since the leaf node has smaller piece of data blocks, there are possibility that sub query thread has range values spread across two or more inner data blocks which requires tree traverse between two child nodes for data search. Once physical address is identified, the queries search duplicate records in the respective data blocks and return the list of matching records. Since this approach featured with b$^+$ tree and braided techniques, helps disjoint parent's child nodes traversal without backtracking results in faster data block search.

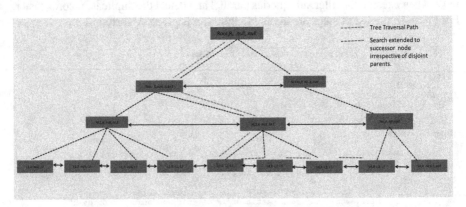

Fig. 4. Braided B$^+$ tree indexing search (Color figure online)

```
Algorithm II: Search

Input:
-Unique composite key uk
-Filter query list fq
-braided B⁺ indexing list BI

Output:
-physical data block address list for query search O

h-=FindIndexingTreeHeight(BI) // Finding height of the braided b+ indexing tree
currentNode=BI.rootNode // Tree traversal starts from the root node
            For i=1 to h-1 do
                    R= currentNode.referenceList(i) // Fetch the list of items in the
        Block identifier list
                    childNode= R.getfirstChildNode(i)

                    For refNode=1 to R.size do  // Traverse the non-leaf nodes
                        if fq .rangeValue<= childNode.RangeValue then
                            currentNode = childNode
                        else
                            childNode = childNode->Next
                    end For
            end For
                if i=h then // Leaf node level
                    R= currentNode.referenceList(i)
                    For refNode=1 to R.size do
                    // Check the CDE's value range till finding the relevant
                    node and next & prev //used for tree traversal irrespective
                    of disjoint parents.
                        if fq .rangeValue<= childNode.RangeValue and
                            childNode->Next.RangeValue <= fq .rangeValue
                            hildNode.>Prev.RangeValue >= fq .rangeValue
                            then
                            addNodeToOutpuList(O,currentNode)
                            exit
                        else if fq .rangeValue<= childNode.RangeValue and
                            childNode->Next.RangeValue <= fq .rangeValue
                            then
                                addNodeToOutpuList(O.currentNode)
                                childNode= childNode->Next
                    End For
                End If

        return O
```

5 Analysis

The duplicate records detection process aims to optimize the time complexity by creating the partition aware filter sub queries in line with horizontal partitioning. In general, range filter query threads perform NxC comparison, when table contains N number of records and C number columns requires time complexity as $O (\log C * N)$. When the S dataset divided into data blocks without high level horizontal partition's knowledge available in data dictionary, creates filter queries which compares each and every record across repository for all query thread and over all time complexity becomes $O (\log C * W)^k$ where W is the total number records present in the repository, C is the total number columns, K is the number filter queries. This partition unaware query generation, increase of data comparisons cumulatively and become the road block of performance, time complexity and worsen search operation. In order to overcome the above mentioned unnecessary data comparison & improve time complexity, we group the datasets based on partition summary and generate filter queries which helps to perform comparisons on relevant datasets. The partition aware filter queries generation relies on high level partitions rather than inner-level data block partitions, since very large dataset overheads the comparison and very small dataset overheads the thread tracking.

If the execution plan for the partition aware filter queries doesn't have indexing then the query thread executes every tuple in high level partitions and worsens the time complexity. So using braided multi-level indexing tree, we traverse to the respective data block and keep the search query in defined number of records. The index tree's node traversal is optimized with maintaining range values in each node for critical business element which helps to find relevant child node rather than whole indexing tree traversal. The Next & Previous links used to traverse between neighbourhoods nodes at each level rather than back track and find the next same level node. And when the query thread filter values fall on two data blocks, the physical address acquiring can be extended easily using braided indexing tree. Overall for W vs S dataset duplicate records detection, we require time complexity as given below:

$$\text{Time complexity} = O\,(\alpha\,\log_b C * N)^k$$

Where,

N   is total number of data records to be searched in horizontal partition
C   is number of data columns
b   is the number of data blocks
k   is the number of subqueries
α is Braided tree indexing search traversal time

The above driven time complexity will vary when the duplicate detection subqueries executed in parallel. And in general, the total number parallel threads execution is depends on the enterprise parallel processing environment setup.

$$\text{Time complexity} = O\,(\alpha\,\log_b C * N)^{k/p}$$

Where,

P   is total number of queries executed in parallel
N   is total number of data records to be searched in horizontal partition
C   is number of data columns
b   is the number of data blocks
k   is the number of subqueries
α is Braided tree indexing search traversal time

6   Conclusion

On the digital age, more and more data getting accumulated on each and every seconds across the globe and complexity of data increases due to multiple electronics gadgets, open source platforms and infrastructures, social media, global business presence, ecommerce centralized systems, inter connected networks, banking transactions, etc. Same way, the importance of quick & reliable decision making also necessary to meet up the speed of evolving digital system through analytical insights with higher quality of data. For reliable solution, Business intelligence team rely on data accuracy which is been affected through unintentional duplicate records insertion and leads to rework, cost and time. The rework can be avoided using the proposed methodology which prevents duplicate records insertion to the enterprise repository. And the proposed method will be best suited for huge data volume integration and providing a better way to store data faster than ever and helps to maintain high quality decision support system for fast growing data volume in analytics.

References

1. B$^+$ Tree. https://en.wikipedia.org/wiki/B%2B_tree. Accessed 22 Aug 2016
2. DBMS Indexing. http://www.tutorialspoint.com/dbms/dbms_indexing.htm. Accessed 22 Aug 2016
3. Ramadan, B., Christen, P., Liang, H.: Dynamic sorted neighborhood indexing for real-time entity resolution. ACM (2015). https://doi.org/10.1145/2816821
4. Kim, J., Jeong, W.-K.: Exploiting massive parallelism for indexing multi-dimensional datasets on the GPU. IEEE (2013). https://doi.org/10.1109/tpds.2014.2347041
5. Deshmukh, P.B., Lokare, Y.B., Katware, A.V., Patil, P.A.: A survey on massively parallelism for indexing multidimensional datasets on the GPU. In: National Conference on Advances in Computing (2015)
6. Data Partitioning Guidance for Patterns and Guidance. https://msdn.microsoft.com/library/dn589795.aspx. Accessed 16 Aug 2016
7. https://azure.microsoft.com/en-in/documentation/articles/best-practices-data-partitioning/. Accessed 16 Aug 2016
8. Best Practices for Data Dictionary Definitions and Usage. v. 1.1 2006-11-14. NED. http://www.pnamp.org/sites/default/files/best_practices_for_data_dictionary_definitions_and_usage_version_1.1_2006-11-14.pdf. Accessed 16 Aug 2016
9. Data Dictionary and Types of Data Dictionary. https://www.tutorialcup.com/dbms/data-dictionary.htm. Accessed 16 Aug 2016
10. Bilenk, M., Mooney, R.J.: Adaptive duplicate detection using learnable string similarity measures. ACM (2003). https://doi.org/10.1145/956750.956759
11. Elmagarmid, A.K., Ipeirotis, P.G., Verykios, V.S.: Duplicate record detection: a survey. Trans. Knowl. Data Eng. **19**(1) (2007). IEEE. https://doi.org/10.1109/tkde.2007.9
12. Ferro, A., Giugno, R., Puglisi, P.L., Pulvirenti, A.: An efficient duplicate record detection using q-grams array inverted index. In: Bach Pedersen, T., Mohania, M.K., Tjoa, A.M. (eds.) DaWaK 2010. LNCS, vol. 6263, pp. 309–323. Springer, Heidelberg (2010). https://doi.org/10.1007/978-3-642-15105-7_25
13. Yousef, A.H.: Cross language duplicate record detection in big data. In: Hassanien, A.E., Azar, A.T., Snasael, V., Kacprzyk, J., Abawajy, J.H. (eds.) Big Data in Complex Systems. SBD, vol. 9, pp. 147–171. Springer, Cham (2015). https://doi.org/10.1007/978-3-319-11056-1_5
14. Sitas, A., Kapidakis, S.: Duplicate detection algorithms of bibliographic descriptions. Libr. Hi Tech **26**(2), 287–301 (2008)
15. Li, M., Wang, H., Li, J., Gao, H.: Efficient duplicate record detection based on similarity estimation. In: Chen, L., Tang, C., Yang, J., Gao, Y. (eds.) WAIM 2010. LNCS, vol. 6184, pp. 595–607. Springer, Heidelberg (2010). https://doi.org/10.1007/978-3-642-14246-8_58

16. Subramaniaswamy, V., Chenthur Pandian, S.: A complete survey of duplicate record detection using data mining techniques. Asian Netw. Sci. Inf. (2012). https://doi.org/10.3923/itj.2012.941.945
17. Mayilvaganan, M., Saipriyanka, M.: Efficient and effective duplicate detection evaluating multiple data using genetic algorithm. Int. J. Innov. Res. Comput. Commun. Eng. **3**(9) (2015)
18. Taniguchi, S.: Duplicate bibliographic record detection with an OCR-converted source of information. J. Inf. Sci. (2012). https://doi.org/10.1177/0165551512459923
19. Dagade, A.A., Mali, M.P.: Survey of data duplication detection and elimination in domain dependent and domain-independent databases. Int. J. Adv. Res. Comput. Sci. Manag. Stud. **4**(5), 1800–1809 (2016)
20. Chen, Q., Zobel, J., Zhang, X., Verspoor, K.: Supervised learning for detection of duplicates in genomic sequence databases. PLOS ONE (2016). https://doi.org/10.1371/journal.pone.0159644
21. Zheng, Y., Fen, X., Xie, X., Peng, S., Fu, J.: Detecting nearly duplicated records in location datasets. ACM (2010). https://doi.org/10.1145/1869790.1869812
22. Liu, W., Zeng, J.: Duplicate literature detection for cross-library search. Cybern. Inf. Technol. **16**(2), 160–178 (2016)
23. Jiang, Y., Lin, C., Meng, W., Yu, C., Cohen, A.M., Smalheiser, N.R.: Rule-Based Deduplication of Article Records from Bibliographic Databases. Oxford University Press, Oxford (2014)
24. Herschel, M., Naumann, F., Szott, S., Taubert, M.: Scalable iterative graph duplicate detection. IEEE Trans. Knowl. Data Eng. **24**(11) (2012). https://doi.org/10.1109/tkde.2011.99
25. Pradeep, A., George, T.: Duplicate record detection in XML using AI techniques. Int. J. Comput. Techn. (IJCT) **2**(3), 55–60 (2015). Published by International Research Group- IRG. ISSN 2394-2231. http://www.ijctjournal.org/

Performance Analysis of Virtual Machines and Docker Containers

Babu Kavitha[✉] and Perumal Varalakshmi

Department of Computer Technology, Anna University, Chennai, India
sridhar.kavitha@gmail.com, varanip@gmail.com

Abstract. Cloud computing is a good paradigm which utilizes virtualization technology to isolate the workloads from one another as well as elastic in nature. Cloud providers possessing multiples of Virtual Machines (VM) to perform the full functionality demanded by the users. Meanwhile, Docker based containers emerged with upgraded performance than VMs. Cloud provider scales up the economic benefits during peak demands for its infrastructure. At the same time it is a taxing issue for the cloud provider to ensure quality of service (QoS) for the clients. By considering all these factors cloud provider can replace VMs by Docker Containers so that overall profit is increased. In this paper we exploit the outstanding performance of the Docker containers in terms of throughput, average response time etc., Here we made a performance test for VM and Docker Container in the same cloud provider namely Amazon Web Service (AWS). To compare the performance of VM and Docker container, a cloud monitoring service called Datadog Agent is integrated with both remote servers to monitor the functionality of resources and an open source testing software tool namely Apache JMeter is employed to perform a load test. The experimental results obtained proves that Docker Container outperforms VMs in almost all metrics.

Keywords: Virtual machine · Docker · Container · Datadog agent · JMeter Throughput · Average response time

1 Introduction

The cloud computing environment offers a restructured computing landscape for the users so that, it is released from overheads in maintaining IT infrastructures. In recent years, almost all the internet services are deployed in the cloud architecture, as it is cost effective, elastic and reliable. Cloud computing provides different services such as Infrastructure as a Service (IaaS), Platform as a Service (PaaS) and Software as a Service (SaaS). Most of the IT people are benefited by IaaS, as the cloud infrastructure is geographically distributed in different areas to serve users. Virtual machines play a major role in cloud computing and it is a synonym to IaaS. Almost all the internet services run inside the VMs. Even PaaS and SaaS providers also deploy on IaaS, running all their workloads inside VMs. VM performance is a challenging element which accounts for the overall cloud performance, since all the cloud workloads are currently running on VMs. As the hypervisor plays an important role in VM virtualization technology,

© Springer Nature Singapore Pte Ltd. 2018
Shriram R and M. Sharma (Eds.): DaSAA 2017, CCIS 804, pp. 99–113, 2018.
https://doi.org/10.1007/978-981-10-8603-8_9

overhead may get imposed which cannot be removed even by any higher layer. In that scenario, such overheads affect the cloud performance. Many studies [1, 2] exposes VM implementation against native execution and this motivates how to improve the performance of VM technology [3, 4].

Container based virtualization establishes an interesting substitute to VM virtualization in the cloud [5]. Before establishing the concept of cloud computing, Virtual Private (VP) server provides utilized containers earlier for a decade. After that they switched over to VMs for delivering consistence performance. Concepts related to container technology like namespaces and cgroups are well known [6].

Container virtualization technology remained lagging until PaaS providers turn to adapt and standardize it, which made a revolution in the use of containers due its isolation and resource control capabilities. Linux is the most preferred operating system (OS) in the cloud as it provides zero price, large ecosystem, better hardware support, good performance and high reliability. Containers are implemented in Linux by the kernel namespace feature and became popular in the recent years [7]. Just before three years, Docker [8] was introduced as a standard run time, image format and build system for Linux containers.

In traditional Unix system, many of the objects such as processes, filesystem and the network stack are globally viewed by all the users leading to the lack of configuration isolation. Due to this drawback, when multiple applications are installed in one OS, the cost of system administration exceeds the software cost itself. This made the administrators and developers to simplify the deployment by installing each application with a separate OS copy, either in a VM or on a dedicated server.

A virtualization system must provide resource isolation which is necessary for cloud infrastructure usage, as the customers wants to get the performance for what they pay. A feature of linux is Kernel Virtual Machine (KVM) [3], in which linux acts as a typical hypervisor [9] and unmodified guest operating system (OS) runs inside a linux process. KVM supports both emulated I/O devices through QEMU [10] and para-virtual I/O devices through Virtio [11]. To minimize the virtualization overhead to very low levels [4], the combination of hardware acceleration and paravirtual I/O is properly designed. KVM also supports live migration of physical server or even whole datacentre, without disturbing the guest OS. Management tool like Libvert [12] can easily use KVM.

As the capacity of VM (in terms of vCPU and vRAM) is limited, its usage is also naturally bounded. The resizing of VM can be done through "hot plugging" and "ballooning" vCPU and vRAM by KVM with support of guest operating system and is rarely followed in the cloud. As each VM is treated as a process, all management facilities like scheduling and cgroups, also apply to VMs. Though it simplifies the overhead of the hypervisor, resource management becomes complicated inside the guest OS. Sometime vCPU can be de-scheduled without notification and vRAM may be swapped out under KVM, causing performance anomalies. While running VMs, two levels of allocation and scheduling, one in the hypervisor and one in the guest OS are executed. These problems are avoided by the cloud provider by not overcommitting resources, which eliminates the scheduling overhead in the hypervisor and also simplifies billing.

Though VM provides excellent isolation still there is overhead in sharing the data between guests or between guest and hypervisor. Also such sharing consumes expensive marshalling and hyper-calls. Storage access by the VM is done through emulated block devices backed by image files. Creation, updation and deployment of disk images are mostly time consuming events and also can waste storage space by duplicating the contents. Measurements [13] have shown that containers can be initiated very quickly than VMs (less than 1 s), as there is no need to boot another copy of the OS. Live migration of containers is performed in theory CRIU [14] also it is much faster to kill the container and start a new one. Containers also removes the distinction between IaaS and "bare metal" non-virtualized servers [15, 16] as it provide control and isolation of VMs.

The paper is organized as follows: Sect. 2 reveals the literature survey. In Sect. 3 problem definition and framework is defined. Section 4 describes the alternative solution and framework. Section 5 discuss about experimental setup and result analysis.

2 Literature Survey

Utility computing infrastructure was built in the 1960s by the Multics [17] project. It created ideas like end-to-end argument and a set of security policies which are still relevant today. IBM introduced VMs in 1970s [18] and then VMs are reinvented on x86 by VMWare [19] in the late 1990s. Again VMs are brought to the open source world in 2000s by Xen [4] and KVM [3]. The overhead in the usage of VMs was high initially and later it was reduced by employing hardware/software optimization [3, 4].

OS level virtualization have crossed a long history. The main purpose of OS is to virtually share the underlying hardware resources, but in the case of unix, it provides traditionally poor isolation as it supports global namespaces for the filesystem, process and the network. Capability based OSes [20] supported container based isolation which is not utilizing global namespace, later it failed out commercially in 1980s. Pre-process file system NS [6] and bind mounts are implemented by Plan-9 which influenced the namespace mechanism that strengthens linux containers. In 2004, Solaris 10 interposed and strongly promoted zones [21] called modernized implementation of containers. IaaS based zones was introduced in 2008 by cloud provider Joyent without any remarkable change in the cloud market. Rudimentary 'jails' has been implemented using Unix chroot() facility and extended by the BSD jails feature.

Linux containers also possess long recorded history. Commercial product Virtuzzo and its version openVZ [7] adopted for web hosting, were merged into Linux. Finally Linux included native containers during 2007 in the form of kernel NS and the Linux Container (LXC) userspace tool to manipulate them.

Heroku which is a PaaS provider innovated the concept of employing containers for efficient deployment of applications [22]. Heroku treated container as a process with additional isolation. The emerging application container faced a little bit overhead, having similar isolation like VMs and resources sharing like normal process. Google also universally acquired application container for its own infrastructure [23]. Later Docker Inc., launched docker [8] as a standard image format and management scheme for application containers. The performance comparison of hypervisor to other hypervisor or non-virtualized execution have been studied [4, 24, 25]. Previous comparisons between VMs and Containers [1, 2, 5, 26, 27] was done utilizing old software like Xen and out-of-tree container patches.

3   Problem Definition and Framework

Traditional VMs are emulated from the underlying infrastructure with the help of hypervisor which is on the top of host OS. Also VMs are created with its own OS by its own memory management device drives, daemons for its applications. Since VM has its own OS, the number of VMs to be virtualized are restricted due to the overhead incurred by the hypervisor. It is also called Hardware Level Virtualization, as it is fully maintained by the hypervisor. VM utilizes quickly a lot of system resource namely CPU cycles and RAM because VMs are created with the motherboard, CPU and memory.

VMs possess many benefits compared to the physical machine such as high availability, scalability, back up with fast recovery, easy cloning and security etc., Server consolidation is the main benefit while using VM. It reaches 50% to 80% utilization than physical server. Since more VMs are hosted on few physical server, it decreases the cost related to hardware maintenance, energy usage and cooling system. As VM needs hypervisor, foot print for RAM and storage becomes bulky. Also VM is slower since it handles two file system, two OSes with strong resource management policy. Amount of memory required for VM is large which restricts the number of VMs to be created. So VMs are considered heavy and expensive.

The start-up time for VM consume few minutes as it depends on the hypervisor. VM runs on the top of physical machine using hypervisor like Xen, Hyper-V etc. VM virtualization has to be redone for every new application or version. This makes it unsuitable for scale out, hybrid cloud, massive clustering and iterative development. Due to heavy weight nature of VM, lack of application portability and slowness in provision of IT resources, performance degradation occurs. At the same time as VMs are fully isolated as it possess high degree of security.

4   Alternative Solution

Instead of using a full OS on virtual hardware, container based virtualization restructures an existing OS to achieve extra isolation. Generally this includes adding a container ID to every process and adding new access control checks to every system call. In practice, Linux provides a container implementation. Linux containers are built with the help of kernel namespaces feature. The most common method of using namespaces is to develop an isolated container which has no access to objects outside the container.

Docker is a popular open source project based on Linux containers that automatically pack, ship and deploy any software application as a light weight container. It is also referred as OS level virtualization as it runs on the userspace on top of OS kernel. Docker make use of Linux kernel's key feature like namespace functionality for complete isolation of an application by means of operating environment, as it includes process trees, networking, user-ID and mounted filesystem. Docker also utilizes cgroups functionality of Linux kernel which permits limitation and prioritization of resources like CPU, memory, block I/O and network etc.

Figure 1 clearly represents the Docker architecture with its main components. Docker basically consists of four components such as *Docker Client, Docker Daemon, Docker registries* and *Containers* as shown in the Fig. 1. Client-Server architecture is employed in Docker. In Docker architecture, Docker registry is the distribution component, Docker Image is the build component and Docker Container is the run component of Docker. The Daemon runs on a host machine. The user cannot interact directly with the Daemon, but through the Docker Client. So the primary user interface to Docker is the Docker Client. It accept commands from the user and communicates with a Docker Daemon.

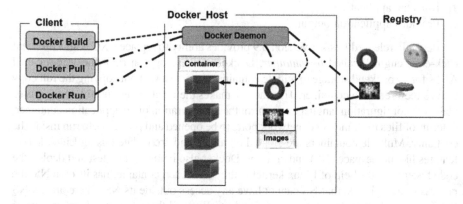

Fig. 1. Docker architecture

Docker Image is a template with read-only property. Docker Registry store images. The registry may be public or private. Public Docker registry provides a service called Docker Hub, which contain thousands of images created by the user or others.

Docker Image is used to create Containers. Container is an isolated secure application platform. Containers can be made to start, run, stop, move and delete. Image has a series of layers. Docker uses union file system which combines these layers into a single image. Every image has a base image. Docker images are built from these layers using set of call instructions. Each instruction forms a new layer on the image. These instructions are placed in a file called *Dockerfile*. So *Dockerfile* is responsible for building images from the base image. Whenever request is made for building an image, Docker reads the *Dockerfile*, executes the instructions and then returns the final image. This image tells the Docker what the container holds, what process to run, and other configuration data. When the container starts a read-write layer is added on the top of the image on which the application can then run. Because of these layers Docker is so light weight compared to VM. If it is necessary to change the Docker image for updating an application to a new version, a new layer can be built, instead of replacing the whole image or rebuilding as done with VM. In this way Docker images are updated or distributed quickly.

Once the containers are created, it becomes the execution environment for applications. After the application is placed in a Container, then it is committed and made it as an image to create multiple containers from it. These containers may be linked together as tiered application architecture.

The Docker Engine client is launched on running a new Container. The Docker Engine performs the following.

a. Pulls the image.
b. Creates a new container.
c. Allocates file system and adds read-write layer to the image.
d. Creates a network interface for the container to communicate with the host.
e. Attaches IP address.
f. Runs the application.
g. Provides application output.

Recently released Docker version 0.9 provides ability to replace LXC with a different back-end "engine" called *libcontainer*. Docker utilizes copy-on right filesystem called AUFs for its backend storage to initiate containers very fast without copying the full copy of files required for a container. This facility makes the Docker very useful. Docker uses plain text configuration language to control the configuration of an application container, in terms of files to be included, network ports to be opened and processes to run inside the container. Multiple containers are created on a host and are isolated using Linux kernel features like namespace (NS) and cgroups. Docker also helps to ship, test and deploy the code faster with the help of Linux kernel features. As each container has its own NS, the process running inside that NS cannot have any access outside its NS. There are six NS in Linux namely *mnt, ipc, net, user, pid* and *uts*. With all these features, Docker is more suitable for virtualization technology and is a cost effective alternative for hypervisor based VMs. Also it supports fast deliver of application, easy deployment and scaling, achieving higher density and running more workloads effectively. There is no memory overhead in Docker container as it needs consumed memory, not provisioned memory. CPU usage of KVM is 1.5 times higher than Docker when idle. Docker shines in the usage of idle resources with good start up and stop times. As there is no hypervisor in Docker architecture, CPU and memory overheads are minimised. Since the containers are created with start-up time less than a second compared to traditional VMs, the Docker container provides potentially better performance than VMs.

5   Experimental Setup and Result Analysis

5.1   Experimental Setup

To compare the performance of VM and Docker Container the configuration set up for both is identical.
CPU: Intel(R) Xeon(R) CPU E5-2670 v2 @ 2.50 GHz, PLATFORM: GNU/Linux, MEMORY: 0.97 GB, FILESYSTEM: 8.32 GB.

Initially VM and Docker Container created and built in Amazon Web Services (AWS) with the above configuration. A monitoring agent may be installed on both target servers, to monitor their functionality and performance. There are many cloud monitoring services like Dockerstats, CAdvisor, Scout, Datadog, Sensu etc. By considering the features like cost, easy of deployment, level of detail, level of aggregation and ability to raise alerts etc., Datadog agent provides more comfortable facility for cloud monitoring. The integration of Datadog agent with VM and Docker container are shown in Fig. 2(a) and (b) respectively.

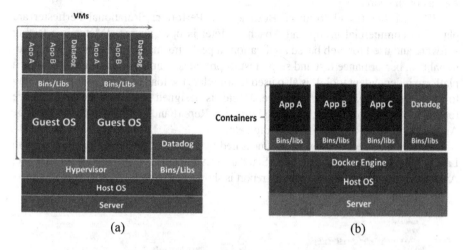

(a)   (b)

Fig. 2. (a) VMs with Datadog (b) Docker containers with Datadog

Datadog is a SaaS based monitoring analytics for IT infrastructure. At one place, it brings together data from servers, databases, tools, application and services. It correlates metrics from all apps, tools, SaaS and cloud providers, with real time dash board in seconds, alert using any metric for a single host or entire cluster, zero time for code changes and team collaboration. Datadog monitors the changes in the host status related to CPU, Memory, Disk, Load and Network etc., and also displays nearly about 68 metrics using dashboards.

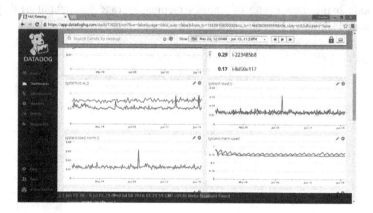

Fig. 3. Snapshot of dashboard of Datadog monitoring tool

Datadog also supports viewing of multiple metrics dashboard on a single window. Figure 3 shows the snapshot of various metrics on a single dashboard of Datadog. In order to compare the performance of VM and Docker container, it is not just enough to monitor the remote servers, instead numerical data related to throughput, response time etc., are required. There are many performance testing tools available commercially as well as open source.

HP perftester (Load Runner), Borland Silk Performer, Relational Perftester are placed in commercial group and Apache JMeter is open source. JMeter is a testing software and used for web based application. It performs many test like load test, functional test, performance test and stress test. It provides simple and intuitive GUI. It is a platform independent tool. It is also used to stimulate the load of many users connecting to the server to measure performance. JMeter is designed to deliver the performance reports in the form of tables, example Summary Report and graphs like Graph Results, Aggregate Graph, Response Time Graph etc.

The summary report show values measured by Jmeter in tabular format, related with Label, Samples, Average, Max, Min, Standard Deviation, Error %, Throughput, KB/Sec, Average Bytes. A sample of summary report is shown in Fig. 4.

Summary Report

Name: Summary Report
Comments:
Write results to file / Read from file
Filename: _____ [Browse...] Log/Display Only: ☐ Errors ☐ Successes [Configure]

Label	# Samples	Average	Min	Max	Std. Dev.	Error %	Throughput	KB/sec	Avg. Bytes
HTTP Reque...	1000	418	163	1412	152.61	0.00%	33.4/sec	134.96	4134.1
HTTP Reque...	1000	397	170	796	128.89	0.00%	33.7/sec	387.54	11767.0
HTTP Reque...	1000	396	165	587	129.67	0.00%	33.8/sec	173.57	5260.0
TOTAL	3000	404	163	1412	137.88	0.00%	97.7/sec	672.91	7053.7

☐ Include group name in label?   [Save Table Data]   ☑ Save Table Header

Fig. 4. Snapshot of summary report.

In the Graph Results, the x-axis denotes n-th sampler and y-axis denotes the time in milliseconds. In the graph the no. of samples, median, average, throughput are displayed as legends and shown in Fig. 5(a) and (b).

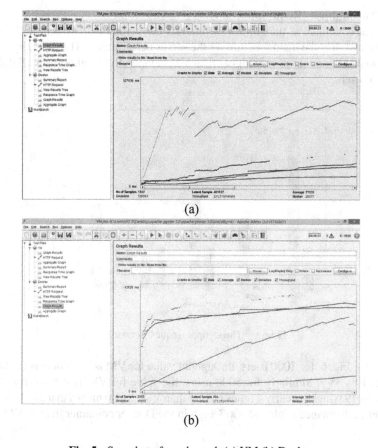

(a)

(b)

Fig. 5. Snapshot of graph result (a) VM (b) Docker

5.2 Steps for Performing Load Test

1. Add a separate thread group name for VM and Docker in test plan.
2. Initialize the number of users.
3. Add HTTP request using Add -> Sampler.
4. Assign IP address and port number for both VM and Docker Container in HTTP request form.
5. Run the test plan.
6. Repeat the test for various number of users.

5.3 Result Analysis

The main contribution in this paper is to analyse the performance of VM and Docker container in terms of throughput (request/sec), average response time, median, 90-95-99 percentile, error rate, standard deviation, average bytes etc.

5.3.1 Throughput (Request/Second)

Throughput is defined as the number of requests per second that are sent to the server during the test. It is the main measure for the server performance. The throughput value for the Docker container is very higher than VM comparatively, almost for all different number of users.

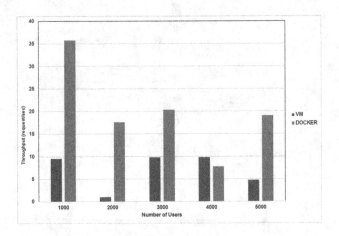

Fig. 6. Throughput (request/second)

From the Fig. 6, for 1000 users, throughput value for VM is 9.5 whereas for Docker container it is 35.7. Similarly for 5000 users, the value for VM is 4.7 and for Docker container is 19 which is nearly 4 times greater than VM. It also means that the throughput i.e. server performance is almost 400% high in the Docker container than in VM.

5.3.2 Average Response Time

It is defined as the average time taken by all samples (users) to execute the particular label (HTTP Request) under the test.

It is measured by the ratio of sum of all sample time to the number of samples. Time is in milliseconds (ms). This metric represents that, when this value is less, the server response is fast otherwise the server response is slow. In the Fig. 7, for thousand users the average response time is 25296 ms for VM and 7633 ms for Docker container, depicting that the Docker container response is very quick. Similarly for 5000 users, for VM the value is 475474 ms whereas for Docker container it is 164232 ms, proving that the time consumed for executing the request is three times greater in VM than Docker. It is clearly proved that the Docker container response is very quick even in user's peak demand environment.

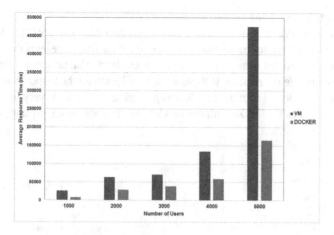

Fig. 7. Average response time

5.3.3 Median

It represents a number which divides the total samples into two equal halves. Half of the samples are smaller than this value and other half is larger than this value. It is also called as 50th percentile. It is better when the average response time is as close as possible with the median value. In the case of 1000 users, the average response time and median value for Docker container are 7633 ms and 7199 ms respectively. But for VM the values are 25296 ms and 21024 ms respectively. For 5000 users the Docker container values are 164232 and 175884, in case of VM it is 475474 and 187212. From the above data and Fig. 8 it is clear that the performance of Docker is consistent and VM is degrading.

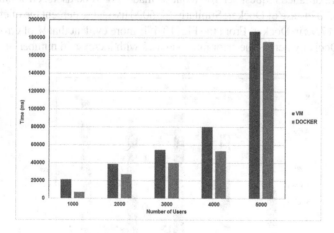

Fig. 8. Median

5.3.4　90%-95%-99% Line

90% line represents that 90% of the samples took less than this time, 95% line denotes that 95% of the samples took not more than this time, also 99% line represents that 99% of the samples took less than this time. All these line proves clearly that how much tine taken by the server to complete the request. If these values are less, then the response of the server is quick, otherwise slow. From the Fig. 9, it is proved that values are very less in Docker than VM. It shows that the Docker outperforms VM in all the stages for any number of users.

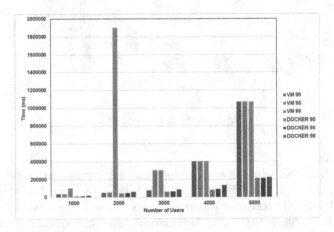

Fig. 9.　90-95-99 percentile

5.3.5　Error Percentage

It is a measure of failed request per 100 requests made. For 1000 users, error rate in VM is 37.10 and 14.30 in case of Docker. Similarly for 5000 users, the percentage of error in VM is 88.08 and 17.92 in Docker. From the Fig. 10, it is more evident that % of error is almost constant in Docker whereas the error rate increases with increase in number of users.

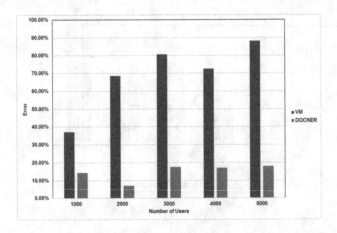

Fig. 10.　Error percentage

5.3.6 Standard Deviation

It is defined as a measure of the variability of a dataset. It is also called as the deviation of the sampled elapsed time. It shows the variation from the average value. It is always preferable to have low standard deviation value for better performance. In the comparison from Fig. 11, it is prominent that the standard deviation values are smaller in Docker than VM, which proves the steady performance of Docker in different situation.

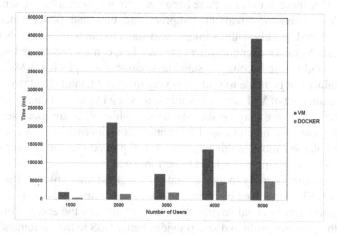

Fig. 11. Standard deviation

5.3.7 Average Bytes

It means average response size. It is defined as the arithmetic mean of response bytes for the samples or it is also called as average size of the sample response in bytes. From the Fig. 12, the average response size falls down in VM when the number of user increases while it remains almost constant in Docker.

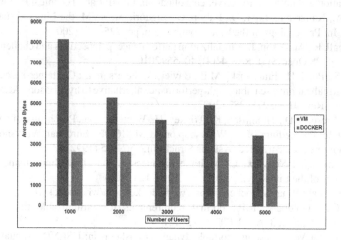

Fig. 12. Average bytes

6 Conclusion

VM supports hardware level virtualization but Docker container supports OS level virtualization. There is an overhead incurred in VM creation and implementation due to hypervisor. Also VM consumes more memory as it has its own Guest OS. Moreover the installation of Guest OS takes time in terms of minutes, which in turn affects rapid deployment. Due these drawbacks there becomes a point to search for the suitable alternative for VM technology without compromising cost and performance. Docker container is created quickly with its images and starts to run within seconds (even less than a second). As the Docker containers are very fast, can also be created in multiples (supports scalability), it becomes a suitable solution for replacing VMs. Moreover Docker container can be made to shutdown very quickly (default shutdown time 10 s), whereas the shutdown of VM takes a few minutes. Since Docker container performs OS level virtualization, there may be security issues, while VMs are more secured. The security issues can also be eliminated by running container inside VM i.e., container based IaaS implementation. In this paper, it is well proved that the Docker containers outperforms VMs in all metrics related to performance.

Docker container is going to play a vital role in cloud infrastructure because of its scalability as well as upgraded performance. So in near future, VMs may get replaced by Docker containers in cloud environment, as it minimizes the energy consumption, maximizes the provider profit and also provides better QoS to the customers.

References

1. Matthews, J.N., Hu, W., Hapuarachchi, M., Deshane, T., Dimatos, D., Hamilton, G., McCabe, M., Owens, J.: Quantifying the performance isolation properties of virtualization system. In: Proceedings of the Workshop on Experimental Computer Science. ACM (2007)
2. Padala, P., Zhu, X., Wang, Z., Singhal, S., Shin, K.G.: Performance evaluation of virtualization technologies for server consolidation. In: HP Labs Technical Report (2007)
3. Kivity, A., Kamay, Y., Laor, D., Lublin, U., Liguori, A.: KVM: the Linux virtual machine monitor. In: Proceedings of the Linux Symposium, pp. 225–230 (2007)
4. McDougall, R., Anderson, J.: Virtualization performance: perspectives and challenges ahead. ACM SIGOPS Oper. Syst. Rev. **44**(4), 40–56 (2010)
5. Soltesz, S., Pötzl, H., Fiuczynski, M.E., Bavier, A., Peterson, L.: Container-based operating system virtualization: a scalable, high-performance alternative to hypervisors. ACM SIGOPS Oper. Syst. Rev. **41**(3), 275–287 (2007)
6. Pike, R., Presotto, D., Thompson, K., Trickey, H., Winterbottom, P.: The use of name spaces in Plan 9. In: Proceedings of the Workshop on ACM SIGOPS European Workshop: Models and Paradigms for Distributed Systems Structuring, pp. 1–5 (1992)
7. Biederman, E.W., Networx, L.: Multiple instances of the global linux namespaces. In: Proceedings of the Linux Symposium, pp. 101–112 (2006)
8. Hykes, S., et al.: What is Docker? https://www.docker.com/whatisdocker/
9. Popek, G.J., Goldberg, R.P.: Formal requirements for virtualizable third generation architectures. Commun. ACM **17**(7), 412–421 (1974)
10. Bellard, F.: QEMU, a fast and portable dynamic translator. In: USENIX Annual Technical Conference, FREENIX Track, Anaheim, CA, USA, pp. 41–46 (2005)

11. Russell, R.: Virtio: towards a de-facto standard for virtual I/O devices. ACM SIGOPS Oper. Syst. Rev. **42**(5), 95–103 (2008)
12. Bolte, M., Sievers, M., Birkenheuer, G., Niehorster, O., Brinkmann, A.: Non-intrusive virtualization management using libvirt. In: Proceedings of the Conference on Design, Automation and Test in Europe, pp. 574–579 (2010)
13. Russell, B.: KVM and Docker LXC Benchmarking with OpenStack (2014)
14. Checkpoint/Restore in Userspace. http://criu.org/
15. SoftLayer introduces bare metal cloud (2009). http://www.softlayer.com/press/release/96/softlayer-introduces-bare-metal-cloud
16. Kontsevoy, E.: On metal: the right way to scale (2014). http://www.rackspace.com/blog/onmetal-the-right-way-to-scale
17. Organick, E.I.: The Multics System: An Examination of Its Structure. MIT Press, Cambridge (1972)
18. Creasy, R.J.: The origin of the VM/370 time-sharing system. IBM J. Res. Dev. **25**(5), 483–490 (1981)
19. Rosenblum, M., Garfinkel, T.: Virtual machine monitors: current technology and future trends. Computer **38**(5), 39–47 (2005)
20. Hardy, N.: KeyKOS architecture. ACM SIGOPS Oper. Syst. Rev. **19**(4), 8–25 (1985)
21. Price, D., Tucker, A.: Solaris zones: operating system support for consolidating commercial workloads. LISA **4**, 241–254 (2004)
22. Lindenbaum, J.: Deployment that just works (2009). https://blog.heroku.com/archives/2009/3/3/deployment_that_just_works
23. Brewer, E.: Robust containers (2014). http://www.slideshare.net/dotCloud/eric-brewer-dockercon-keynote
24. Huber, N., von Quast, M., Hauck, M., Kounev S.: Evaluating and modeling virtualization performance overhead for cloud environments. In: CLOSER, pp. 563–573 (2011)
25. Hwang, J., Zeng, S., y Wu, F., Wood, T.: A component-based performance comparison of four hypervisors. In: IFIP/IEEE International Symposium on Integrated Network Management, pp. 269–276 (2013)
26. Shea, R., Liu, J.: Understanding the impact of denial of service attacks on virtual machines. In: Proceedings of the IEEE 20th International Workshop on Quality of Service (2012)
27. Xavier, M.G., Neves, M.V., Rossi, F.D., Ferreto, T.C., Lange, T., De Rose, C.A.: Performance evaluation of container-based virtualization for high performance computing environments. In: 21st Euromicro International Conference on Parallel, Distributed, and Network-Based Processing, pp. 233–240 (2013)

Content Based Image Retrieval with Enhanced Privacy in Cloud Using Apache Spark

Sathishkumar Easwaramoorthy[1]([✉]), Usha Moorthy[1], Chunduru Anil Kumar[2],
S. Bharath Bhushan[1], and Vishnupriya Sadagopan[3]

[1] SITE, VIT University, Vellore, India
srisathishkumarve@gmail.com
[2] SCOPE, VIT University, Vellore, India
[3] Accenture, Bangalore, India

Abstract. Content Based Image Retrieval (CBIR) is the application through the integration of various traditional computer vision techniques to the image retrieval problem. CBIR usually contains high volume of personal and authenticated information which makes image privacy as a major concern. The proposed scheme for privacy allows the data owner to outsource the image database and the CBIR service to the cloud, without revealing the actual content of the database to the cloud server. The system uses only the index of the query image to prevent revealing the content of the image. Second, the image is encrypted using the session key generated between the client and the cloud server and then sent to the server for computation. Being the reduced information, it is computing stiff for the server to know the client's interest. The proposed architecture also uses a novel framework called Apache Spark which is considered to 100x faster than MapReduce in certain applications. Result shown Apache Spark is in-memory computations which helps a lot in the retrieval of similar images. Apache Spark framework has been used when the images are newly inserted into the Cloud storage at the point of which features are extracted from the image using transformation and action functionalities and stored in the feature database.

Keywords: MapReduce · Apache spark · Image privacy

1 Introduction

The methodology based on the computer vision for Content Based Image Retrieval (CBIR) and it has been applied to the image retrieval problem, that is, the problem of investigating for digital images in large databases. Because of large amounts of image data, all the image dataset are moved to cloud and processed in the cloud as an on demand service. Since the images have to be moved to the cloud, the privacy of the images becomes a major concern. The privacy scheme should allow the data owner to outsource the image database to the cloud without revealing pattern the actual content of the image database. Content-based image retrieval (CBIR), also called query by image content (QBIC) and content-based visual information retrieval (CBVIR) is the application of computer vision methods to the image retrieval problem, that is, the problem of

© Springer Nature Singapore Pte Ltd. 2018
Shriram R and M. Sharma (Eds.): DaSAA 2017, CCIS 804, pp. 114–128, 2018.
https://doi.org/10.1007/978-981-10-8603-8_10

investigating for digital images in huge databases [1]. The context might pass on to colors, shapes, textures, or any extra information that can be derived from the image itself. Image content can be classified into visual and semantic contents. Visual content can be very general or domain specific. General visual content include color, texture, shape, spatial relationship and so on. Domain specific visual content, similar to human faces, is application dependent and may engage field knowledge.

Image retrieval depended on color means retrieval on color descriptors. Most commonly used color descriptors such as color histogram, color layout, color coherence vector, color correlogram, and color moments [2]. The color histogram [3] serves as an effective representation of the color content of an image if the color pattern is unique compared with the remaining data set. The color histogram is easy to manipulate and effective in characterizing both the global and local distribution of colors in an image. Being any pixel in the image can be described by three modules in a certain color space (such as red, green, and blue modules in RGB space, or hue, saturation, and value in HSV space), a histogram, i.e., the distribution of the number of pixels for each quantized bin, can be defined for each module. Clearly, the more bins a color histogram contains, the more discrimination efficient it has. However, a histogram with a large number of bins will not only gain the manipulating cost, but will also be inappropriate for building efficient indexes for image databases.

Texture of an image is visual patterns that an image possesses and how they are spatially defined. Textures are defined by texels [3], which are then placed into a number of sets, depending on how many textures are detected in the image. These sets not only define the texture, but also where in the image the texture is located. Statistical analysis method such as co-occurrence Matrices can be used for quantitative measure of the arrangement of intensities in a particular region. To get texture information of image directional features were pulled out. The six image texture properties coarseness, regularity, directionality, contrast, line likeness and roughness. Structural methods describe texture by identifying structural primitives and their placement rules using morphological operator and adjacency graph. They deal with the arrangement of image primitives, presence of parallel or regularly spaced objects.

Statistical analysis methods utilizes statistical distribution of the image intensity to characterize the texture by the popular co-occurrence matrix, Fourier power spectra, Shift invariant principal component analysis (SPCA), Tamura feature, Multiresolution filtering method such as Gabor and wavelet transform [4]. Tamura features have six characteristics which are coarseness, line-likeness, contrast, roughness, regularity and directionality. Initial three characteristics proved to be noteworthy in CBIR systems such as QBIC. Coarseness is defined as a texture granularity, contrast is computed from statistical methods of moment invariants such as kurtosis and variance of the entire image and directionality is computed from convolution of images.

This work outsources the image database and the proposed CBIR with enhanced privacy service to the cloud, without revealing pattern the actual content of the database to the cloud server using Spark framework. Spark takes MapReduce to the next level with smaller amount expensive shuffles in the data processing [5]. The features of all the images in the image dataset are acquired, encrypted and stored in cloud. The system accepts a query image and finds similarity between query image feature and image dataset features in the cloud and returns the similar images to the cloud user.

The report is organized as follows. Section 2 discusses the related works and literature survey. Section 3 discusses the proposed system in detail. The Privacy preserving architecture of the proposed system is discussed in Sect. 4. Section 5 discusses about experimental results and performance analysis.

2 Literature Survey

Weng et al. [6] proposed a privacy protection framework for large-scale content-based information retrieval. It offers two hands of protection. One hand, robust hash values are used as queries to prevent revealing pattern original content or features while on the another hand, the client can choose to omit certain bits in a hash value to further increase the ambiguity for the server. The server will return the hash values of all possible candidates to the client. Then the client performs a search within the candidate list to find the most favorable match. Since only hash values are exchanged between the client and the server, the privacy of both parties is protected.

Xia et al. [7] proposed a privacy-preserving content-based image retrieval scheme, which allows the data owner to outsource the image database and CBIR service to the cloud, without revealing the actual content of the database to the cloud server. Local features are utilized to represent the images, and earth mover's distance (EMD) is employed to evaluate the similarity of images. This scheme transforms the EMD problem in such a way that the cloud server can solve it without learning the sensitive information. The main advantage is that the image is segmented and the features are computed locally which improves the efficiency of the image retrieval. The disadvantage is that there is burden on both the data owner and the user as it is implemented locally on a single machine.

VikasMaral et al. [8] proposed a distributed computing environment using cloud computing, where Relevance Feedback Techniques is used to integrate user's perception and Machine Learning Techniques to associate low level features with high level concepts. The bottleneck of current CBIR systems is the semantic gap between low level image features and high level user semantic concepts. In order to avoid this bottleneck, a relevance feedback mechanism was introduced to get input from the user about the similarity comparison which is used to improve the image retrieval. However, this technique requires large amount of computing efficient, which may not be obtainable with client machine. Therefore cloud environment is used for the image retrieval process to improve the speed and computation of the retrieval process.

Mushtaq et al. [9] proposed a framework that implements an in-memory distributed version of the GATK pipeline using Apache Spark. It presents a big data framework to parallelize the various stages of the GATK pipeline using Apache Spark. The framework uses an independent data set segmentation approach in order to make scalability. The approach is able to efficiently utilize the available computational resources by combining the different analysis stages into a single and high performance tightly integrated computational pipeline are runs on a custom-made high-performance computing (HPC) cluster. The framework reduced execution time by keeping data active in the memory between the maps and reduce algorithm. In addition, it has a dynamic load balancing algorithm utilizes system performance using runtime statistics of the active workload.

Elsebakhi et al. [10] explained the exponential growth of biomedical data along with the complexities of managing high dimensionality, imbalanced distribution, sparse attributes instigates a tough challenge of effectively applying functional networks as a new large-scale predictive modeling in healthcare and biomedicine. Spark is a huge-scale platform supporting many algorithms, like genetic algorithms and particle swarm optimization, between others. The main focus is to use Spark with biomedical platforms to solve the problems of applying big data to functional networks based on maximum likelihood estimation. The problems mainly stem from a classifier computation bottle-neck of estimating the parameters of the model, which are complex matrix computations involving matrix multiplications, transposition, and inversion.

Sun et al. [11] proposed an in-memory computing framework to address the fast development of remote sensing techniques; the volume of acquired data that grows exponentially. On the Spark based on platform, data loaded into memory in the primary iteration can be reused in the subsequent iterations. The experiments are carried out on massive remote sensing data using multi-iteration Singular Value Decomposition (SVD) algorithm. The advantage is that Spark-based SVD can obtain significantly faster computation time than MapReduce, typically by one order of magnitude.

Zhou et al. [12], investigated many Cloud Computing system providers about their concerns on security and privacy issues. Those concerns are not adequate and more should be added in terms of five phases (i.e., availability, confidentiality, data integrity, control, audit) for security. Multi located data storage and services (i.e., applications) in the Cloud, make privacy problems even though worse. Cloud computing systems have significant implications for the privacy of personal information whereas for the confidentiality of business and governmental information. That's because any information is moved from local computers to the Cloud Computing systems.

Murala et al. [13] proposed an image indexing and retrieval algorithm using local tetra patterns (LTrPs) for content-based image retrieval (CBIR). The standard local binary pattern (LBP) and local ternary pattern (LTP) encode the relationship among the referenced pixel and its surrounding neighbors through computing gray-level difference. The proposed method encodes the relationship among the referenced pixel and its neighbors, based on the directions that are manipulated using the first-order derivatives in vertical and horizontal directions. Furthermore, a generic approach to calculate nth-order LTrP using (n − 1)th-order horizontal and vertical derivatives for efficient CBIR and analyze the effectiveness of algorithm by hybriding it with the Gabor transform.

Jalaja et al. [14] proposed structural methods of texture analysis for CBIR in view of their closeness to human perception and description of texture. In variety of structural analysis, local patterns are the key point and when used as features perhaps expected to return more relevant images in CBIR. One method to describe local patterns in computationally simple terms is texture spectrum proposed by Heand Wang. The extension of He and Wang's texture spectrum to larger and more major windows, along with new structural features that capture local patterns such as horizontal and vertical stripes, alternating dark and bright spots, etc.

3 Content Based Image Retrieval with Enhanced Privacy

The proposed system extracts features from all the images in the image dataset, creates an index and centroid database and encrypts the database to enforce privacy in the cloud. When the user wants to search for the query image, an UI has been created using Bootstrap and AngularJS, and Dropwizard framework is used to accept RestAPI calls at the cloud server and process the user query. Once the user uploads the query image, a session key is created using Diffie-Hellman key exchange algorithm, then the features of the image are extracted and then homomorphically encrypted and sent to the cloud server. The cloud server compares the centroid of the query image to that of the centroid database in the cloud server and then returns the image indexes that belongs to the same cluster to the user side. Now distance is computed using Euclidian distance between the query image index and other indexes obtained from the cloud server. The distances are then sent to the cloud server which performs the distance check with all the indexes from the database and returns the top 15 images. The images are then returned to the user. The above process does not leak any information regarding the query image, as the image is not really uploaded, only the centroid of the image is used for computation at the server and also any information regarding the image dataset is not known to the cloud server as the images are encrypted and the index database is also encrypted and all the computations are done homo morphically. The index creation and the searching of images are implemented using apache spark framework.

A. *System Modules*

The modules mentioned in Fig. 1 are explained below:

(1) *Image database:* Cloud storage where the images are stored. Images can be dynamically added and removed from the cloud storage
(2) *Image Segmentation:* Partitioning a digital image into multiple segments (sets of pixels, also known as superpixels). The goal of segmentation is to simplify and/or change the representation of an image into something that is more meaningful and easier to analyze.
(3) *Feature Extraction:* All CBIR systems view the query image and the target images as a collection of features. These features, or image signatures, characterize the content of the image. The advantages of using image features instead of the original image pixels appear in image representation and comparison for retrieving. When we use the image features for matching, we almost do compression for the image and use the most important content of the image. This bridges the gaps between the semantic meaning of the image and the pixel representation.

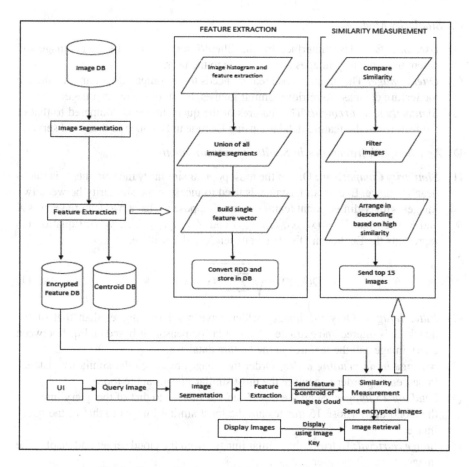

Fig. 1. Proposed system architecture using Apache Spark

B. *Spark Framework in Feature Extraction*

(1) *Image Histogram and texture extraction:* This is a transformation function where the partitioned image features including histogram and texture corresponding to the partition. The result will be stored as Resilient Distributed Dataset (RDD).

(2) *Union of image segments:* The segmented image features are transformed(union) into a single image feature separately for both histogram and texture.

(3) *Build single feature vector:* Both histogram and texture feature is combined together into a single image feature and stored in the feature database for future reference.

　(i) *Convert RDD and store in feature database:* RDD is converted into normal value which can be used for other operations and the value is stored in the feature database.

　(ii) *Feature database:* Database which consists of all the extracted image features and the data is stored in encrypted format in the cloud. Several other features of the image are also stored in the feature database.

C. Similarity Module

(1) **User interface:** User interface for the Client/User to select the query image and where the similarity images are displayed to the user.

(2) **Query image:** The image whose feature needs to be compared with the features in the feature database to retrieve similar images to that of the query image.

(3) **Similarity measurement:** The features of the query image is compared to that of the features in the feature database using Euclidean Distance in the cloud server.

D. Apache spark framework in Similarity measurement

(1) **Similarity Comparison:** One of the most popular similarity measurements is Euclidean Distance. Euclidean Distance is used to measure the similarity between two images with N-dimensional feature vector. Suppose we have two feature vectors X and Y such that $X = (x_0, x_1, \ldots, x_{N-1})$ and $Y = (y_0, y_1, \ldots, y_{N-1})$. Equation (1) represents the Euclidean Distance between X and Y will be:

$$D(X, Y) = \sqrt[2]{\sum_{i=0}^{N-1} (x_i - y_i)^2} \tag{1}$$

(2) **Filter images:** Only the images which have similarity higher than that of the threshold is filtered and extracted, the similarity measure is based on Eq. 1 between query image and the features in the feature database.

(3) **Arrange in descending order:** Order the images based on the similarity distance in descending order to acquire the most similar images at the top.

(4) **Send top 15 images:** Send the top 15 similar images to that of the query image to the cloud user. Those 15 images are the most similar images to that of the query image.

(5) **Image retrieval:** Retrieve the similar images from the cloud server and display the images to the cloud user.

(6) **Send top 15 images:** Send the top 15 similar images to that of the query image to the cloud user. Those 15 images are the most similar images to that of the query image.

(7) **Image retrieval:** Retrieve the similar images from the cloud server and display the images to the cloud user.

4 Privacy Preserving Architecture

See Fig. 2.

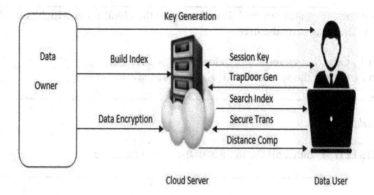

Fig. 2. Privacy preserving architecture of the proposed system

A. Initializing and Creating Database

ALGORITHM:

Step 1: Upload all the images to the cloud.

Step 2: Images are split into image divisions to find the signatures of the image.

$$s_t = \{(c^{(t)}_1, w^{(t)}_1), ..., (c^{(t)}_i, w^{(t)}_i), ..., (c^{(t)}_{kt}, w^{(t)}_{kt})\}$$

where c_i denotes a cluster center, w_i is the number of local features that are clustered to the class centered by c_i.

Step 3: Create a signature database by extracting signature from all the images as above.

Step 4: Create a centroid database by finding the centroid for all the images individually using

$$\xi_t = \sum_{i=1}^{kt} c_i^{(t)} w_i^{(t)}$$

where c_i denotes a cluster center, w_i is the number oflocal features that are clustered to the class centered by c_i.

Step 5: Encrypt the databases and randomize such that the cloud server can do computations without knowing the sensitive information.

B. Key Generation

ALGORITHM : K←KeyGen(1^κ)

> Data owner generates key and distributes it to the cloud users which is used to decrypt the images by the user.
>
> **Step 1** : Generate secret keys randomly $K_M, K_S, K_\Xi, \{K_j\}^L_{j=1}$
> **Step 2** : Output the secret key $K_M, K_S, K_\Xi, \{K_j\}^L_{j=1}$

C. Build Index

ALGORITHM: Index all the images in the image database.

> **Input:** The centroid database Ξ, the set of hash functions $\{g_i\}L_{i=q}$, the set of keys for hash value $\{Ki\}L_{i=q}$, the one wayhash function ϕ.
> **Output:** Secure index I.
> **Step 1:** For each $j = 1, \cdots, L$, data owner builds the j-th hash table by applying function g_j over all the elements in centroid database.
>
> **Step 2:** For each $j = 1, \cdots, L$, data owner picks a random key K_j and replaces each LSH hash digest $B_{j,i}, i = 1, \cdots, N_j$ in the j-th hash table with $\phi(K_j, B_{j,i}, i)$.
> **Return:** Index I consists of L secure hash tables. Hash tables are randomized using bit-plane randomization to prevent direct use of the hash values.

D. Data Encryption

ALGORITHM: $\{M', S'\}$←DataEnc(M, S, K_M, K_S)

> **Step 1:** Encrypt all the image $m_t \in M$ with secure key K_M, generating encrypted image set M';
>
> **Step 2:** Encrypt all the image $s_t \in S$ with secure key K_S, generating encrypted image set S';
>
> **Step 3:** Output$\{M', S'\}$

E. Session Key Generation

Use Diffie-Helman Key exchange to exchange secure keys between the cloud server and the user. Key is computed as follows:

$$\textbf{Server:} \quad K = B^a \ (mod \ p) = (\ g^b)^a \ (mod \ p)$$
$$\textbf{User:} \quad K = A^b \ (mod \ p) = (\ g^a)^b \ (mod \ p)$$

F. Trap Door Generation

Trap door function is used for security purposes where the session key is used to decrypt the trap-function by the cloud server, man in the middle attack is avoided by the use of trap door function.

ALGORITHM: $T_q \leftarrow$ **TrapdoorGen(s_q, ξ_q)**

Step 1: For query signature s_q, compute its centroid ξ_q.

Step 2: For each hash function generate the trapdoor $T_q j = \phi(K_j, g_j(\xi_q))$

Step 3: Output T_q.

G. Search Index

The index of the query image is compared with the index of the all the images in the dataset.

ALGORITHM:

Step 1: Use the session key to decrypt the trapdoor function.
Step 2: Compare the centroid value of the query image with all the hash tables in centroid database to get the relevant images.
Step 3: Retrieve the signatures of all the relevant images.
Step 4: Output retrieval encrypted signature set S'_q.

H. Compute Similar Images

ALGORITHM:

> **Step 1:** Decrypt all the retrieved signature set S'_q.
> **Step 2:** Compare all the signature set with the signature of the query image S_q.
> **Step 3:** Compute the Euclidian distance using equation (1) between the two signature vectors.
> **Step 4:** Send the computed distance to the server.

I. Distance Computation

ALGORITHM:

> **Step 1:** Use the distance from the retrieved set to find all the signature that are relevant to the query image.
> **Step 2:** Rank the images based on the Euclidian distance based on equation (1).
> **Step 3:** Send the top 15 images to the user.

5   Experimental Results

The application created is a web based application using Bootstrap and AngularJs [15]. LIRE (Lucene Image REtrieval) is used to extract low level features such as Color layout, FCTH, RGB and Tamura texture. The application connects to the Cloud server using RestAPI calls which is handled in the server side with Dropwizard and Jersey framework. The cloud environment is created using Open Nebula cloud. The user first exchanges session key to create a secure session between themselves and the cloud server. Then the user selects the query image and the index of the image is computed at the user side and the index is encrypted using the session key and is sent to the cloud server. The cloud server analyses the index of the query image and finds similarity between the query image index and the index database in the cloud server to find similar images. Then the top 15 similar images are found and sent to the cloud user.

The experiments were carried on in Apache Spark frame work [16] with real-world image database; Corel Image Set [17] with and the performance graph has been put. The graph has been plotted with different number of images each time and the time taken for index creation and image retrieval process with different number of cloud worker nodes.

5.1 Accuracy of Image Retrieval Using Different Image Retrieval Techniques

Here the graph Fig. 3 is plotted between number of images on x-axis and accuracy of different image retrieval techniques on the y-axis, the accuracy has been calculated for different dataset size and the graph is plotted (Table 1).

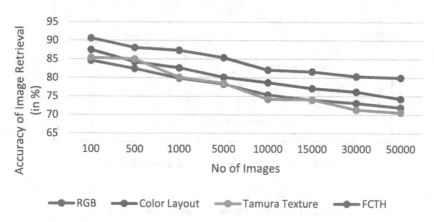

Fig. 3. Comparison of Accuracy using Different Image Retrieval Techniques

Table 1. Accuracy of image retrieval for different image features

S. No.	No. of images	Image retrieval techniques			
		RGB	Color layout	Tamura texture	FCTH
1	100	84.56	87.47	85.37	90.58
2	500	82.41	84.23	85.00	88.06
3	1000	79.85	82.63	80.12	87.35
4	5000	78.27	80.12	78.48	85.37
5	10000	75.38	78.69	74.16	82.06
6	15000	74.00	77.15	74.08	81.63
7	30000	73.14	76.25	71.37	80.36
8	50000	71.95	74.28	70.58	80.00

5.2 Time for Secure Transformation of Images

Here the graph Fig. 4 is plotted between number of images on x-axis and time taken for the secure transformation of images using hashing tables in seconds on the y-axis. The time taken with Centroid database for image retrieval is reduced by about 40% (Table 2).

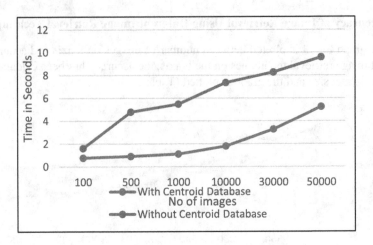

Fig. 4. Time for Secure Transformation of Images

Table 2. Time taken for secure transmission of images

S. No.	No. of images	With centroid database	Without centroid database
1	100	0.76	1.6
2	500	0.9	4.79
3	1000	1.1	5.48
4	10000	1.79	7.36
5	30000	3.26	8.26
6	50000	5.25	9.58

Table 3. Performance comparison between Apache Spark and MapReduce framework

S. No.	No. of images	Framework (Time in Seconds)	
		Apache Spark	MapReduce
1	1000	0.0399	0.1149
2	5000	1.5509	2.5959
3	10000	3.0049	4.1729
4	25000	7.00532	9.11532
5	50000	9.00024	11.24324

5.3 Performance Between Apache Spark and MapReduce Framework

Here the graph Fig. 5 is plotted between number of images on x-axis and time taken in seconds at the y-axis. This is the performance comparison between map reduce and apache spark framework in cloud (Table 3).

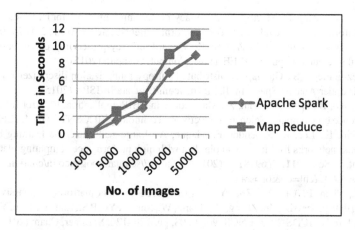

Fig. 5. Performance comparison between Apache Spark and MapReduce framework

6   Conclusion

The proposed scheme for privacy allows the data owner to outsource the image database and the CBIR service to the cloud, without revealing the actual content of the database to the cloud server. The privacy of the query image is completely preserved by homomorphically encrypting the index of the query image and all the computations in the cloud server are done without revealing any information to the server. With the help of Centroid database the retrieval time of the images are reduced by 40%. Apache Spark framework improves the retrieval of the images from the server than that of using Map-Reduce. Thus the spark framework can be used in cloud for Content Based Image Retrieval (CBIR) and the top 15 images are retrieved from the server, which is efficient than map reduce by 15%. This scheme can be extended by deploying on the public cloud environment (e.g., Amazon EC2) and scalability performance can be checked. The apache spark framework can be further improved by modifying at the framework level for the image, then the size of the encryption can be further reduced by modifying the algorithm.

References

1. Bhute, A.N., Meshram, B.B.: Content Based Image Indexing and Retrieval. arXiv preprint arXiv:1401.1742 (2014)
2. Kodituwakku, S.R., Selvarajah, S.: Comparison of color features for image retrieval. Indian J. Comput. Sci. Eng. **1**(3), 207–211 (2004)
3. Feng, D., Siu, W.-C., Zhang, H.J. (eds.): Multimedia information retrieval and management: Technological fundamentals and applications. Springer Science & Business Media, Heidelberg (2013)
4. Karaa, W.B.A. (ed.): Biomedical Image Analysis and Mining Techniques for Improved Health Outcomes. IGI Global (2015)
5. Zaharia, M., Chowdhury, M., Franklin, M.J., Shenker, S., Stoica, I.: Spark: cluster computing with working sets. HotCloud **10**(10–10), 95 (2010)

6. Weng, L., Amsaleg, L., Morton, A.: A privacy-preserving framework for large-scale content-based information retrieval. IEEE Trans. Inform. Forensics Secur. **10**, 152–167 (2015)

7. Xia, Z., Zhu, Y., Sun, X., Qin, Z., Ren, K.: Towards privacy-preserving content-based image retrieval in cloud computing. IEEE Trans. Comput. Comput. (2015)

8. Ramirez-Gallego, S., García, S.: Distributed entropy minimization discretizer for big data analysis under Apache Spark. In: IEEETrustcom/BigDataSE/ISPA (2015)

9. Shi, L., Wu, B., Wang, B., Yan, X.: Map/reduce in CBIR application. In: 2011 International Conference on Computer Science and Network Technology (ICCSNT), vol. 4. IEEE (2011)

10. Elsebakhi, E., Lee, F., Schendel, E., Haque, A.: Large-scale machine learning based on functional networks for biomedical big data with high performance computing platforms. J. Comput. Sci. **11**, 69–81 (2015). https://scholar.google.co.in/citations?user=A-ExtXkAAAAJ&hl=en&oi=sra

11. Sun, Z., Chen, F., Chi, M., Zhu, Y.: A spark-based big data platform for massive remote sensing data processing. In: Zhang, C., Huang, W., Shi, Y., Yu, P.S., Zhu, Y., Tian, Y., Zhang, P., He, J. (eds.) ICDS 2015. LNCS, vol. 9208, pp. 120–126. Springer, Cham (2015). https://doi.org/10.1007/978-3-319-24474-7_17

12. Shankarwar, M.U., Pawar, A.V.: Security and privacy in cloud computing: a survey. In: Satapathy, S.C., Biswal, B.N., Udgata, S.K., Mandal, J.K. (eds.) Proceedings of the 3rd International Conference on Frontiers of Intelligent Computing: Theory and Applications (FICTA) 2014. AISC, vol. 328, pp. 1–11. Springer, Cham (2015). https://doi.org/10.1007/978-3-319-12012-6_1

13. Murala, S., Maheshwari, R.P., Balasubramanian, R.: Local tetra patterns: a new feature descriptor for content-based image retrieval. IEEE Trans. Image Process. **21**(5), 2874–2886 (2012). https://scholar.google.co.in/citations?user=_RZpISEAAAAJ&hl=en&oi=sra

14. Jalaja, K., Bhagvati, C., Deekshatulu, B.L.: Texture element feature characterizations for CBIR. In: Proceedings, 2005 IEEE International Geoscience and Remote Sensing Symposium, IGARSS 2005, vol. 2. IEEE (2005)

15. LIRE: www.semanticmetadata.net/lire/

16. Apache Spark: spark.apache.org

17. Wang, J.Z., Li, J., Wiederhold, G.: Simplicity: semantics - sensitive integrated matching for picture libraries. IEEE Trans. Pattern Anal. Mach. Intell. **23**(9), 947–963 (2001)

Remote Continuous Health Monitoring
System for Patients

D. Jagadish[✉], N. Priya, and R. Suganya

Department of Information Technology, Vel Tech High Tech Dr. Rangarajan
Dr. Sakunthala Engineering College, Anna University, Chennai, India
jagadishmitindia@gmail.com, priya.nanthakumar05@gmail.com,
suganyaramesh95@gmail.com

Abstract. Recent advances in Internet of Things (IoT) leads to the development of several applications. Some of these applications are related to smart healthcare monitoring though there are several applications for healthcare and monitoring it does not fully address the ability to satisfy the patient's needs, doctor convenience and the automation of system to act according to the status of the patient. In this paper, we implemented an algorithm for (a) the continuous health monitoring and frequent update to the hospital server which notifies the doctor. It also supports the mobility of patient, (b) acts according to the critical levels of patient which is safe, intermediate or emergency through cloud processing, (c) ability of the doctor to view enormous sensor record in comprehend form using the visualization and analysis and (d) Drug management system to deliver drugs to the patient on time and without the presence of the nurse using stored data in the server. Raspberry pi 2 is used to transmit the bio-sensed data of patient directly to the cloud by using the internet of smart phone or PC where based on the critical level sends a notification to the doctor through hospital server, caretaker and/or Ambulance service.

Keywords: Health monitoring · IoT · Diverse emergency situation
Tele-medicine

1 Introduction

The emerging issues in health management are to take care of their health as well as the individuals who are dependent on them. Over the past decades, people have more interest in buying wearable sensors which provides the digitized & accurate measurement of their health status [1, 2]. The measurement of sensor data can be done automatically without even doing the manual intervention such as the key press. Recent invents provides the caretaker and doctor to guide the patient or the patient can consult the doctor without physically being visiting them which can be provided securely.

Some other systems provide the setup to alert caretaker in abnormal condition [3]. This kind of system provides the feature to connect to the database of the patient's health records. Thus makes the doctor to better prognosis and recommend the treatment at an earlier stage. It drastically reduces the impact of diseases in an advanced stage. These innovations are just the start, there are many systems developed to facilitate the handling

Shriram R and M. Sharma (Eds.): DaSAA 2017, CCIS 804, pp. 129–138, 2018.
https://doi.org/10.1007/978-981-10-8603-8_11

of voluminous sensor data. The enormous data is generated because of the huge population of people who need to be in observation and the tendency of the people to buy those devices [4].

Technologically, the above-described vision will be feasible for few years from now in clinical practice. Yet the system is not fully automatic and cost effective. The existing systems are not affordable in real time emergency situation. In this paper, we are focused on continuous monitoring and update of sensor data to the hospital server to keep track of health records with the algorithm to implement timely measures during massive situations and the drug management is made possible. We are sectioned our paper into: Sect. 2 highlights some background work for this paper. In Sect. 3, we outline the high-level architecture of the proposed system based on connected bio-sensors, transmission, storage and the action undertaken with particular sensor results. Section 4, 5, 6 describes the components in each phase of the architecture. In Sect. 7, we conclude the paper with limitations and future work of our paper.

2 Background

Most proposed systems of home-based health monitoring have the manual intervention for taking the sensor measurement. [3] proposed the system to take the continuous measurement of sensor values and sends it to the phone or PC for tracking their status and also used to save the patient records. It uses the PIC controller to receive the bio-signals from various sensor units and transmit to PC using the Bluetooth. This system alerts the caretaker in case of abnormality in patient's record. [5] also proposed the system to measure medical parameters continuously and transmits the gathered data using ZigBee. This system also equipped with alert notification to the doctor when he is not present in the hospital but it is difficult to track the location of the patient during an emergency situation.

In [6], Personal Health Device is used to monitor the patient remotely using the internet and hence, doctor consultation is also done remotely. There is no security or privacy provided with this IEEE11073 standard. [7] designed a system obtains the sensor data and processed using an ARM7 controller and is transmitted to an android application created in smartphone of Doctor or caretaker using any of low range transceivers such as ZigBee, Bluetooth, GSM or GPRS. The SMS alert is sent to Doctor's Pc in the case of emergency.

In addition to the medical sensors which is used in most of the papers, it is necessary to measure the environmental sensor such as Gas detection, Piezoelectric and temperature sensor to maintain oxygen & temperature level and also to detect the fall or collapse of the patient. The alert is given to Smartphone of doctor or caretaker based on the emergency level [8].

As the advent of IoT is developed from healthcare centre to home, thus allows this type of the system to be used even in clinics where the patient has to undergo the registration for the RFID tag for the first time by physically visiting the health centre to record the vital organs. This RFID tag connects with RFID reader which is near the hospital server from where the health records are transferred to the doctor. The patient can press the RFID tag to sense their medical parameter with the previously recorded status of patient and the doctor provide the medical adherence remotely [9].

3   High-Level Architecture

The Fig. 1 illustrates the high-level architecture of continuous monitoring and update of remote patient health record for massive emergency situation which describes different phases of system and its components.

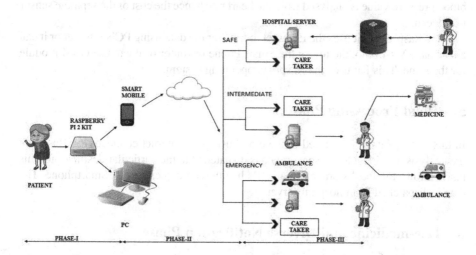

Fig. 1. Architecture of IOT based remote health monitoring for massive emergency situation

Sensor data composition phases used to collect the data from the various sensor unit to monitor different medical parameters such as Body temperature, blood oxygen saturation level, blood pressure, etc. and it is connected to the Microcontroller.

In Data transfer phase, the gathered sensor data is sent to the hospital server, doctor, ambulance or caretaker based on the critical level using the internet of the smart phone, PC or through GSM module.

Cloud processing and diverse notification phase allows to process the gathered data and determines the abnormality. Based on the change in a normal level of each biosensor data, the primitive action is taken by sending the data to the caretaker ambulance and the doctor after visualization and analysis through hospital server. In the following section, we considered the components of each phase of the high-level architecture.

4   Sensor Composition Phase

Medical parameters of patient's health are necessary to analyse the abnormality of the patient by comparing the sensor data with the threshold values. These sensors should be connected to the controller for providing such capability. The microcontroller can be stand-alone to transmit itself without using some other device like smart phone or PC.

In this paper, we are using the raspberry pi 2B kit to connect the various sensors. It consists of an ARM11 processor, 1 GB RAM and also has 40 pin extended GPIO with 4 USB ports, 4 pole Stereo output and Composite video port Full-size HDMI. Here we are connecting the heart rate, temperature and blood pressure sensor.

Temperature sensor gives analogue output but the raspberry pi accepts and sends the data in digital form, hence, an ADC is deployed between them. The MCP3208 Analogue to Digital Converter has 16 pin, 12 bit, 8 channel, Serial Peripheral Interface (SPI). The blood pressure value is analysed from the heart rate hence the cost of the separate sensor is reduced.

This Raspberry kit uses the Ethernet to transfer the data using PC's internet or it can either have Wi-Fi module to use the Smart Phone or router or it can use GSM module for the same. This Kit uses the Raspbian operating system.

5   Cloud Processing Phase

In this phase, data is forwarded to the cloud using the internet connectivity. Based on the analysis of critical level, sensor data is dispatched to the particular destination. This phase allows the local storage of patient's health record such as PC, Smartphone. The data is dispatched from hospital server.

6   Tele-medicine and Diverse Notification Phase

In this phase, we are doing the processing of gathered sensor data by Analytics and visualisation method which is used to compare the sensor data with the previous record for prognosis and provides the ability to view enormous sensor record in comprehending form for the doctor. So that the doctor can concentrate only on critical issues instead of going through all records thus saves the time and energy [4]. Here we have designed three critical levels based on which the data is dispatched are as follows:

A. *Safe Level*:

The patient is said to be in safe level when he/she maintains the normal level till their appointed regular check-up date. Based on the analysis of patient's health record, the doctor will prescribe the medicine to the patient using the big data concept. This concept helps the critical patient to take those medicine for a particular symptom. The prescribed medicine is sent to the patient as well as caretaker which also stored in hospital server.

B. *Intermediate Level*:

In this level the patient's bio-signal value changes to slight abnormal value then the information is passed to the doctor and caretaker. Here the doctor decides whether to call for an ambulance or suggest the patient to take some other medicine, the same information is passed also to the caretaker.

C. *Cemergency Level*:

This level denotes critical situation of the patient where the automated call for an ambulance is done initially. Then the information is passed to the doctor & the caretaker.

7 Prototype Implementation

In our prototype implementation, we are having several sensors in sensor composition phase to determine heart rate variability, respiratory level, position and temperature of the patient and is connected to the raspberry pi kit along with Ethernet for internet connectivity is developed as described in Fig. 2.

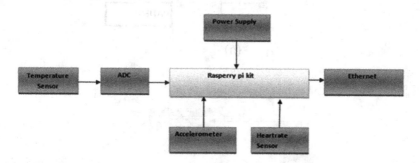

Fig. 2. Block diagram of sensor composition phase

In the cloud processing phase, the bio-medical parameters of the patient are transformed to the hospital server, from which the actual process starts. The hospital server analyses the critical level along with the update of patient's record. The updated patient record is then represented in graphical form and is illustrated in Fig. 3. The analysed critical level action will be reflected in next phase.

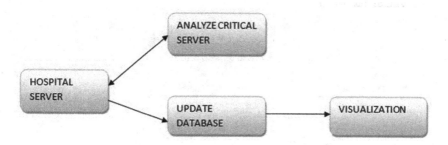

Fig. 3. Block diagram of cloud processing phase

LEVEL 1: SAFE

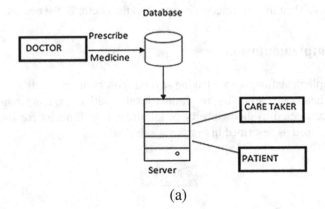

(a)

LEVEL 2: INTERMEDIATE

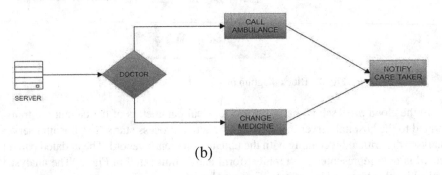

(b)

LEVEL 3: EMERGENCY

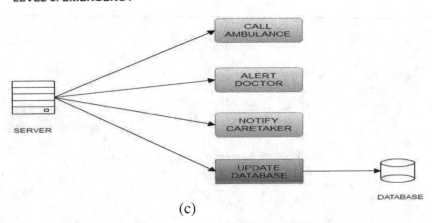

(c)

Fig. 4. (a) Block diagram of safe level in tele-medicine and diverse notification phase, (b) Block diagram of intermediate level in tele-medicine and diverse notification phase, (c) Block diagram of emergency level in tele-medicine and diverse notification phase

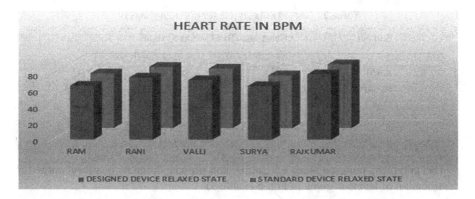

Fig. 5. Comparison of Heart rate values of different subjects of standard and designed device

In the telemedicine and diverse notification phase, the alert is given to different destination based on the analysed critical levels. In all the levels the doctor and caretaker will get notified about the patient. The database will also be updated at every level. In addition to that, the emergency level has an automatic call to the ambulance, intermediate level allows the doctor to decide whether to execute safe or emergency level and safe level allows the doctor to prescribe medicine which will be reflected in the database. The prescribed medicine will also be sent as a mail to the caretaker. These processes are explained in the following Figs. 4(a), (b) and (c).

8 Experimental Analysis and Results

We aim at providing fully automated health monitoring without manual intervention to support all type of sensors in a compact manner. We are also providing better flexibility and mobility for the patient. Several devices have been deployed in the market for the effective usage of the patient like the smart watch. Even though smart phone addresses many problems it does not have the ability to sense the respiratory level. The Table 1 shows the sensor usage in different health monitoring device

Table 1. List of sensors in existing and proposed system

Monitoring device/Sensors	Heart rate monitor	Accelerometer	Temperature sensor	Pressure analyzer
Samsung Galaxy S3	✓	✓	–	✓
Moto G2	✓	✓	–	–
Designed Device	✓	✓	✓	✓

The experimentation is conducted on different patients in which the designed device provides more accurate result compared to the traditional medical equipment. As a sample, we have provided the heart rate reading of various patients. Table 2 provides the record of sensed data of designed and existing device.

Table 2. Record of heart rate for different subjects

Subject	Heart rate (BPM)-relaxed state	
	Designed device	Standard device
RAM	65	66
RANI	75	74
VALLI	72	72
SURYA	65	64
RAJKUMAR	79	77

The graphical representation of comparison among different heartbeat rates for identification of levels is given in Fig. 6 (Table 3).

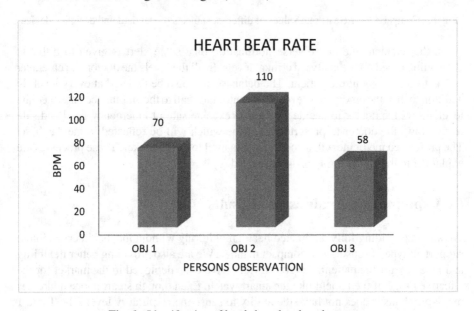

Fig. 6. Identification of levels based on heartbeat rates

Table 3. Comparison of different heartbeat rates for identification of levels

Name	Heart rate (Normal rate = 70–10 BPM)
OBJ 1	70
OBJ 2	110
OBJ 3	58

The variation with the standard device and the accuracy of designed device is better represented in Fig. 5 as follows. Here we have compared the leading smart watch with our kit based on the performance as shown in Table 4 as follows,

Table 4. Performance comparison

Monitoring device	Performance in MHZ
Samsung gear s3 smart watch	800
Raspberry pi Kit	900

The graphical representation of performance comparison between Samsung galaxy gear s3 smart watch and our designed device is given in Fig. 7.

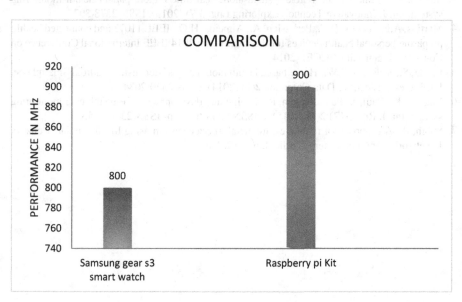

Fig. 7. Performance comparison with leading health monitor

9 Conclusion and Future Enhancement

In this paper, we reviewed some of the existing tools and technologies and also proposed the system to provide fully automated and better flexible kit to support the sensor data updating continuously to the hospital server. We have also implemented the drug management system which records the drugs prescribed & distribute it to the patient remotely. Since, there are many devices which incorporate controller and sensor together such as the smart watch, fitness tracker but still these do not support the feature of connecting all sensors together especially respiratory sensor. With advance research in this aspect, there can be an advancement in our proposed system and can change the medical monitoring system.

References

1. Varma, D., Shete, V.V., Somani, S.B.: Development of home health care self-monitoring system. Int. J. Adv. Res. Comput. Commun. Eng. **4**(6), 253–255 (2015)
2. Hassanalieragh, M., Page, A., Soyata, T., Sharma, G., Aktas, M., Mateos, G., Kantarci, B., Andreescu, S.: Health monitoring and management using Internet-of-things (IoT) sensing with cloud-based processing: opportunities and challenges. In: IEEE International Conference on Services Computing (2015)
3. Shaikh, R.A., Shaikh, S.: Wireless stand-alone real time remote patient health monitoring system. Int. J. Innovative Technol. Exploring Eng. **3**(7) (2013). ISSN 2278-3075
4. Martins, A.F., Santos, D.F., Perkusich, A., Almeida, H.O.: IEEE 11073 and connected health: preparing personal health devices for the internet. In: 2014 IEEE International Conference on Consumer Electronics (ICCE) (2014)
5. Pawar, S., Kulkarni, P.W.: Home based health monitoring system using Android Smartphone. Int. J. Electr. Electron. Data Commun. **2**(2) (2014). ISSN 2320-2084
6. Raghav, K., Paul, J., Pandurangan, R.: Design and development of e-health care monitoring system. Int. J. Res. (IJR) **2**(4) (2015). e-ISSN 2348-6848, p- ISSN 2348-795X
7. Singh, R.: A proposal for mobile e-care health service system using IoT for Indian scenario. J. Network Commun. Emerg. Technol. **6**(1) (2016)

Secure Data Archiving Using Enhanced Data Retention Policies

H. Sabireen, S. Kirthica[✉] [iD], and Rajeswari Sridhar

Department of Computer Science and Engineering,
College of Engineering, Anna University, Chennai 600025, India
sabireen2000@gmail.com, s.kirthica@gmail.com, rajisridhar@gmail.com

Abstract. With the increase in the number of applications that are deployed and executed in a cloud, cloud service providers face several maintenance related issues due to the high volume of data involved. The inability to effectively organize the information for decision making can have a serious impact on business decision making. The use of a cloud's storage facilities for data backup and archiving provides flexibility and data preservation features at a very low cost. In this paper, we present an efficient data management system that can archive, store and manage information effectively. The massive amount of data in the cloud is grouped based on Jaccard Similarity into six different buckets. Two sets of data retention policies are proposed for the cloud archive framework. These policies are applied to each of the buckets individually to identify the data to be archived. Additionally, homomorphic encryption is applied to provide a level of security to the data to be archived. This data is archived into the cloud to provide a data storage environment as a service that is optimized for long term data retention, security and that is compliant with the data retention policy. This framework eventually improves the availability, confidentiality and reduces the access latency significantly.

Keywords: Cloud archiving · Jaccard similarity
Homomorphic encryption

1 Introduction

Organizations today are challenged with huge volumes of inactive structured and unstructured data [1]. Both public and private organizations deal with large amount of information in paper and electronic form. Furthermore, it is not uncommon for records to have retention periods of several tens of years, becoming historic records that need to be kept indefinitely [2]. Industries struggle with the ever-present, ever-increasing cost of managing this massive amount of data. Such high volumes of data are leading to scalability and maintenance issues. The inability to effectively locate, organize and leverage information for decision making has a serious impact on business decision making [1]. Hence, an

© Springer Nature Singapore Pte Ltd. 2018
Shriram R and M. Sharma (Eds.): DaSAA 2017, CCIS 804, pp. 139–152, 2018.
https://doi.org/10.1007/978-981-10-8603-8_12

efficient data management system that can archive, store and manage information effectively can help to manage data in a better manner.

In the current scenario huge volumes of data are stored on clouds, enjoying the benefits that Cloud Computing has to offer, while requiring low effort on the part of the cloud customer to manage the necessary resources [3]. Data management in a cloud is critical to an organization's success. An important part of data management is the data retention policy which is used to archive the data. Unfortunately, such a policy is not given as much importance in the commercial sector as is required. It is either not in use or not properly enforced where used. Such a policy will be effective only if it covers all data irrespective of its form or residence.

Archiving service solutions generally provide cost reduction, storage, backup and management of data for e-discovery and compliance. In addition to archiving e-mail and instant messages, organizations are beginning to look for archiving numerous other contents. Archive infrastructure must support high volumes of data at low cost, extended data retention and periodic high volume searching.

Data archiving is not just located in the past, it occurs in the present, and it impacts the future. In order to help meet the current and future long-term storage requirements, an archive storage system should be capable of storing and managing multiple billions of documents over the deployment lifetime of the system.

In this paper, we propose an efficient data management system that can archive, store and manage information effectively. The archival of the data is done in a secure and scalable manner by designing and applying efficient data retention policies and encryption techniques to efficiently manage and archive the data. We also present the results of our evaluation of the proposed work.

The rest of the paper is organized as follows: The background and related work are explained in Sect. 2. In Sect. 3, the architecture of the proposed data archival framework and the analysis of the proposed algorithms are discussed. In Sect. 4, the design of experiments and the performance analysis of our system are discussed. The conclusion and future work are explained in Sect. 5.

2   Problem Statement and Related Work

Compared to local drives, cloud storage offers higher availability, unlimited space, and lower cost. Though, such a storage is convenient, it becomes highly vulnerable. Also, there is heavy dependence on specific protocols and tools of a particular cloud vendor which may make future migration difficult and costly. This is demonstrated in the shutdown of Mega upload [4] where though service providers guaranteed availability, there was a possibility of users losing their valuable digital assets [5].

2.1   Related Work

Storage of data that is no longer actively used adds to maintenance costs. Such data can be moved to a separate storage device for long-term retention and this process is called data archiving. Data archival in a cloud is becoming increasingly popular due to its agility and ease of management. Though the archive data is old, it may be needed for future reference and is therefore important [6]. The computing and storage facilities offered by a cloud solve many problems related to long-term image archives [7].

Data retention belongs to a class of data policies, called action policies that specify what to do under the current situation. However, these actions or policies are not explicitly specified. Data management should be as per the agreed upon data management policies to ensure compliance with regulatory policies such as the Data Protection Directive under EU privacy law, HIPAA, and PCI-DSS. These high-level policies are often translated to low-level enforceable actions relating to data availability, data integrity, data migration, data retention, and data access [8,9].

Internet Archive, one of the earliest archive systems, preserves comprehensive snapshots of the Internet. Other institutional archivists are either domain-centric, e.g. UK Web Archive (preserves UK websites), or topic-centric, e.g. Human Rights Web Archive at Columbia University (preserves websites related to human rights) [10]. Hewlett-Packard (HP) uses the Grid architecture for medical image archive services [11]. The aim of a similar work [12] is to help people to keep their own health data on the cloud archive and refer the data for future use and allow patients or caregiver with the same diseases to interact with each other. However, no information is provided on safeguarding the health related records and who can access the data.

The current archiving systems [13–15] deal with vendor lock-in problem which poses a challenge in data migration and data loss when a cloud service provider ceases to exist. For historic records that need indefinite retention, Cloud-based backup and archival services use large tape libraries to store them for cost-effectiveness. These services leverage duplication to reduce the disk storage capacity required by their customer data sets [16]. This tends to re-duplicate the data when moving it from disk to tape.

To summarize the issues of the existing works, the systems do not explain about the policies they have adopted for archival and focus only on archiving heritage, medical images, etc. Security also seems to be a bottleneck. Since the data available in the cloud is massive it needs to be grouped based on analysis and then archived to improve performance. Also, these systems focus on policies based on time and are not application specific. The proposed system focuses on archiving e-commerce data by grouping different types of data available in the cloud and then a generic framework of data retention policy is proposed to archive the data and also to provide security to confidential information.

3   Proposed Data Archival Framework

To determine which and what kind of data are to be archived, firstly, it is required to group the data based on similarity. The grouping is done based on Jaccard Similarity algorithm. It is necessary to determine the importance of the data for current and future operations, so as to determine the time for retaining the data, if it does not fall under any industry requirement or state and federal regulations.

Secondly, a data retention policy is framed to identify the data to be archived from the grouped data. Finally, the data to be archived is secured using homomorphic encryption and the entire data is archived into the cloud. This archive storage system will provide data integrity, scalability and power management at competitive pricing.

3.1   System Architecture Framework

The system aims at archiving e-commerce data from both user and server side and is given in Fig. 1.

First, the massive amount of data available in the cloud is pre-processed by pre-processing techniques like data cleaning, data transformation and data retention. This pre-processed data is then placed in the cloud from the perspective of cloud admin who will be archiving the required user data and server data. The huge amount of data available is grouped based on Jaccard similarity algorithm.

The given data is grouped into 6 different buckets namely frequent users and frequent buyers, frequent users and no frequent buyers, calculative shoppers, no shows, region wise and product wise based on different features. To the grouped bucket 2 policies are applied namely fTUBA based on frequency Time Usage Based and Access and TR^2P based on Time Regions Reviews and Products in order to identify the data which is to be archived. From each respective bucket, the required data to be archived is obtained based on the policies. Before archiving the data, it is essential to provide security to the transaction data as it

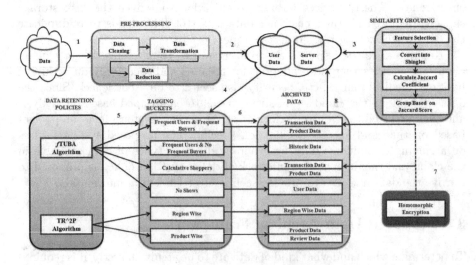

Fig. 1. Data archival architecture

contains confidential information. The given transaction data is encrypted using homomorphic algorithm and archived. The archived data is stored on the cloud.

3.2 Jaccard Similarity

The Jaccard Similarity algorithm takes as input the processed data and groups users into four different buckets namely frequent users and frequent buyers, frequent users and not frequent buyers, no shows are those users who have logged into the system but have not used any of the services and Calculative shoppers are those users who spend miserly but shop excess. Similarity for keywords is applied in [17]. In a similar manner, different features between users are taken for each of the buckets and the Jaccard coefficient is calculated as in Eq. 1 to identify similar kind of users belonging to the same bucket.

$$sf(x, y) = \frac{Tf(x) \cap Tf(y)}{Tf(x) \cup Tf(y)} \tag{1}$$

The Jaccard coefficient obtained between users is then compared with the Jaccard score, if it satisfies the score it belongs to the respective bucket. The process is carried out for all of the users and hence unique similar users are obtained in each of the respective buckets.

3.3 Data Retention Policies Using fTUBA and TR^2P

A data retention policy is a set of guidelines that describe which data will be archived and the duration for which it will be kept. The data retention algorithm given in Algorithm 1 generates rules based on the proposed policies.

The data archived in the cloud should also be kept secure. The buckets obtained from Jaccard algorithm namely frequent users and frequent buyers, frequent users and not buyers, no shows, calculative shoppers, region wise and product wise are grouped based on similarity and each of the buckets contain massive amount of information some of which would never be used. Establishing such a policy for cloud data has the following advantages,

1. makes production systems run better,
2. uses less resources,
3. reduces overall storage costs,
4. backup and recovery runs faster,
5. disaster recovery is less costly,
6. systems are easier to manage,
7. data moved into archives is stored at lower cost.

Hence, DRP is proposed to identify the data that would not be used i.e. the data is to be archived. The proposed DRP consists of two sets namely fTUBA and TR^2P, the first one is applied to user data and the later one is applied to server data. The fTUBA policy algorithm which is applied to user data identifies what kind of data is to be archived from each of the buckets. The policy is proposed based on frequency, time, usage based and access. The TR^2P policy is based on time, regions, reviews and products. This policy is applied to Region wise and Product wise bucket.

Algorithm 1. Data Retention Policy

Input: Rules R, Buckets B (classified data D)
Output: Data to be archived A
1: **foreach** bucket B **do**
2:     Create a single or a combination of rules r_j, that will predict data to be archived
3:     **foreach** B $\in$ classified Data D **do**
4:         Apply rules $r_j \in$ R based on fTUBA to B
5:         Call fTUBA B_i
6:         **if** return(fTUBA($r_i \rightarrow B_i$)) is Transaction data **then**
7:             Call Homo()
8:         **end if**
9:         Apply rules $sr_i \in$ R based on TR^2P to B
10:        Call $TR^2P(sB_i)$
11:        **if** return(find($sr_i \rightarrow B$)) $\in$ Transaction data **then**
12:            Call Homo()
13:        **end if**
14:    **end for**
15:    Transaction data $\in$ A is encrypted
16:    Transaction data and other archival data A obtained from fTUBA and TR^2P
       is archived respectively
17: **end for**

3.4 Rule Based Policies

The fTUBA policy when applied to FUFB bucket identifies that users belonging to this bucket frequently interact with system and use the services of the system, therefore, only their previous transactional history and products purchased is identified to be archived. When the fTUBA is applied to FUBNB bucket it identifies that these users have been interacting with the system but have not used the services from a particular period of time. Henceforth, all the historic data relevant to the user is identified to be archived.

The fTUBA policy specified in Algorithm 2, when applied to no shows bucket where users have just used the system initially but have neither used the system nor its services from a long period of time with very low access and frequency identifies that the entire data with respect to user needs to be archived. Similarly when the policy is applied to calculative shoppers who spend miserly but shop excess identifies based on the time, usage and access that transactional data and product data of those users needs to be archived.

The TR^2P policy, specified in Algorithm 3, is applied to region wise bucket based on time and regions, it identifies which of the regions have not had excess product import and export for a prolonged period of time with respect to a region baseline and identifies those regions and their details to be archived.

The TR^2P policy when applied to product wise bucket identifies the products which are least sold and also the products which have not been accessed, out of stock, products no more manufactured for a prolonged period of time, it also obtains the different reviews with respect to these products to be archived. Hence, the above 2 policies identifies the data to be archived from each of the buckets.

Algorithm 2. fTUBA

Input: fTUBA (DataSet D)
1: RuleSet $= \varphi$
2: **foreach** Bucket $b_i \in B$ **do**
3:     newRuleSet $=$ LearnRules(D,b_i)
4:     Remove tuples covered by newRuleSet from D
5:     Ruleset $+=$ newRuleSet
6: **end for**
7: **return** RuleSet

`LearnRules(D,b`$_i$`)`
1: **foreach** $b_i \in B$ **do**
2:     **if** A_i is frequent $\in$ users, buyers with regular access **then**
3:         **if** the rule fully covers Instance I of the user data **then**
4:             **return** transaction data and product data
5:         **end if**
6:         **if** the rule partially covers Instance I of the user data with min (amount) **then**
7:             **return** product data and transaction data
8:         **end if**
9:     **end if**
10:     **if** (A_i is initial login with low access and frequency **then**
11:         **if** the rule is covered for Instance I **then**
12:             **return** historic data
13:         **end if**
14:         **if** the rule is fully covered with no access and no frequency **then**
15:             **return** user data
16:         **end if**
17:     **end if**
18: **end for**

Algorithm 3. TR^2P

Input: TR^2P (DataSet D)
1: **while** (region (sales) <0) and (products sold intersection that region $= 0$) **do**
2:     **foreach** Instance A_i **do**
3:         Obtain the corresponding tuple satisfying the criteria
4:     **end for**
5: **end while**
6: **return** regions with less sales
7: **if** (product (sales) is rarely sold) and (products $= 0$ which belongs to each region) **then**
8:     **return** product data
9: **end if**

3.5   Homomorphic Encryption

Homomorphic encryption is an encryption scheme which performs operations on encrypted data which when decrypted gives the same result as that of the original plain text. The principle of homomorphic encryption is a cryptographic technique based on mathematical problem computational complexity theory. This encryption is applied to the transactional data which is obtained after applying the policies to further secure the data. It operates directly on the encrypted data without affecting the confidentiality of the systems and ensures privacy. To the data, multiplicative homomorphic encryption is applied [18] as in Eq. 2.

$$C_1.C_2 = m_1^e.m_2^e \ mod \ n = (m_1.m_2)^e \ mod \ n \tag{2}$$

It is the encryption of the already encrypted data (rather than of the original data) which provides the same result as is done on plain text. And, the complex mathematical operations can be performed on the cipher text without changing the nature of the encryption [19].

3.6   Storage of Archived Data

The archived data which is obtained by applying the DRP and then homomorphic encryption to the transactional data is stored in the cloud. This archived data is made available in the cloud as it would be easy to maintain high volumes of data at low cost. The cloud archiving provides a way to manage the data for long-term retention and compliance while improving performance and hiding complexity and technical details.

4   Implementation and Performance Analysis

4.1   Experimental SetUp

The implementation is carried out by deploying the data in the cloud. The input datasets are taken from Amazon Web Services containing user details, transactional data of the user, products purchased by the user. It also contains product details like product Id, product descriptions, product price, regional data with respect to products and also the various reviews on different products. This dataset is deployed in Eucalyptus cloud to achieve the archival data using proposed data retention policies and grouping based on Jaccard Similarity by securing the transactional data using homomorphic encryption.

4.2   Bucketization Metric

This metric is used to measure the efficiency of grouping data based on similarity using Jaccard coefficient. The precision, recall and f-measure are calculated to group based on Jaccard Index [17]. Equations 3, 4 and 5 respectively discuss precision, recall and f-measure.

$$Precision, P = \frac{true \ positive}{true \ positive + false \ positive} \tag{3}$$

$$Recall, R = \frac{true\ positive}{true\ positive + false\ negative} \qquad (4)$$

$$F - measure, F = \frac{2 \times P \times R}{P + R} \qquad (5)$$

The total number of users is 1357 of which 1123 are classified using Jaccard index. The remaining 234 users are randomly distributed in the buckets as shown in Table 1.

Table 1. Distribution of users

Buckets	Users
BUCKET 1	277 + 34
BUCKET 2	725 + 150
BUCKET 3	110 + 46
BUCKET 4	11 + 4

The randomly distributed users in each bucket are further grouped into the remaining four buckets as illustrated in Fig. 2.

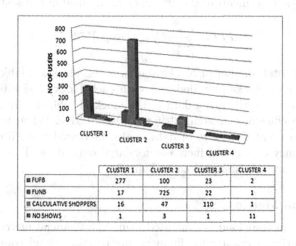

	CLUSTER 1	CLUSTER 2	CLUSTER 3	CLUSTER 4
■ FUFB	277	100	23	2
■ FUNB	17	725	22	1
■ CALCULATIVE SHOPPERS	16	47	110	1
■ NO SHOWS	1	3	1	11

Fig. 2. Distribution of users in each bucket

After the distribution of the users, the respective Precision and Recall is calculated for each bucket. Figure 3 illustrates the graph on Precision and Recall. Precision greater than 70% indicates that Jaccard Similarity returns substantially relevant results than irrelevant. Recall greater than 50% indicates that relevant results are retrieved.

F-measure greater than 0.9 indicates the effectiveness of the corresponding grouping based on Jaccard Similarity and is listed in Table 2.

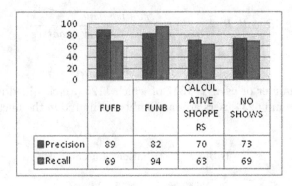

Fig. 3. Precision and Recall

Table 2. F-Measure

	FUFB	FUNB	Calculative shoppers	No shows
F-Measure	1.13	0.93	1.05	1.03

4.3 Archival Efficiency

This metric is used to measure the efficiency of archival of the system.

$$eff = \sum_{i=0}^{n} nC_i \ p_0^i (1 - p_0)^{n-i} \qquad (6)$$

where, n is the total number of blocks and p_0 is the block available for storage.

The number of blocks provided is 5 with each block of size 65 KB. Upon applying the policy to the given data in the blocks 1.5 blocks are available. On calculating the efficiency of archival it achieves 77.31%. When the number of blocks is increased and the size of data is also increased in each of the blocks then the efficiency of archival increases for large scale data. The results of the workload summary are summarized in Table 3.

4.4 Financial Metric

Archiving data in the cloud is evaluated using the financial metric [20]. Based on the information necessary for financial metrics and cloud computing criteria, evaluation strategies are proposed for the evaluation of cloud. The strategy implies the use of cost benefit analysis, return on investment and total cost of ownership in order to provide a combined metric for calculation. The formula of the metric is:

$$V_T = \frac{\sum_{i=1}^{r} \frac{Benefit}{(1+r)^t} - InitialCost - \sum_{i=1}^{r}(DirectCost_t + IndirectCost_t)}{\sum_{i=1}^{r}(DirectCost_t + IndirectCost_t) + InitialCost} \qquad (7)$$

Table 3. Workload summary

Workload	Size and percentage
Input size	303 KB
No. of files	7
File size	15–65 KB
Archival data size	85 KB
Total data occupies	218 KB
Available space for storage	5 KB
Percentage of space used	71.9%
Percentage of space available	28%
Archival efficiency	77.31%

where, V_T is the percent of the return on investments at a specified time moment T, r is the discount rate and t is the year.

The metric is evaluated between two alternatives: cloud and tradition magnetic tape and suggests one with the higher percentage. The costs for the cloud storage pricing [21] and magnetic tape cost [22,23] are listed. Let the initial investment for each year be 1500. And it is assumed to be the same for all years and all the rates in USD hypothetically. The standard pricing of cloud is listed in Table 4.

Table 4. Cloud pricing and benefits

Time (years)	Total Cost ($)	Initial Cost ($)	Direct Cost ($)	Indirect Cost ($)	Benefit ($)	Discount ($)	Total Benefit ($)
1	700	300	300	100	800	0	800
2	400	N/A	300	100	1100	800	1900
3	400	N/A	300	100	1100	1100	2200
4	400	N/A	300	100	1100	1100	2200
5	400	N/A	300	100	1100	1100	2200
6	500	N/A	300	200	1000	1100	2100
7	400	N/A	300	100	1100	1000	2100
8	400	N/A	300	100	1100	900	2000
9	300	N/A	200	100	1200	1100	2300
10	300	N/A	200	100	1200	1200	2400

Figures 4 and 5 respectively indicate the comparison of tape with total cost and total benefit.

It is observed that when the above metric is applied. The Returns on tape is only 13.5% and the returns on cloud is 78%. Hence the cloud gives a better return on investment with lower maintenance costs.

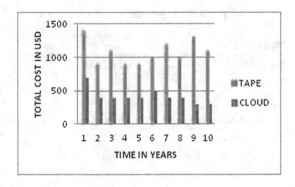

Fig. 4. Comparison of Total Cost for Cloud vs Tape

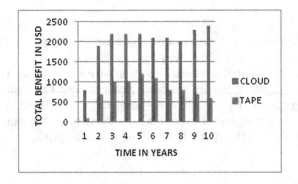

Fig. 5. Comparison of Total Benefit between Cloud vs Tape

5   Conclusion and Future Work

In this paper, we present redefined data retention policies - fTUBA and TR^2P - which help to archive the data in the cloud for securing it in order to improve scalability, maintainability and to reduce latency of accessed data. The decision to deploy a cloud-based archiving solution enables a trade-off between upfront implementation costs for software/hardware and ongoing IT management. The design and implementation of this framework demonstrates the feasibility of using the cloud computing platform to provide a long-term archive solution. It has the potential to lower the cost of storage and management and to increase disaster recoverability. Jaccard similarity algorithm is therefore suitably sufficient to be employed in user similarity. Additional security is provided through homomorphic encryption before archiving the data.

The proposed policies focus not only on time but also other factors to focus on retention of data for a longer period of time. The policies are designed and implemented on different types of data to identify the type of data to be archived efficiently. Further, the policies could be designed to be domain independent of data handling.

References

1. IBM Global Technology Services. http://www.ibm.com/services/be/en/it-services/ Cloud_based_data_archiving_service.pdf
2. Prom, C.: Requirements for electronic records management systems (2011). Accessed 24 Mar 2012 (2011)
3. Hall, P.: Opportunities for CSPs in enterprise-grade public cloud computing. OVUM, May 2012
4. Megaupload file-sharing site shut down. http://www.bbc.com/news/technology-16642369
5. Qiu, S., Zhou, J., Yang, T.: Versioned file backup and synchronization for storage clouds. In: 2013 13th IEEE/ACM International Symposium on Cluster, Cloud and Grid Computing (CCGrid), pp. 302–310. IEEE (2013)
6. Data archiving. http://searchdatabackup.techtarget.com/definition/data-archiving
7. Liu, B., Cao, F., Zhou, M., Mogel, G., Documet, L.: Trends in PACS image storage and archive. Comput. Med. Imaging Graph. 27(2), 165–174 (2003)
8. Kephart, J.O., Walsh, W.E.: An artificial intelligence perspective on autonomic computing policies. In: Fifth IEEE International Workshop on Policies for Distributed Systems and Networks, POLICY 2004, Proceedings, pp. 3–12. IEEE (2004)
9. Li, J., Stephenson, B., Motahari-Nezhad, H.R., Singhal, S.: GEODAC: a data assurance policy specification and enforcement framework for outsourced services. IEEE Trans. Serv. Comput. 4(4), 340–354 (2011)
10. Teevan, J.: How people re-find information when the web changes (2004)
11. Teng, C.C., Mitchell, J., Walker, C., Swan, A., Davila, C., Howard, D., Needham, T.: A medical image archive solution in the cloud. In: 2010 IEEE International Conference on Software Engineering and Service Sciences, pp. 431–434. IEEE (2010)
12. Huang, L.C., Liu, W.C., Chou, S.C.T.: Howcare: a personal health cloud archive and care-partners' community. In: 2013 IEEE/ACM International Conference on Advances in Social Networks Analysis and Mining (ASONAM), pp. 1237–1241. IEEE (2013)
13. http://insiteone.com/news-pressreleases.php?newsID=63
14. Amazon S3. https://aws.amazon.com/s3/
15. Jaeger, P.T., Lin, J., Grimes, J.M.: Cloud computing and information policy: computing in a policy cloud? J. Inform. Technol. Politics 5(3), 269–283 (2008)
16. Gharaibeh, A., Constantinescu, C., Lu, M., Sharma, A., Routray, R.R., Sarkar, P., Pease, D., Ripeanu, M.: CloudDT: efficient tape resource management using deduplication in cloud backup and archival services. In: Proceedings of the 8th International Conference on Network and Service Management, pp. 169–173. International Federation for Information Processing (2012)
17. Niwattanakul, S., Singthongchai, J., Naenudorn, E., Wanapu, S.: Using of Jaccard coefficient for keywords similarity. In: Proceedings of the International MultiConference of Engineers and Computer Scientists, vol. 1, pp. 13–15 (2013)
18. Tebaa, M., El Hajji, S., El Ghazi, A.: Homomorphic encryption applied to the cloud computing security. In: Proceedings of the World Congress on Engineering, vol. 1, pp. 4–6 (2012)
19. Boneh, D., Goh, E.-J., Nissim, K.: Evaluating 2-DNF formulas on ciphertexts. In: Kilian, J. (ed.) TCC 2005. LNCS, vol. 3378, pp. 325–341. Springer, Heidelberg (2005). https://doi.org/10.1007/978-3-540-30576-7_18

20. Kornevs, M., Minkevica, V., Holm, M.: Cloud computing evaluation based on financial metrics. Inf. Technol. Manage. Sci. **15**(1), 87–92 (2012)
21. Amazon S3 Pricing. https://aws.amazon.com/s3/pricing/
22. http://www.3phw.com/faq/faq.shtml
23. Keeping Data For A Long Time. http://www.forbes.com/forbes/welcome/

Silhouette Based Human Action Recognition Using an Efficient Transformation Technique

T. Subetha[✉] and S. Chitrakala[✉]

Anna University, Chennai, India
subethathankaraj@gmail.com, au.chitras@gmail.com

Abstract. Human Action Recognition (HAR) aims to understand and identifies the human action based on features extracted from human poses in a video. The major difficulty in Human Action Recognition is to detect the foreground and identify the actions despite varying background conditions and also to process the action recognition task with the high dimensional data. In this paper, the background subtraction issue is resolved using an adaptive Gaussian Mixture Model which is combined with the contour saliency to detect the efficient silhouettes in dynamic backgrounds and also in identifying the human even if they are latent for two to three frames. Here the system is proposed to introduce an efficient transformation technique named Reduced Variant tSNE (rv-tSNE) to transform the high dimensional feature space data to a low dimensional feature space data. This method is inspired from tSNE where the crowding problem is eliminated but variation in the obtained low dimensional space is high. The proposed algorithm rv-tSNE reduces the variation and eliminates the Data discrimination problem. The proposed system also identifies the actions of two actors performing different existing actions. Finally the actions are recognized and classified using a multi class Support Vector Machine. Experimental results show the higher recognition rate achieved compared to the existing tSNE for various actions using the bench-marking datasets such as Kinect Interaction dataset and Gaming dataset. The proposed Human Action Recognition system finds its application in human-machine interaction, intelligent video surveillance, sports event analysis, and content-based video Retrieval and others.

Keywords: Human action recognition · Adaptive gaussian mixture model
Contour saliency · Multi class support vector machine · Reduced variant tSNE

1 Introduction

In recent times, Human Action Recognition (HAR) is playing an indispensable role in various applications like Visual Surveillance, Ambient Assisted Living, Ambient Intelligence, Human Behavior Analysis, Vandalism deterrence and Human Computer Interaction. The main intention of this action recognition is the automated scrutiny or explications of current events and their context from video data. This application comprises a multi-type of systems that involves interactions between humans and electronic devices such as Human-Computer Interfaces. Majority of these applications demand

© Springer Nature Singapore Pte Ltd. 2018
Shriram R and M. Sharma (Eds.): DaSAA 2017, CCIS 804, pp. 153–162, 2018.
https://doi.org/10.1007/978-981-10-8603-8_13

recollection of high level activities repeatedly composed of numerous elementary actions of persons.

Human Action Recognition can be considered as one of the most demanding and dynamic fields. Due to its immense growth in the recent times top-notch universities like Boston University, Staffordshire University, Video Sense, HCI lab, University of Manitoba have been staunchly working for further improvements in this area. Identifying the actions being accomplished by the human in the video sequence automatically and tagging their actions is the prime functionality of intelligent video systems. HAR seeks to recognize or interpret human actions that depend upon features extracted from human posture sequences.

There are generally four major processing steps as given in Fig. 1 that are required for recognizing the actions at different degrees of generalization. In the first phase generally known as the background subtraction phase the foreground is detected from the background using some background subtraction techniques. The most popular background subtraction techniques are ViBE, Kalman filter, Adaptive Gaussian Mixture, RectGauss, Local Binary Similarity Pattern etc. This phase is affected by various conditions like dynamic backgrounds, cluttered backgrounds, identifying the latent human etc. The detected foreground is given to the Feature Extraction phase where the mandatory features are extracted for further processing. The extracted features are transformed and fed into tracking phase where human features are continuously tracked and classified using an appropriate classifier algorithm.

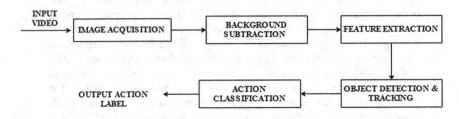

Fig. 1. General framework of HAR

In this paper, silhouettes of human are extracted as feature of human action through adaptive background subtraction mixture model. The extraction of the human elementary structure involves a multilevel learning, where both the spatial and temporal features of human motion between each frame is maintained. Since multilevel learning is employed, the curse-of-dimensionality problem can also be handled efficiently. In general human action involves a high spatio-temporal complexity therefore the time sequence information between each frame is maintained by spatio-temporal domain and temporal correlation. There are many classifiers in machine learning for the training phase of action recognition. Among those classifiers a hybrid SVM-NN classifier is used to enhance the recognition accuracy. Initially, SVM is used to classify the input features. Some of these features are correctly classified while few are not. Such, wrongly classified feature set are fed into the K-NN classifier. By using this approach, it has been found this is more efficient compared to other action recognition model.

This paper is structured as follows. Section 2 depicts the allied works in HAR. Section 3 outlines the proposed work. Section 4 describes the experimental evaluation followed by the conclusion in Sect. 5.

2 Related Works

Jian et al. [1] proposed a model that endorses human action from the extracted human silhouette sequences. A new method is depicted for maximizing the distance between frames which are similar in appearance but belongs to different classes by taking the temporal information into consideration. A general framework known as graph embedding along with linearization, kernelization and ternsorization is proposed to provide an unified perspective of the manifold learning algorithms.

Jian et al. [2] recognizes human actions from the extracted human silhouette sequences. st-tSNE is proposed for learning the underlying relationship between action frames in a manifold. st-tSNE is evolved from the variants of SNE. st-tSNE is developed from Manifold Oriented Stochastic Neighbor Projection (MSNP) and Discriminative Stochastic Neighbor Embedding (DSNE). MSNP makes use of geometric measure for finding out pairwise similarity and linear projection of the underlying non-linear pattern structure. DSNE based on MSNP utilizes class labels for maximizing the inter class distance and minimizing the intra class distance. But the system fails in data discrimination and in obtaining the complete silhouettes in low contrast background conditions.

Bo et al. [3] addresses the problem of human behavior recognition from video sequences using fuzzy-based systems. Fuzzy logic is used to handle the uncertainties in the behavior. A behavior model is computed, each output degree is represented by the likelihood occurs in between the behavior in current frame and the trained behavior model in the knowledge base. Selecting the candidate model which has the highest output degree is based on classifier. This system can be extended to support behavioral similarities, occlusion, illumination and shadow problems.

Khan et al. [4] converts the video sequences to frames and applies adaptive background subtraction algorithm. R transform is used to extract symmetric, scale and translation invariant features from silhouettes. KDA on R-transform features increases the variation among different classes of activities better than Hidden Markov Model. The system fails in handling in many actions only 6 actions are identified in this paper. This paper is applicable only for the specific dataset.

Weiyao et al. [5] proposed a network based model to find the activity. People in the scene are modeled as packages, while human activities can be modeled as the process of package transmission in the network. These specific package are analyzed by the transmission processes thereby analyzing and identifying the activities of human. This system works well for identifying group activity and detecting the abnormal activities of human. But the system lacks in multi-view activity recognition process.

3   The Proposed rv-tSNE Based Human Action Recognition

A novel transformation technique named rv-tSNE is proposed for increasing the accuracy of Action Recognition thereby reducing the misclassification rate. The proposed algorithm eliminates the data discrimination problem and the variation in the data is reduced to a greater extent by taking a joint probability distribution with covariance matrix. In this paper an efficient silhouettes are obtained by combining adaptive Gaussian Mixture Model and Contour Saliency Map. This removes the dynamic backgrounds and identifies the human even if they are latent for two to three frames. SURF (Speeded Up Robust Features) feature detection technique is used to extract the features from the detected silhouettes. The extracted features are stored in the repository as gesture profile descriptor. The major difficulty in transformation technique is to transform the high quality feature space to a low quality feature space. Hence the proposed algorithm rv-tSNE is applied on the extracted features to switch over from a high quality feature space to a low quality feature space to eradicate the curse of dimensionality problem. These transformed low dimensional points are fed to the SVM-NN classifier to identify the action label. The overall architecture of the proposed system is depicted in Fig. 2.

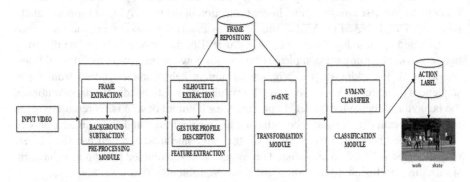

Fig. 2.   System architecture

3.1   Preprocessing

Preprocessing module is the initial stage for processing any video. This module acquires video as the input and does the following processes like frame extraction, background subtraction and silhouette extraction which is given to the later stages for further processing of video. Frame Extraction is the basic and foremost step involved in video processing. In frame extraction, each frame in the given input video is extracted individually. The extracted frames will contain both foreground and background environment. To detect the foreground various background subtraction methodologies are proposed. Stauffer and Grimson [6, 7] proposed a pixel based background model called Gaussian Mixture Model. This model pursues a multimodal distribution but fails in segmenting the objects that are latent for a while in their movement. Hence in this paper we utilized the combination of both Adaptive Gaussian Mixture Model (AGMM) proposed by Suo [8] that can detect the objects even if the objects are latent for a while.

AGMM is combined with Contour Saliency to extract efficient silhouettes from the video sequences. The pseudo code for AGMM is given in Table 1.

Table 1. Pseudo code for silhouette extraction

```
Begin
For the first obtained value X₁, initialize all the K Gaussians with the same
parameters
N_c=1, μ_{k,1}=X₁, σ_{k,1}=σ_0, ω_{k,1}=1/k
For a new pixel value X_t, check against the first N_c Gaussian distributions in turn.
           Loop a:
                if ω_i/σ_i >ω_{i-1}/σ_{i-1}
                    exchange positions
                    i=i-1
                if i!=1 or !(ω_i/σ_i<ω_{i-1}/σ_{i-1})
                    call a
                if no matching model,
                    let N_c=  ⎧ N_c+1  if N_c<K ⎫
                              ⎩ K      if N_c=K ⎭
After learning L frames, apply contour saliency to extract the contour silhouettes
Calculate the distance of each pixel to the rest of pixels in the same frame.
                Contour saliency=∑| I_k- I₁|
End
```

3.2 Feature Extraction

The next stage after preprocessing module is the feature extraction phase which contains Silhouette Extraction, SURF feature detection and gesture profile descriptor. The frames with its foreground information are converted into a silhouette image for efficient processing. After the proper silhouette extraction the mandatory features must be extracted from the foreground obtained. SURF features are used in this proposed system to extract the mandatory features as it is proven to be better than the SIFT features which is the Scale Invariant Feature Transform. Because of its robustness SURF features are applied in the proposed system that detects and save the requisite features in the feature repository. After extracting the features points (i.e.) movement descriptors gesture Profiles are constructed. Gesture profile descriptor describes the movements of the body parts like hand, leg and the entire body. These points are extracted and stored as gesture profile descriptor. These feature points are in high dimension and have to be reduced in dimension for the ease of computation and further processing.

3.3 Transformation

The obtained features are in high dimensions and cannot be processed as such. So there is a need for an efficient transformation algorithm for better processing of data. There are numerous transformation algorithms for the conversion of high dimensional feature space to a low dimensional feature space. But the major issues faced by these algorithms are crowding problem, data discrimination and high variation in data even after trans-formation. To resolve the above aforementioned problems a novel transformation algo-rithm named rv-tSNE which is a variant of tSNE is proposed for reducing the high dimensional data into a low dimensional data and the proposed methods has been proved better than the existing algorithms.

rv-tSNE

SNE is recent method in dimensionality reduction process. This method converts the Euclidean distance between data points in high dimension to low dimension using the conditional probability distribution that is the pair wise similarity and this probability is maintained during dimensionality reduction. t-SNE- is a variant of SNE where instead of conditional probability it employs joint probability distribution for efficient cost function. The pair wise similarity is determined with the following Eq. 1

$$p_{ij} = \sum P_j | i + P_i | j / 2n \tag{1}$$

The gradients are computed using the Eq. 2

$$\delta C(Y)/\delta y_i = 4 \sum (p_{ij} - q_{ij})(y_i - y_j)(1 + \left\| y_i - y_j \right\|^2)^{-1} \tag{2}$$

The divergence between the two probability distributions are calculated using the Eq. 3

$$y^{(n)} = y^{(n-1)} + \frac{\eta \delta c}{\delta y} + \alpha(t)y^{(n-1)} + y^{(n-2)} \tag{3}$$

As the silhouette features are taken for efficient processing maximum spatio-temporal dissimilarity embedding method is applied to differentiate similar actions by increasing the distance between the frames and also temporal labels are included by adding the similarity relation information to the frame. The tSNE method transforms points efficiently from high dimensional to low dimensional space with the help of joint probability in contrast to SNE which uses conditional probability. Although an obtained tSNE result solves the infamous crowding problem, the variance obtained after applying tSNE seemed to be very high, which leads to divergence of data points in space. To avoid this, covariance matrix is computed for the data obtained from tSNE, which proves to avoid the problem of divergence of data in low dimensionality space. The proposed algorithm also resolves the data discrimination problem. rv-tSNE obtains the orthogonal basis of the matrix and the Eigen values. To perform this calculation SURF Feature points is given as the input which is obtained from the feature extraction module. Then the joint probability is calculated and the covariance matrix and eigenvectors are computed with the output obtained to transform x, y points in low dimensional space. The pseudocode of rv-tSNE is given in Table 2.

Table 2. Proposed rv-tSNE algorithm

```
Begin
Obtain the random vector population x of features as x =(x₁,…xₙ)
Sample initial low dimensional data as Y⁽⁰⁾ = {y₁,y₂,y₃,…yₙ} where N ∈{0,10⁻⁴}
Iterate for all the points
  for i= 1 : N  do
    Compute the joint probability Pᵢ,ⱼ , from eq (2).
    Construct a matrix, Obtain the Covariance  matrix from equation
        Vᵢ,ⱼ= E{(Cᵢ,ⱼ- μ) (Cᵢ,ⱼ-μ)ᵀ}
    From Vᵢⱼ covariance matrix is obtained to get the orthogonal basis by finding
    its Eigen value from the sample x₁,x₂,x₃,…xₙ. as, Cₓeᵢ = λᵢeᵢ, i=1,2,3…n.
        Y = A(Cᵢ,ⱼ- μ) where A is the Eigen Vector
        X = Aᵀy + μ
            end
Return X,Y
End
```

3.4 Classification Using SVM-NN

The transformed feature which contains the transformed value of the feature descriptor is stored in the repository. These transformed values are given as the input to the Support Vector Machine for training. Usually, a Support vector machine can have only two class, so that it will be able to differentiate easily. But as the proposed system deals with two actors performing different existing actions in the same frame a multiclass Support Vector Machine is used, which can classify more than two actions. In multiclass SVM, we construct a set of binary classifier, each trained to separate one class from the rest. By doing this, we can get the multiclass classifier, which can classify more than two actions. By constructing, hypersphere, instead of the hyperplane, the multiclass SVM can group the classes and classify different action. So while, training phase, the classifier will be made to group the action using the k-means clustering algorithm and classify them to a particular class. While testing, based on the grouping, the action class can be identified. The recognized action label is depicted in Fig. 3.

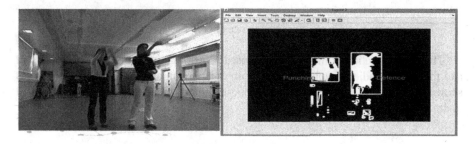

Fig. 3. Action label

4 Experimental Evaluation

The effectiveness of the proposed system is assessed by performing several experiments with the two prominent datasets such as Gaming dataset [9] and Kinect dataset [10]. The tested video has a minimum of 20 key frames. These frames are extracted from the video and stored. The background subtraction is applied on these frames to get the foreground object. Each frame would generate a minimum of 20 SURF points. Therefore, for 20 frames, 400 points will be generated and stored. These points are difficult to process at high dimensional space. Therefore, transformation needs to be applied for dimensionality reduction. In transformation, a new approach rv-tSNE is applied which is a extended algorithm of tSNE. This method also helps in effective identification of the action performed by the human by classifying appropriately. The transformed low dimensional data are given to SVM-NN hybrid classifier that can group and classify the action, by recognizing the concentration of data points. Various parameters like Precision, Recall given in Eqs. 4 and 5 are used to evaluate our proposed system. The recognition rate of different actions by the classifier is shown in Fig. 4.

$$\text{precision} = \frac{\text{No of instances of correct positive recognition}}{\text{Total no of positive recognition}} \quad (4)$$

$$\text{recall} = \frac{\text{No of instances of positive recognition found}}{\text{Total no of relevant input instances}} \quad (5)$$

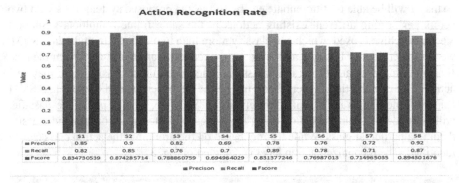

Fig. 4. Recognition rate of proposed system

The transformation points of the proposed transformation algorithm are found out and the corresponding graph is plotted with comparison of the existing algorithm as shown in Fig. 5 which proves that our proposed algorithm is more effective compared to other existing transformations.

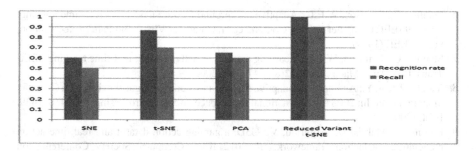

Fig. 5. Comparison chart for the proposed algorithm with the existing algorithms

5   Conclusion and Future Works

A novel method is proposed to recognize the actions of the human efficiently by applying the better transformation algorithm named rv-tSNE. Silhouette based identification of action is proven to be more effective than other model-based algorithms. The gesture profile descriptor is created and used to track the human at each frame that can be effectively used to identify the action performed by the human in the given video. The transformation module reduces the high dimensional feature to low dimension, therefore enabling effective embedding of all the information got from each frame of the video. By reducing the dimension, the processing of data gets reduced and hence the classifier can easily group the action to different class, enabling fast processing and classification. The proposed algorithm is tested using the benchmarking datasets such as Kinect inter-action and Gaming Dataset. The algorithm accuracy is compared with the existing algorithm using various parameters like precision, recall and the system shows higher recognition rate achieved for various complex actions. The system is tested only for Human Action Recognition. In future we planned to extend the system for handling the activities of humans by analyzing and interpreting the interactions between two humans.

References

1. Cheng, J., Liu, H., Li, H.: Silhouette analysis for human action recognition based on maximum spatio-temporal dissimilarity embedding. Mach. Vis. Appl. **25**(4), 1007–1018 (2014)
2. Cheng, J., Liu, H., Wang, F., Li, H., Zhu, C.: Silhouette analysis for human action recognition based on supervised temporal t-SNE and incremental learning. IEEE Trans. Image Process. **24**(10), 3203–3217 (2015)
3. Yao, B., Hagras, H., Alhaddad, M.J., Alghazzawi, D.: A fuzzy logic based system for the automation of human behavior recognition using machine vision in intelligent environments. Soft. Comput. **19**(2), 499–506 (2015)
4. Khan, Z., Sohn, W.: Hierarchical human activity recognition system based on R-transform and nonlinear kernel discriminant features. Electron. Lett. **48**(18), 1119–1120 (2012)
5. Lin, W., Chen, Y., Wu, J., Wang, H., Sheng, B., Li, H.: A new network-based algorithm for human activity recognition in videos. IEEE Trans. Circuits Syst. Video Technol. **24**(5), 826–841 (2014)

6. Stauffer, C., Grimson, W.E.L.: Adaptive background mixture models for real-time tracking. In: 1999 IEEE Computer Society Conference on Computer Vision and Pattern Recognition, vol. 2. IEEE (1999)
7. Stauffer, C., Grimson, W.E.L.: Learning patterns of activity using real-time tracking. IEEE Trans. Patt. Anal. Mach. Intell. **22**(8), 747–757 (2000)
8. Suo, P., Wang, Y.: An improved adaptive background modeling algorithm based on Gaussian mixture model. In: 2008 9th International Conference on Signal Processing, pp. 1436–1439. IEEE (2008)
9. Bloom, V., Makris, D., Argyriou, V.: G3D: a gaming action dataset and real time action recognition evaluation framework. In: 2012 IEEE Computer Society Conference on Computer Vision and Pattern Recognition Workshops, pp. 7–12, June 2012
10. Yun, K., Honorio, J., Chattopadhyay, D., Berg, T.L., Samaras, D.: Two-person interaction detection using body-pose features and multiple instance learning. In: 2012 IEEE Computer Society Conference on Computer Vision and Pattern Recognition Workshops (CVPRW). IEEE (2012)

Towards Secure DNA Based Cryptosystem

M. Thangavel[1]([✉]) [iD], P. Varalakshmi[2] [iD], R. Sindhuja[2]([✉]) [iD], and S. Sridhar[2]

[1] Department of Information Technology, Thiagarajar College of Engineering,
Madurai 625015, Tamilnadu, India
thangavelmuruganme@gmail.com
[2] Department of Computer Technology, Anna University, MIT Campus,
Chennai 600044, Tamilnadu, India
varanip@gmail.com, sindhurajendran16@gmail.com,
veerasri.492@gmail.com

Abstract. Cryptography is an art of secret writing. To ensure data security in both data transfer and data storage cryptographic techniques are used for the data we handle in our day to day activities. The need for cryptographic techniques exists from the period of 150 B.C. till date. Though there are too many cryptographic algorithms, an algorithm with reduced complexity and utmost security is needed. And so, DNA cryptography paves a way towards satisfying the needs with its own biological properties. DNA has greater capacity to store, process and secure data. The existing DNA cryptographic algorithm does not have a standardized approach that involves both biological and arithmetic processes. To meet out the standardized framework we propose a novel DNA based cryptosystem comprising key generation, encoding, and encryption, decryption methodologies. The detailed performance and security analysis with their results are shown to support the strength of our algorithm towards reducing the computational complexity as well as the storage complexity and thereby achieving an enhanced security.

Keywords: DNA cryptography · DNA encoding · DNA computing · Encryption
Decryption · Key generation · DNA based encoding

1 Introduction

Cryptography is a technique used for encrypting the plaintext to achieve data confidentiality. Traditional cryptographic algorithms like DES, AES and RSA are less secure as it could be broken with increased computational power and also it involves with greater computations to preserve data security. To minimize the computational complexity and also to achieve maximum security an alternate method of cryptography is needed.

DNA (Deoxyribo Nucleic Acid) is a molecule in the living organisms that carries the genetic information used for the growth and development of the organism. DNA molecules have a double helix structure made up of two strands of polynucleotides. The four nucleotides of DNA molecule are Adenine (A), Guanine (G), Cytosine (C) and Thymine (T). These DNA nucleotides form complementary pairs as Adenine is paired with Thymine and Guanine is paired with Cytosine and vice versa.

© Springer Nature Singapore Pte Ltd. 2018
Shriram R and M. Sharma (Eds.): DaSAA 2017, CCIS 804, pp. 163–177, 2018.
https://doi.org/10.1007/978-981-10-8603-8_14

These DNA molecules were proved for its significance of massive computational speed, less computational power and greater storage capacity through the work of Leonard Adleman. In 1994, he used DNA molecules to compute solution for the NP complete problem. From then, the field of DNA computing came into existence. Through various research works, the capability of DNA molecules were studied, analyzed and it evolved the area of DNA cryptography where DNA molecules hides the original data to provide enhanced data security.

There are many DNA sequences available in various sources like EBI database, NCBI database and DDBJ database. The sequences can be selected in random based on the user needs. Still the DNA sequences can be synthesized in artificial manner through the basic nucleotides. DNA cryptographic techniques use these DNA sequences to construct an efficient cryptosystem.

An efficient cryptosystem with novel ideas should also consider certain measures like minimum encryption time, decryption time and increased cryptanalysis time. The algorithm should also support the plaintext of larger file size. Ultimately, all the metrics can be ensured only if the process of encoding and encryption is dynamic for every user on his every access. In our proposed work, the above said criteria are mete out with unique generation of encoding table mapping with unique values dynamically. It involves both the biological processes like transcription, translation, etc. and arithmetic processes like XOR, XNOR operations, etc. The performance analysis with respect to time and storage space taken for encoding, decoding, encryption and decryption processes reveals the result obtained for our algorithmic implementation.

The further sections of this paper is organized in a way such as, Sect. 2 describes the related work in the field of DNA cryptography. Section 3 describes the methodology of our proposed DNA cryptosystem and its architecture. Section 4 describes the proposed algorithm solved with an example. Section 5 describes the performance analysis and the results obtained.

2   Related Work

DNA cryptography evolved based on the properties and nature of DNA molecules. The fundamental concept of DNA nucleotides is exploited in every DNA cryptosystem in order to hide the original message thereby enhancing confidentiality of data. DNA nucleotide bases are Adenine (A), Guanine (G), Cytosine (C) and Thymine (T). In general, these four bases are replaced with the binary values such as 00, 01, 10 and 11 to convert the original plaintext to binary values and further transforms into a DNA sequence.

The concept of amino acids in protein synthesis is used to convert the computed DNA cipher text into a collated cipher text using a defined character set. The high storage space, computational speed of DNA strengthens DNA cryptosystem by providing quick data access, biological process oriented approach and provides security against attackers in a digital computing environment.

Hussain [1] proposed a novel DNA cryptographic technique that emphasizes the importance of dynamicity in generating encoding table and in encryption process. Here, the six properties for an ideal DNA cryptosystem are identified. The novel idea of work lies in the generation of encoding table that converts the plaintext characters into unique DNA sequences. In encryption process, it uses the properties of DNA and amino acids to generate the cipher text dynamically. The computational time becomes higher in this approach thereby increasing complexity in the system. A cryptosystem was proposed to secure the password sent for authentication process [2]. It involves two levels of encryption techniques, first level of encryption was done by Elgamal encryption and the second level of encryption was done by DNA encryption. The time taken to perform both encryption techniques is quite high. But the sharing of secret values is tedious.

Mono Sabry [3] performs AES technique using DNA sequences. This framework takes much time to compute the required cipher text [4]. Similarly, Aich [5] proposes a symmetric key cryptography technique using DNA sequence as OTP key. It performs two levels of encryption for the given plaintext. Initially, a process of encryption is done to generate an OTP (One Time Pad) key. Then, encryption is performed to produce the cipher text of DNA sequence. It has higher computational complexity when the size of the plaintext increases. Mandge [6] proposed a DNA encryption algorithm using matrices where the plaintext is converted into a 4×4 matrix [7] and then converted to DNA sequence but the biological properties of DNA are not widely used. In general, matrices are used to achieve robustness in the proposed work through row or column level transformations [8].

The properties of DNA molecules are used with the RGB colour coding values in a proposed DNA cryptographic system [9]. Initially, the plaintext is encoded in a UNICODE format. Then it is encrypted using the RGB colour values which are converted into binary, then getting split into two parts forming the message and the key. Operation like XOR operation is performed between the key and the message. The key is again encrypted using RSA algorithm, whereas the message is converted into DNA sequences forming the cipher text. Another approach of UNICODE and colour based DNA cryptographic algorithm was proposed [10]. It substitutes the plaintext characters with the hexadecimal values and colours.

Lu Ming Xin [11] proposes that the encryption process is done through the fabrication of a specially designed DNA chip and the decryption process is done through DNA hybridization. Similarly, the primers are used to hide the data where the plaintext is converted into binary form. DES encryption is performed on the binary values. It is then separated into odd and even sequences and is appended with the former and rear primers which are then mixed to form microdots of cipher text [12]. It reduces the feasibility of real time implementation as it involves biological resources.

Majumdar [13] proposed a DNA cryptography involving two phases. In the first phase, encryption of the plaintext is done using the key of 256 bits in length. In the second phase, it is embedded in an image that acts as the carrier of the message [14]. The sharing of the secret keys is quite challenging [15, 16]. Misbahuddin [17] proposed a DNA based cryptosystem based on central dogma of molecular biology [18, 19] techniques such as splicing, transcription and translation. It hides the cipher text within the primers that were appended. It is hard to intrude but a larger plaintext needs a larger key which is not easily available in the repository.

Among various proposed DNA based cryptosystems, the effective mechanism is provided when it achieves both arithmetic process and biological process. At the same time, to prevent from cryptanalysis it has to perform dynamic encoding and encryption process [20]. Thus, the time and cost to break the cipher should be higher than the time taken for the normal transmission of the original cipher text. All these criteria has been satisfied in our proposed work with reduced complexity.

3   Proposed Work

DNA cryptography enriches data security by hiding the original message within the DNA molecules based on the significance of its biological properties. In general, DNA based cryptosystem takes less time for computation than the traditional cryptosystem because of the high parallelism, storage and computational power of the DNA molecules. But rather the time taken to perform cryptanalysis is computationally high. Among various DNA cryptosystems, the challenges were to incorporate both the biological operations and the arithmetic operations in an optimal manner. It is ensured through the six properties for any DNA based cryptosystem. They are,

- DNA encoding of complete character set fulfillment
- Dynamic encoding table generation
- Unique sequence for encoding of every character of plaintext to DNA sequence
- Robustness of encoding
- Biological process simulation
- Dynamicity of encryption process

Our DNA based cryptosystem satisfies the above needed properties and provides security to the data. The proposed system comprises of algorithms for Key generation, Encryption and Decryption.

3.1   Key Generation

Key generation is the initial process of our DNA cryptosystem. In key generation, the date and time values are taken as the input along with the 10 digit random number. These 22 digits are converted into binary values. From the binary value each two digit binary values are taken and are replaced with a single DNA nucleotide. This sequence is known as the intron sequence and it is used as the key for our cryptosystem. The pseudo code for key generation is,

---

Key_Generation (d,m,h,min,sec,rand)
Input: date **d**, month **m**, year y, hour **h**, minute **min**, second **sec**, random number
  rand
Output: intron sequence **i_seq**
Procedure:

  Get the values for **d, m, y, h, min** and **sec**
  Get **rand**
  Append all these values
  Convert it into binary values
  Transform to a DNA sequence forming **i_seq**

3.2 Encoding Table Generation

The novelty of our proposed DNA based cryptosystem lies in the generation of the encoding table. Initially, the amino acid table is generated with the three DNA collating sequences given by the user that forms a matrix of 64 amino sequences where each sequence is mapped with an amino acid. The tRNA sequence is split into sequences, where each tRNA sequence has three nucleotides. It is then mapped with the amino acid value in the table. Then based on the positioning value given by the user, the mapped amino acid value is positioned within the tRNA sequence. Each tRNA sequence obtained is mapped with the character set comprising of 26 lowercase alphabets, 6 uppercase alphabets and 32 symbols. It forms the encoding table. The pseudo code for generating the encoding table is,

---

DNA_Encoding_Table (cs1, cs2, cs3, pv, seq$_{tRNA}$, cset)
Input: collating sequence 1 **cs1**, collating sequence 2 **cs2**, collating sequence 3
  cs3, positioning value **pv**, tRNA sequence **seq$_{tRNA}$**, character set **cset**
Output: encoding table **etable**
Method Variables: amino acid lookup table **amino$_{lookup}$**
Procedure:

  Get **cs1, cs2, cs3**
  Generate **amino$_{lookup}$** with **cs1, cs2, cs3** and amino acid values
  Split **seq$_{tRNA}$** into sequences having three nucleotides in each
  Map each sequence with **amino$_{lookup}$** values
  Get **pv**
  Position the mapped value in each split sequence at **pv**
  Map each of the obtained sequence with **cset** to form **etable**

3.3 Encryption

The pseudo code for the encryption process is,

DNA_Encryption (pt, i_seq, etable)
Input: plaintext **pt**, intron sequence **i_seq**, encoding table **etable**
Output: cipher text **ct**
Method Variables: binary plaintext pt_b, left half of sequence **lh**, right half of
sequence **rh**, binary sequence seq_b, DNA sequence seq_{DNA},
mRNA sequence seq_{mRNA}, tRNA sequence seq_{tRNA}
Procedure:
Convert **pt** into ASCII
Convert ASCII into binary values pt_b
XNOR pt_b and **i_seq**
Split it into **lh** and **rh**
Do one bit left circular shift for **lh** and do one bit right circular shift
for **rh**
Combine the resulting **lh** and **rh**
XOR the above sequence and **i_seq**
Append **i_seq** with the previous result to form seq_b
Convert seq_b into DNA sequence as seq_{DNA}
Convert seq_{DNA} into mRNA sequence as seq_{mRNA}
Convert seq_{mRNA} into tRNA sequence as seq_{tRNA}
Map the values with the generated **etable** values to generate **ct**

The process of DNA encryption is described in Fig. 1. Encryption process is performed by taking the plaintext and converting it into ASCII values. Then the ASCII values are converted into binary form. The binary values of the plaintext and the intron sequence generated in key generation process are performed an XNOR operation. The result of the XNOR operation is divided into two equal halves namely left half and right half. Left half value is performed an one bit left circular shift and the right half is performed an one bit right circular shift. After shift operation, left and right halves of values are combined together. Now XOR operation is performed between the intron sequence and the combined value. The result of XOR operation is concatenated with the intron sequence. The resultant sequence is converted from binary values into DNA sequence by mapping the unique combination of binary values to a unique DNA nucleotide like 00 mapped with A, 01 mapped with T, 10 mapped with C and 11 mapped with G. The DNA sequence is then converted into mRNA sequence by replacing Thymine (T) with Uracil (U). Then the mRNA sequence is converted into tRNA sequence by replacing every nucleotide with its corresponding complementary pairs like A complements T and C complements G and vice versa. The tRNA sequence is considered by splitting it into sequences having three nucleotides in each. Every sequence is replaced with the corresponding encoding table value. The resultant value forms the cipher text.

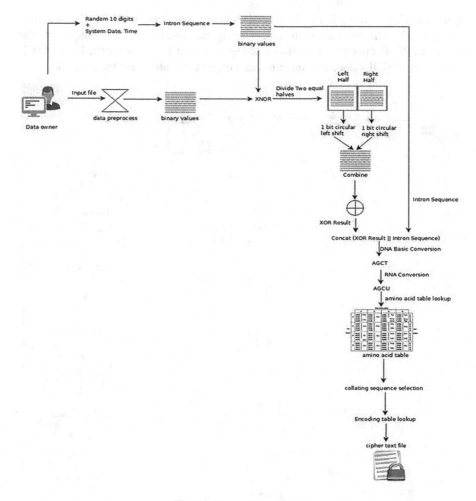

Fig. 1. Encryption process

3.4   Decryption

The receiver on receiving the cipher text performs the DNA decryption process as shown in Fig. 2. The receiver generates the amino acid table using the three collating sequences. From the above values the encoding table is generated and lookup operation is performed for the cipher text values. It results in obtaining the tRNA sequence. The tRNA sequence is converted into a mRNA sequence by replacing with the complementary pairs. Further, the mRNA sequence is converted into a DNA sequence by replacing Uracil (U) with Thymine (T). Resultant DNA sequence is converted into binary form. The intron sequence is extracted from the binary sequence. The remaining binary sequence is performed an XOR operation with the intron sequence. The resultant XOR value is divided into two halves. The left half sequence is performed an one bit right circular shift operation. The right half sequence is performed an one bit left circular shift operation. The resulting left and right half sequences are combined together and then perform an XNOR operation with the intron sequence and the combined sequence. The result of XNOR operation is a binary sequence which is then converted into ASCII values. The ASCII values are converted into original plaintext sent by the sender.

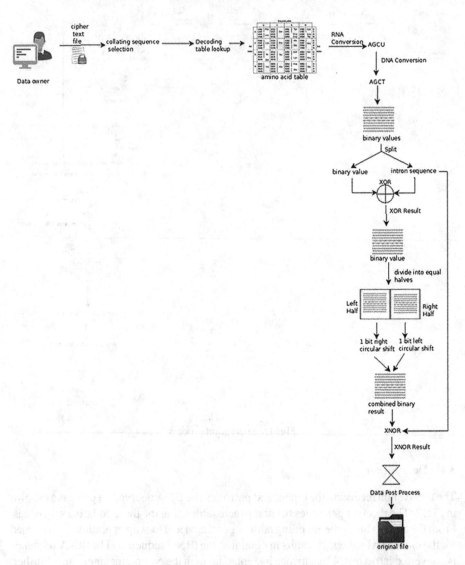

Fig. 2. Decryption process

The pseudo code for decryption is,

DNA_Decryption (ct, etable)
Input: cipher text ct, encoding table etable
Output: plaintext pt
Method Variables: binary plaintext pt_b, intron sequence i_seq, left half of
        sequence lh, right half of sequence rh, binary sequence seq_b,
        DNA sequence seq_{DNA}, mRNA sequence seq_{mRNA}, tRNA
        sequence seq_{tRNA}
Procedure:
        Map ct with the generated etable values
        Combine the obtained sequences to form seq_{tRNA}
        Convert seq_{tRNA} into mRNA sequence seq_{mRNA}
        Convert seq_{mRNA} into DNA sequence as seq_{DNA}
        Transform seq_{DNA} into binary sequence seq_b
        Extract i_seq from seq_b
        XOR i_seq and the remaining seq_b
        Split the resulting sequence into lh and rh
        Do one bit right circular shift for lh and one bit left circular shift for
        rh
        Combine the resulting lh and rh
        XNOR i_seq and the above sequence to form pt_b
        Convert pt_b into ASCII
        Convert ASCII values into pt

4   Example

In this example, the sender chooses the plaintext as "tce". Initially, the sender performs key generation process. The values for date and time is chosen as 10/12/2016 12:10:20 and the random value as 1928739281. These two values are combined and converted into binary format as 00001010000011001111 1011100000011000000101000010100111001011110110001110011101 0001. This binary value is converted into DNA sequence with the corresponding DNA nucleotide. The DNA sequence generated for the obtained binary value is formed as AACCAAGAGGCGCAATCAATTAACCTGACGGTCAGCTGTAT. This intron sequence forms the key.

Sender converts the plaintext into ASCII characters as 116 99 101. These ASCII values are converted into binary form as 01110100 01100011 0110010. As the plaintext length is lesser than the length of intron sequence it is balanced to the length of the plaintext by padding the sequence with the bit '1'. The balanced plaintext becomes   01110100011000110110010111111111111111111111111111111111111111111 1111111111111111111111 1111. Then, XNOR operation is performed between the binary value of the intron sequence and the balanced plaintext's binary value. The result is, 10000001100100000110000110000001100000010100001010011100101 1

1101100011100111010001. It is divided into two equal halves. Perform one bit left circular shift by shifting the first digit to its last place that becomes 00000011001000001100001100000011000000101.

Similarly, the right half is taken and one bit right circular shift is performed by moving the last digit to its first place and the right half is obtained as 11000010100111001011110110001110011101000.

The left and right half values are then combined and performed XOR with the binary intron sequence. The sequence becomes 00001001001011000 0111000100000101000001110100011110100101110001101001001010100111001. Further it is concatenated with the intron sequence as, 000010010010 110000111000100000101000001110100011110100101110001101001001010111 001000010100000110011111011100000011000000101000010100011100101111101 100011100111010001.

The result is converted into DNA sequence based on the binary values mapped with the DNA nucleotides as, AACTACGAAGCACAACCAAGCCAGGTACGCA GTACT-TAGCTAACCAAGAGGCGCAATCAATTAACCTGACGGTCAGCTGTT. This DNA sequence is converted into mRNA sequence by replacing Thymine with Uracil and the sequence is converted into tRNA sequence as UUGAUG CUUCGUGUUGGUUCGGUC-CAUGCGUCAUGAAUCGAUUGGUUCUCCGCGUUAGUUAAUUGGACUGCCA-GUCGACAUA. Then the sender gives three collating sequence values as UCAG, CAUG, GUCA which is used to generate an encoding table. Every three nucleotides of the tRNA sequence is taken and a lookup is performed with the encoding table values to form the final cipher text. The final cipher text obtained is $, %5- = d.upc3*O4"bp#-y4in97uB which is sent to the receiver. The receiver receives the cipher text and performs the decryption process to identify the original text from the cipher text. It is the complete reverse process of encryption.

5   Performance Analysis

An algorithm meets its significance when it is proved for efficiency. Here, our DNA cryptosystem is analyzed by comparing it with the results obtained in the prior work of Rahman [1]. The time taken to perform encoding and decoding of the range of words as input is compared between both the cryptosystems as shown in Table 1. Thus, from the results, it is proved that the time complexity has been reduced in our framework. Also, the time factor increases linearly with the increase in the number of words. The comparison graphs are shown in Figs. 3 and 4.

Table 1. Word count vs encoding and decoding time

Word count	Encoding time in our framework (ms)	Encoding time in prior framework (ms)	Decoding time in our framework (ms)	Decoding time in prior framework (ms)
500	0.000006	0.000006	0.000019	0.000102
1000	0.000184	0.000209	0.00022	0.00027
2000	0.00056	0.000868	0.000875	0.000929
4000	0.00194	0.003872	0.00296	0.003361
6000	0.00321	0.010531	0.00976	0.011246
8000	0.010264	0.023422	0.01121	0.020673
10000	0.02783	0.03894	0.02883	0.029886

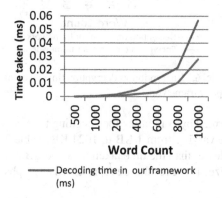

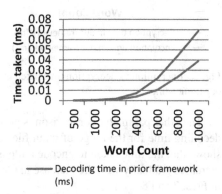

Fig. 3. Encoding vs decoding time taken in our framework

Fig. 4. Encoding vs decoding time taken in prior framework

Table 2. Word count vs encryption and decryption time

Word count	Encryption time in our framework (ms)	Encryption time in prior framework (ms)	Decryption time in our framework (ms)	Decryption time in prior framework (ms)
500	0.00011	0.00015	0.00009	0.000173
1000	0.00023	0.000313	0.00018	0.000371
2000	0.00032	0.000963	0.00030	0.001037
4000	0.00254	0.004175	0.00230	0.004735
6000	0.00989	0.012813	0.00914	0.013377
8000	0.01041	0.024362	0.00980	0.021547
10000	0.02051	0.040071	0.01782	0.032520

Similarly, the encryption and decryption time for the range of words are computed for the proposed framework and it is compared with the results of the prior framework [20] as shown in Table 2. Thus, the results prove that our proposed framework has reduced computational time and complexity when compared to the prior work. At the same time, the time taken for cryptanalysis is high and so our algorithm provides enhanced security to data with less complexity. The graphs comparing encryption time and decryption time for both the proposed framework and prior framework is shown in Figs. 5 and 6.

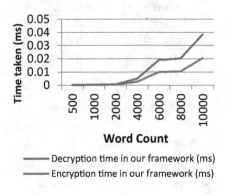

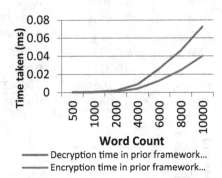

Fig. 5. Encryption vs decryption time taken in our framework

Fig. 6. Encryption vs decryption time taken in prior framework

The other parameter comparison is performed by computing the encoding time and decoding time for the range of input file size varying from 1 KB to 1024 KB. Table 3 shows that the time taken to encode a file is lesser than the time taken to decode. But it increases gradually with the increase in file size. These results are represented as graphs in Figs. 7 and 8.

Table 3. File size vs encoding and decoding time

File size (KB)	Encoding time (ms)	Decoding time (ms)
1	0.000001	0.000001
2	0.000005	0.000008
4	0.000009	0.000012
8	0.000017	0.00002
16	0.00032	0.0004
32	0.00049	0.00062
64	0.0012	0.0019
128	0.002	0.0027
256	0.0095	0.0162
512	0.0236	0.0311
1024	1.235	1.854

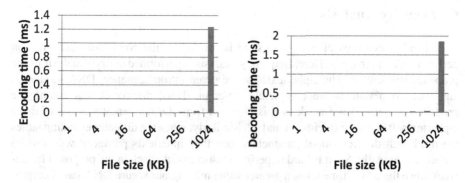

Fig. 7. Encoding time taken for the corresponding file size

Fig. 8. Decoding time taken for the corresponding file size

Similarly, the encryption time and decryption time are compared with the increase in file size that results with increase in decryption time whereas the encryption time is less than that, as shown in Table 4. The above results prove that our proposed framework has reduced storage time and complexity. It is represented as graphs in Figs. 9 and 10.

Table 4. File size vs encryption and decryption time

File size (KB)	Encryption time (ms)	Decryption time (ms)
1	0.00001	0.00006
2	0.00005	0.00008
4	0.00009	0.00013
8	0.00016	0.0002
16	0.00023	0.00029
32	0.00135	0.001039
64	0.0048	0.0069
128	0.01975	0.0287
256	1.741	2.098
512	2.211	2.423
1024	4.652	4.935

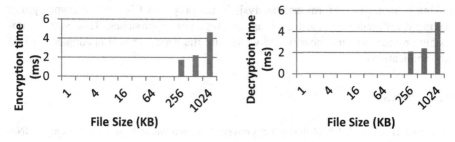

Fig. 9. Encryption time taken for the corresponding file size

Fig. 10. Decryption time taken for the corresponding file size

6   Security Analysis

The security measures of a cryptosystem is proved by the complexity achieved on performing cryptanalysis. Here, frequency analysis is performed as cryptanalysis of the proposed framework. The ciphertexts for the given intron sequence, DNA sequences and the two plaintexts are completely different. Thus, the correlation among the produced ciphertexts are weak as it is obtained from the frequency analysis of those ciphertexts. It is shown in Figs. 11 and 12. Similarly, when the different encoding tables are used with different input parameters then the ciphertexts produced will also be different eventually. So, it is hard to perform a successful attack in the proposed framework since the attack time takes a greater value making our secure DNA based cryptosystem to meet out all the security requirements.

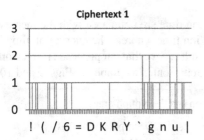
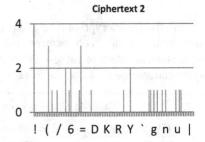

Fig. 11. Frequency analysis of Ciphertext 1   **Fig. 12.** Frequency analysis of Ciphertext 2

7   Conclusion

Our secure DNA based cryptosystem performs dynamic generation of encoding table, encryption and decryption techniques to ensure confidentiality of secure communication. It meets out the security requirements by satisfying the properties of robustness, unique character mapping and dynamic cryptosystem. The computational and storage complexity is completely reduced in the proposed framework thereby producing a better enhanced performance of the cryptosystem. It is highly impossible for the unintended users to detect the intron sequence and the plain text from the encrypted cipher text thus making it harder to perform cryptanalysis in the proposed DNA based cryptosystem making it different from the traditional cryptographic approaches. Thus, our cryptosystem provides greater security and would suit the needs when it is adopted for real time applications.

References

1. Noorul Hussain, U., Chithralekha, T.: A novel DNA encoding technique and system for DNA cryptography. India Patent 5107, CHE (2012)
2. Raju, P.S.V.N., Parwekar, P.: DNA encryption based dual server password authentication. Adv. Intell. Syst. Comput. **248**, 29–37 (2014)

3. Sabry, M., Hashem, M., Nazmy, T., Khalifa, M.E.: Design of DNA based advanced encryption standard (AES). In: International Conference on Intelligent Computing and Information Systems (ICICIS), pp. 390–397. IEEE (2015)
4. Cui, G., Han, D., Wang, Y., Wang, Y., Wang, Z.: An improved method of DNA information encryption. In: Pan, L., Păun, G., Pérez-Jiménez, Mario J., Song, T. (eds.) BIC-TA 2014. CCIS, vol. 472, pp. 73–77. Springer, Heidelberg (2014). https://doi.org/10.1007/978-3-662-45049-9_12
5. Aich, A., Sen, A., Ranjan Das, S., Dehuri, S.: A symmetric key cryptosystem using DNA sequence with OTP key. Inf. Syst. Des. Intell. Appl. **340**, 207–215 (2015)
6. Mandge, T., Vijay, C.: A DNA encryption technique based on matrix manipulation and secure key generation scheme. In: Information Communication and Embedded systems (ICICES), pp. 47–52. IEEE (2013)
7. Jain, S., Bhatnagar, V.: A novel DNA sequence dictionary method for securing data in DNA using spiral approach and framework of DNA cryptography. In: ICAETR, pp. 1–5. IEEE (2014)
8. Al-Wattar, A.H., Mahmod, R., Zukarnain, Z.A., Udzir, N.: A new DNA based approach of generating key-dependent mix columns transformation. Int. J. Comput. Netw. Commun. (IJCNC) **7**, 93–102 (2015)
9. Panchami, V., Fasila, K.A.: A multilevel security scheme based on UNICODE and RGB color model using DNA cryptography. In: ICETT Proceedings (2012)
10. Suryavanshi, H., Bansal, P: An improved cryptographic algorithm using UNICODE and universal colors. In: WOCN, pp. 1–3. IEEE (2012)
11. Mingxin, L.U., Xuejia, L., Guozhen, X., Lei, Q.: Symmetric-key cryptosystem with DNA technology. Sci. China Ser. F Inf. Sci. **50**, 325–333 (2007)
12. Cui, G., Wang, Y., Han, D., Wang, Y., Wang, Z., Wu, Y.: An encryption scheme based on DNA microdots technology. In: Pan, L., Păun, G., Pérez-Jiménez, M.J., Song, T. (eds.) BIC-TA 2014. CCIS, vol. 472, pp. 78–82. Springer, Heidelberg (2014). https://doi.org/10.1007/978-3-662-45049-9_13
13. Majumdar, A., Podder, T., Majumder, A., Kar, N., Sharma, M.: DNA based cryptographic approach toward information security. Adv. Intell. Syst. Comput. **308**, 209–219 (2015)
14. Gugnani, G., Ghrera, S.P., Gupta, P.K., Malekian, R., Maharaj, B.T.J.: Implementing DNA encryption technique in web services to embed confidentiality in cloud. In: Satapathy, S.C., Raju, K.Srujan, Mandal, J.K., Bhateja, V. (eds.) Proceedings of the Second International Conference on Computer and Communication Technologies. AISC, vol. 381, pp. 407–415. Springer, New Delhi (2016). https://doi.org/10.1007/978-81-322-2526-3_42
15. Prajapati Ashishkumar, B., Barkha, P.: Implementation of DNA cryptography in cloud computing and using socket programming. In: ICCCI. IEEE (2016)
16. Kazuo, T., Akimitsu, O., Isao, S.: Public-key system using DNA as a one-way function for key distribution. Biosystems **81**, 25–29 (2005)
17. Misbahuddin, M., Mohammed Hashim, N.P., Sreeja, C.S.: DNA for information security: a survey on DNA computing and a pseudo DNA method based on central dogma of molecular biology. In: ICCCT, pp. 1–6. IEEE (2014)
18. Wang, X., Zhang, Q.: DNA computing-based cryptography. In: IEEE, pp. 67–69 (2009)
19. Dhawan, S., Saini, A.: A new DNA encryption technique for secure data transmission. In: IJETCAS, pp. 36–42 (2012)
20. Rahman, N.H.U., Chithralekha, B., Rajapandian, M.: A novel DNA computing based encryption and decryption algorithm. Procedia Comput. Sci. ICICT **46**, 463–475 (2014)

Trust Management Model Based on Malicious Filtered Feedback in Cloud

P. Varalakshmi, T. Judgi, and D. Balaji[✉]

Department of Computer Technology, Anna University, Chennai, India
varanip@gmail.com, judginagarajan6@gmail.com,
d.balajikkdi@gmail.com

Abstract. Cloud is designed to provide scalable IT resources remotely and requires less infrastructure management. The services of untrustworthy provider may cause the cost loss and dissatisfaction to the Cloud User (CU). Moreover, the Service Level Agreement (SLA) has not been found consistent among the communicating entities in the cloud environment. The selection of best provider is a challenging task in an untrusted environment like cloud. Therefore, we developed a Cloud Broker (CB) framework which helps consumers to select the ideal Cloud Provider (CP) for processing their request in a trustworthy environment. Since feedback is a good source to evaluate the trust of the provider, the trustworthiness of the feedback should be analyzed. So the proposed framework efficiently and accurately evaluates the trust of the CP by analyzing various attacks including sybil and collusive attack. As a result, CB can select the best CP only based on true feedback which provides valid service to the requested CU. Our proposed framework improves job success rate and reduces cost loss to the user in a cloud environment.

Keywords: Cloud · Trust · Sybil attack · Collusive attack

1 Introduction

Cloud can provide scalable resources and manage the tremendous amount of customers request, especially, during a peak time. It also provides Anything as a Service (XaaS) which includes Infrastructure as a Service (IaaS), Software as a Service (Saas) and Platform as a Service (PaaS). The customer request is outsourced and processed in third party server in an Internet based computing environment, like cloud. The process of user request with untrustworthy provider may cause high job failure rate, more cost loss and less satisfaction to the CU. Therefore, the selection of trustworthy provider plays a vital role where the customers in a position to select an ideal service provider for processing their request. Without trust evaluation, it is difficult to identify the best cloud provider. Previous work addressed the problem of selection of trustworthy provider through many trust evaluation approach or framework. Yet, these methods are considered the feedback directly without analyzing the trustworthiness of the feedback. As discussed in [1] a cloud broker should have the ability to manage the trust issues and support the customers in choosing the best service provider. So there is a strong need of trusted broker to

© Springer Nature Singapore Pte Ltd. 2018
Shriram R and M. Sharma (Eds.): DaSAA 2017, CCIS 804, pp. 178–187, 2018.
https://doi.org/10.1007/978-981-10-8603-8_15

support CUs for their successful completion of the submitted request. Following this, the present work proposes a broker framework called Cloud Broker, which effectively estimates the trust value of the Cloud Provider (CP). Moreover, the feedback from the malicious users are identified and discarded to find the accurate trust value of the provider. To discard the malicious feedback, we performed analysis over various attacks, including sybil and collusive attack. Finally, trust of the CP is evaluated by considering the true feedback alone. The performance of the proposed framework is analyzed in various aspects such as with malicious feedback and without malicious feedback. The present framework ensures CU to identify the best CP and increases the user satisfaction and also job success rate.

Salient features of the proposed work are given as follows,

1. True feedback alone is considered for evaluating the trust of the provider.
2. The credibility of the feedback was analyzed.
3. Fuzzy based approach is used for accurate selection and allocation of trustworthy provider.
4. Three methods, namely without trust, with trust value and trust with fuzzy were considered in the analysis part of our proposed framework.
5. The proposed model increases user satisfaction and job success rate of cloud provider.

The rest of this paper is organized as follows: Sect. 2 gives an overview of related work. The cloud broker framework is described in Sect. 3. Section 4 gives the detailed description about the trust evaluation of cloud providers. Section 5 discusses about results and implementation. Finally, Sect. 6 summarizes this work and suggests some future directions.

2 Related Work

This section gives a detailed description about the existing mechanisms on trust evaluation schemes in cloud computing. Determining the trustworthiness of cloud service provider is a major issue. Li et al. (2015) proposed Service Operator-aware Trust (SOT) scheme in [1] which evaluates trust value of cloud resources by considering multiple trust factors. This approach overcomes the limitation where the trusted attributes are weighted subjectively. It does not take into account user feedback on computing the trustworthiness of a resource. Li et al. (2015) proposed trust aware brokering architecture in [2], where broker acts as a trusted third party where trust is calculated on the basis of dynamic service behavior. It also monitors the service of resource providers. This approach overcomes the limitation where attributes of cloud resources are weighted manually. But they did not analyze the credibility of the feedback.

Chunsheng et al. (2015) proposed Authenticated Trust and Reputation Calculation and Management (ATRCM) framework in [3] based on the consideration of authentication, requirements, cost, trust and reputation of CSP and Service Network Providers. The proposed work avoids malicious spoofing attacks by authenticating, calculates and manages the trust and reputation of a service, but does not consider the feedback for computing and helps cloud users to select desirable CSP and with the help of CSP selects the SNP.

Huang et al. (2015) provides a reputation measurement approach in [4] to address the behavior of nodes by using both virgin and non-virgin approach. Malicious feedback affects the nodes' reputation scores. This approach avoids the malicious feedback ratings that may lower the reputation scores and helps users in selecting the service. Since trust depends on users feedback, Soon-Keow et al. (2014) in [5] calculates the trustworthiness of users by applying Beta filtering technique which distinguishes the malicious feedback and the trustworthy feedback. Trust is evaluated based on multi-attribute decision making system and the approach also detects the security threats which affects the trust information.

Rajendran et al. (2015) proposed a hybrid model in [6] to calculate trust based on compliance and reputation. User feedback and reputation of the service provider is used to compute the overall trust. But does not consider the trustworthiness of the feedback in trust evaluation. Lack of trust between CU and CP is a major issue. Agheli et al. (2014) in [7] provides a model where the services are prioritized so that the user can select the services of their choices by calculating trust value. Direct experiences, reputational values and feedback are considered in calculating the trust value.

Qu et al. (2014) in [8] proposed a trust evaluation system which is based on fuzzy to select a cloud service. Fuzzy inference system take into account user preferences and requirements to derive trust levels and providing a service that meet all the requirements. Naseer et al. (2014) in [9] gives a trust model to select the trustworthy CP based on user feedback and performance of cloud service providers in its past. The attributes such as security measures, compliance, uptime, downtime, customer support, performance and response time are all considered while selecting a CP because users' needs and requirements may vary.

Singh et al. (2014) in [10] used a distributed framework which calculates trust value based on users self-trust, friend's trust and feedback trust. Weight is assigned for each type of trust. The limit of fuzzy set theory is overcome by sole membership degree. Recommendation and feedback plays a major role in calculating the final trust. Thus the literature study clearly shows that the trust management system is still lagging in calculating the trust value of the CP. Most of the above models are evaluated the trust by considering the feedback directly without analyzing the feedback. The present work overcomes this issue by filtering the malicious feedback and used true feedback only to calculate the trust value of cloud provider.

3 Proposed Work

Figure 1 illustrates the CB framework which effectively calculates the trust of a CP based on the genuine user feedback. This framework constitutes modules, including malicious feedback filtering module and trust evaluation module.

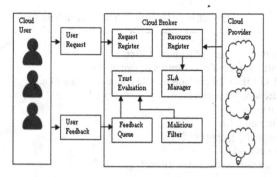

Fig. 1. Cloud Broker Framework

CU sends request to the CB, who has the overall control in the proposed framework, is trusted to assess and expose the risk of cloud services on behalf of the users upon request. CB is a third-party individual that acts as an intermediary between the CU and CP. It helps CU to choose the appropriate trustworthy provider based on the trust value of the CP. CB has a mutual agreement with various CPs, where if selected, provides more testable, less cost and faster deployment of resources. It maintains user requests, user feedback, SLAs, malicious user details and trust value of the CP. Also, CU gives feedback for the last transaction of the CPs which is stored in the feedback queue. The malicious filtered feedback are considered for trust evaluation by analyzing various attack which is described in Sect. 4. CP has the resources to provide as a service to the CU based on their request through the internet. CP should register their resources with the broker. After completion of transaction, they receive the service cost from the CU. SLA is an agreement between two or more parties, where one is the CU and the other is CP, that specifies the details of the service, which is managed by the CB. It assures customer satisfaction and trust to some extent.

4 Trust Evaluation

In this section, a trust of the provider is evaluated based on the filtered malicious feedback. Since user feedback is a good source to evaluate the trust of the provider reality of the feedback should be analyzed. To identify the malicious feedback, the analysis over the various attacks including, sybil and collusive attacks are performed.

4.1 Sybil Attack Detection

Sybil attack rises when malicious users increase the users count by creating the multi identity recognition for the group of people. They do this to either promote the value of particular CP or slander the value of the particular CP, thereby modifying the end trust value of the CP as good or bad. It is detected using the multi identity technique.

Algorithm 1. Occurrence of user attributes

> **Input:** the attributes of particular userid
> **Output:** number of occurrences of that attributes
> **Step 1:**Get the user credentials data count and store in n.
> **Step 2:**count the occurrence
> For I in range 1,n
> For k in range 1,m
> If credentials[i][k]==user[k]
> count=count+1
> **Step 3:**return the occurrence count

Algorithm 2. Sybil attack detection

> **Input**: userid, count of user id and m attributes.
> **Output**: Filtered users of sybil attack
> **Step 1:**Calculate the sybil attack detection factor.
> sdf=m/count
> **Step 2:**Calculate the sybil attack detection value of the user.
> For k in userid
> For t = 1 to m
> sum=occurence(k[m])
> temp=sum/count
> sd[k]=1 - temp
> **Step 3:**Calculate the filtered users of sybil attack g.
> For k in userid
> if(sd[k]==sdf)
> G=sd[k]

Algorithm 2 filters the malicious CU who performs the sybil attack either self-promoting or slandering. We need to calculate the Sybil attack detection factor first which is done by dividing the total user attributed divided by the total records in the user credentials. Then the sybil attack detection value for each user is computed which is done by checking the number of times of occurrences of the user attributes (Algorithm 1) divided by the total number of identity records. Then the Sybil attack detection factor and Sybil attack detection value of each user is matched to get the filtered users of Sybil attack.

4.2   Collusive Attack Detection

Collusive attack occur when malicious users collaborate together to give misleading feedback to increase the trust result of CPs (i.e., a self-promoting attack) or to decrease the trust result of CPs (i.e., a slandering attack). Now the output of sybil attack detection, i.e., the consumers with unique credentials are taken as input to eliminate the collusion attackers using the feedback density method. Now malicious users who give fake feedback to change the trust results for CPs is needed to be identified. A threshold is set to identify the collusive attackers, so that any user who give feedback more than this threshold is considered to be suspicious.

Algorithm 3. Count feedback

Input:userid and cspid
Output:number of feedbacks given by userid to cspid
Step 1: Get the user feedbacks data.
Step 2:count the feedbacks given by userid to cspid
For i in feedback
If i.userid==userid
If i.cspid==cspid
Count=count+1
Step 3:return the count of the feedback

Algorithm 4. Collusion attack detection

Input: Filtered users of sybil attack G.
Output: Filtered users of both sybil attack and collusion attack
Step 1: Get the threshold of filtered users for all CSP Th.
Step 2: Calculate the collusion attack detection value
For t in G
for p in CSP
ct=countfeedback(t,p)
if(ct>Th(t,p))
val=1
else
val=0
temp=val/countcspfeedback(p)
sum+=temp
cd[t]=sum
Step 3: Calculate the filtered users of both sybil and collusive attack FU
for t in G
if(cd[t]==0)
FU=t

Algorithm 5. Count CSP feedback

Input:thecsp id
Output:number of feedbacks received by the csp.
Step 1: Get the user feedbacks data.
Step 2:count the feedbacks with csp id
For i in feedback
If i.cspid==cspid
Count=count+1
Step 3:return the count of feedback

Algorithm 4 determines the malicious CU who performs the Collusion attack either self-promoting or slandering. First, get the threshold value for single user for each CSP. Calculate the feedback count of user for the CSP (Algorithm 3). If the feedback count exceeds the threshold value of the user for that CSP, then the value is set to 1, otherwise 0. Then that value is divided by the total 25 number of feedback for the CSP (Algorithm 5) to compute the collusion attack detection value of the user. If the collusion attack detection value is 0, then the user is genuine, who is free from sybil and collusion attack. Finally, the trust of the provider is evaluated only based on the malicious filtered feedback. The following Eq. (1) shows the trust value of the particular provider p_i.

$$T(P_i) = \frac{\sum_1^n Gf}{t} \qquad (1)$$

Where, $T(P_i)$ is a trust of the ith provider, Gf is the genuine feedback and t is the total number of transactions. Implementation and performance analysis are described in the following section.

5   Implementation and Results

This section gives a detailed description about the implementation of proposed work, its analysis and results. To evaluate the proposed CB framework, cloud is setup using the Cloudsim 3.0.3. CloudSim is a toolkit for simulation of cloud computing scenarios. A cloudlet specifies a set of user requests. In the framework, one cloud broker, ten data centers were created which were considered as ten CPs along with the host. The programming language Java is used with netbeans IDE and MYSQL database is used in our proposed framework. We considered two methods, namely with malicious feedback and without malicious feedback and also the comparison with the earlier model listed in references for the analysis part of our proposed work. The job success rate for the number of jobs for the two methods are measured and their results are shown in Fig. 2 which shows that job success rate achieves better performance on trust calculated without malicious feedback. Here X axis represents the number of jobs in the range as 100, 200, 300, 400, 500 and the Y axis represents the job success rate in percentile. Also the cost loss for the number of jobs for the two methods are measured and plotted as a graph which is shown in Fig. 3. Based on Fig. 3, the cost loss is reduced on trust calculated without malicious feedback. Here X axis represents the number of jobs in the range as 100, 200, 300, 400, 500 and the Y axis represents the cost loss in rupees.

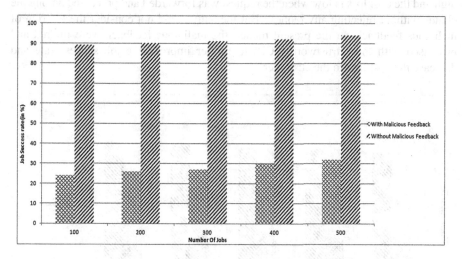

Fig. 2. Job success rate with 50% malicious feedback

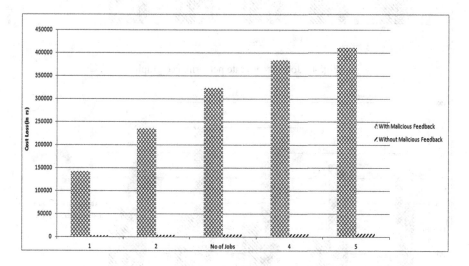

Fig. 3. Cost loss with 50% malicious feedback

While introducing 50% malicious feedback, job success rate for with malicious feedback lies between 24 to 32%, and for without malicious feedback lies around 89 to 95% which is shown in Fig. 3.

In the presence of 50% malicious feedback, cost loss is minimum even though the number of jobs (in 100 s) increases because only more trusted CPs are allocated to complete user jobs while using without malicious feedback as more accurate trust value is evaluated.

Figures 4 and 5 depicts the comparison graph of the earlier TLA-based trust model [11] and the present trust management model. In the earlier model, job success rate is high and the cost loss is low when the request was forwarded and processed among the clouds without rejecting any request. But the authors did not consider the filtering of malicious feedback. In the present model, the malicious feedback were filtered and processed with more trustworthy CPs to further improve the job success rate and decrease the cost loss to the customer.

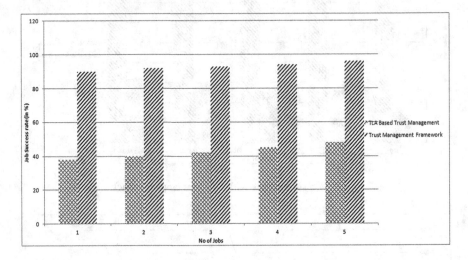

Fig. 4. Job success rate performance graph

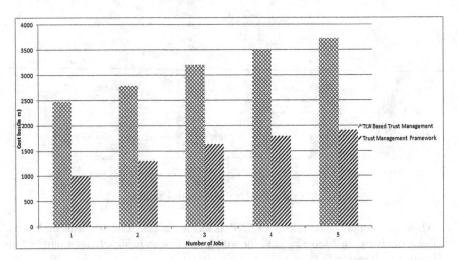

Fig. 5. Cost loss performance graph

6 Conclusion and Future Work

Cloud is an emerging computing market where cloud providers, brokers, and users share, mediate, and consume computing resource. To overcome the issue of selecting the best CP, we have proposed a CB framework for effective evaluation of trust of the CP using filtered malicious feedback. Sybil attack and collusive attack as malicious users may give misleading feedback which increase or decrease the overall trust. Therefore, the analysis over Sybil and collusive attack is performed to check the credibility of the user feedback. Based on this analysis, CB able to select an ideal CP for processing the user request. The experimental results ensure an effective and accurate trust evaluation of CP. Besides, the proposed framework helps CU in terms of cost loss and job success rate.

Our future work can be extended to be applied in mobile clouds. The parameters like time and delay can be further taken into account for more accurate trust evaluation of resources.

References

1. Li, X., Ma, H., Zhou, F., Gui, X.: Service operator-aware trust scheme for resource matchmaking across multiple clouds. IEEE Trans. Parallel Distrib. Syst. **26**(5), 1419–1429 (2015)
2. Li, X., Ma, H., Zhou, F., Yao, W.: T-broker: a trust-aware service brokering scheme for multiple cloud collaborative services. IEEE Trans. Inf. Forensics Secur. **10**(7), 1402–1415 (2015)
3. Chunsheng, Z., Nicanfar, H., Leung, V.C.M., Yang, L.T.: An authenticated trust and reputation calculation and management system for cloud and sensor networks integration. IEEE Trans. Inf. Forensics Secur. **10**(1), 118–131 (2015)
4. Huang, L., Wang, S., Hsu, C.H., Zhang, J., Yang, F.: Using reputation measurement to defend mobile social networks against malicious feedback ratings. J. Supercomput. **71**(6), 2190–2203 (2015)
5. Soon-Keow, C., JemalAbawajy, M.A., Hamid, I.A.: Enhancing trust management in cloud environment. Procedia Soc. Behav. Sci. **129**, 314–321 (2014)
6. Rajendran, V.V., Swamynathan, S.: Hybrid model for dynamic evaluation of trust in cloud services. Wirel. Netw. **22**(6), 1 – 6 (2015)
7. Agheli, N., Hosseini, B., Shojaee, A.: A trust evaluation model for selecting service provider in cloud environment. In: 4th International eConference on IEEE Computer and Knowledge Engineering, pp. 251–255 (2014)
8. Qu, C., Buyya, R.: A cloud trust evaluation system using hierarchical fuzzy inference system for service selection. In: IEEE 28th International Conference on Advanced Information Networking and Applications, pp. 850–857. IEEE (2014)
9. Naseer, M.K., Jabbar, S., Zafar, I.: A novel trust model for selection of cloud service provider. In: World Symposium on Computer Applications & Research, pp. 1–6. IEEE (2014)
10. Singh, S., Chand, D.: Trust evaluation in cloud based on friends and third party's recommendations. In: Recent Advances in Engineering and Computational Sciences, pp. 1–6. IEEE (2014)
11. Judgi, T., Varalakshmi, P., Vivek, S.: TLA based trust management in collaborative cloud. In: International Conference on Next Generation Computing and Communication Technologies (ICNGCCT 2015) (2015)

Using Online Metadata to Enhance Religious Video Search

Eunice Tan, Iris Seaman, and Yiu-Kai Ng[⊠]

Computer Science Department, Brigham Young University, Provo, UT 84602, USA
eunicetzc@gmail.com, irisrseaman@gmail.com, ng@compsci.byu.edu

Abstract. Online videos are on the path to become the future of content marketing. Many church organizations have produced online videos, hosting them on their domains as well as on YouTube, as a communication media for establishing public relations. Searching these online religious videos, however, tends to be challenging due to their inadequate retrieval and ranking strategies and the lack of textual description toward videos. These shortcomings apply to the religious and YouTube search engines, which rely on user-provided keywords to search online videos. Moreover, ranking of these online videos appears to be arbitrary and at time the retrieved videos do not seem to have any bearing to the original query compared with its thumbnails, titles, and categorization. We propose to develop a new search and ranking engine, called VSeek, to circumvent the problem by tapping into the online community through the use of the social media data of videos, which include their title, tags, description, comments, view count, and like/dislike count. The performance evaluation clearly demonstrates the effectiveness of VSeek, and its recommended videos were preferred over videos suggestions by YouTube and MormonChannel.org.

Keywords: Religious videos · Online data sources · Ranking

1 Introduction

According to [8], about 84% of the world's population have religious beliefs, with over majority of them belonging to one of the five largest religious groups—Christianity, Islam, Hinduism, Buddhism, and forms of folk religion. Different religious organizations have taught people to adopt and develop higher quality of life: endurance, honesty, generosity, kindness, etc., and they have invested their time and efforts in preaching their beliefs through multimedia, such as video, audio, printed materials, images, and animation. With the explosion of media use, online videos have moved from obscurity to the main stream [6]. Realizing the popularity of social media and its capability to reach out to huge audience, many religious organizations, including The Church of Jesus Christ of Latter-Day Saints (LDS), have recently begun to produce and offer high quality videos with compelling real life stories, targeting both the church members as well as non-members to share

© Springer Nature Singapore Pte Ltd. 2018
Shriram R and M. Sharma (Eds.): DaSAA 2017, CCIS 804, pp. 188–203, 2018.
https://doi.org/10.1007/978-981-10-8603-8_16

its faith globally.[1] However, producing high quality videos that appeal to an audience is only part of the equation. The other part relies heavily on the ability of the users to find and view videos that are relevant to their needs. As a result, retrieval effectiveness is very critical to the success of online video search.

Online videos comprise of stories created through the use of different camera techniques and shots. Even though an online video is a form of image data, its structure lacks resemblance from a textual document. The structure of an online video is a series of frames of moving graphics, with each frame being comprised of an image, and each image is described by millions of smallest addressable color dot, called pixel. This structure poses many challenges to traditional information retrieval (IR) methods in searching and ranking online videos, since traditional IR search algorithms were designed to optimize textual search through the use of proximity search, text relevance, and page link analysis. However, these IR techniques are mainly developed for textual analysis, not image analysis.

Due to the advancement in technology and break-through in utilizing horizontal clustering to boost search efficiency, existing web search engines offer the options of searches by text as well as by images. Despite the quantum leap in the web search technology, the search by image option only allows a single image search at a time. Unlike text and single image, online video is made up of fame of still images, which cannot be processed by web search engines. In view of the limitation faced by existing web search methods, we propose to develop a video search engine, called *VSeek*, which enhances the current search experiences of users.

VSeek is designed to retrieve religious videos by tapping into the power of online data sources, such as YouTube, a popular social website that archives user-generated videos. VSeek incorporates various features of an online video, including its (i) *title* and (ii) *tags*, which describe the *content* and *context* of the video, respectively, (iii) *topic*, which indicate the particular type, such as forgiveness, family unity, obedience, and affliction, to name a few, to which the video belongs, (iv) *views count*, which measure the video's popularity, (v) *like/dislike opinions*, which allow a user to express their support or disapproval of the video, and (vi) *sentiment* of user's comments on the video, which are publicly available through online reputable websites.

The remaining of this paper is organized as follows. In Sect. 2, we discuss the recent development in searching online videos. In Sect. 3, we detail the design methodology of VSeek. In Sect. 4, we present the results of the empirical study conducted to evaluate the performance of VSeek and verify the preference expressed by end users on its suggestions. In Sect. 5, we give a conclusion.

2   Related Work

Mislove et al. [15] introduce an integrated web search and social network to improve user search experience through locating useful content by combining

---

[1] The LDS church hosts its online videos under its domains, the media library section of www.lds.org and www.mormonchannel.org, as well as on YouTube, a highly popular social site, to spread important gospel messages.

hyperlinks mined from social network that fall outside of Google's index. Inferring social links between users or offering either a global or custom ranking to specific social group remains a challenge, since users might participate in various social network circles. As opposed to mining information within a social network group, VSeek exploits the online data sources through the use of the social metadata.

Cheng et al. [5] consider various YouTube videos' statistics, such as video category, file size, bit rate, upload date, play length, and total views of videos to determine the video growth trend and its active life span window. They provide network traffic engineers with potential network traffic growth rate through the statistics of YouTube videos for the building of a more robust and scalable network, which achieves a different mission compared with VSeek that analyzes online video metadata to improve a video user's search experience.

Based on existing user's click-through data, Chen et al. [4] construct a user-query graph, which identifies the queries issued by a user, and a query-video graph, which indicates the videos retrieved as results of a user's query. The relationships among users, videos, and queries are captured by using a tripartite graph. In order to construct such a tripartite graph, however, it requires the access to user's query logs, which is a constraint imposed on this recommendation strategy, since users' query logs are not widely available nor accessible.

Siersdorfer et al. [17] mine YouTube's comments to study the comment rating behaviors and analyze the connection between sentiments in comments. The goals of their research were to filter unrated comments and to predict the rating of unrated comments, and their work is not directly applicable for either searching or ranking of videos.

Zhou et al. [18] analyze YouTube's search and recommendation system and seek to educate users by performing a study on the causation for driving the popularity (video views) of a YouTube video. VSeek, on the other hand, is a video search engine designed through the use of online metadata.

Bian et al. [1] propose a robust social media ranking solution by introducing a machine learning-based ranking framework through incorporating user interactions and detecting spam in vote. However, their research is mainly based on community Q&A and its voting environment, which is differed from VSeek, since the latter is a holistic approach by considering various online metadata.

3   Our Video Searching and Ranking System

In an attempt to retrieve relevant videos and provide accurately-ranked videos, VSeek collects online religious videos through the Web. For example, LDS videos and its social metadata, denoted YLDS, can be downloaded from YouTube using YouTube Data API v3.0., Mormon Channel(.org), LDS General Conference, Mormon Newsroom, Mormon.org, and FamilySearch, etc. VSeek utilizes online social features, which include titles, tags, comments, view count, and like/dislike count of videos, in addition to the inferred *topic* to which a religious video belongs, to compute an individual *ranking* score for each retrieved video based on

Table 1. Features used by VSeek in two (out of 10) different videos ranked and recommended for the user query "Trust and Mercy"

Title	Tags	Topic	View count	Like/dislike count	Publication date	Comments
Bullying - stop it	Bully, mercy, forgiveness, prevent, bullying, ...	Changing the heart	3,380,655	68,159/1,505	02/28/2014	Stand up to a bully, it should stop, great, thanks, the sermon, ...
Good things to come	Christianity, faith, trust, blessings, trial, ...	Tithing	1,111,497	6,237/306	06/14/2010	Beautiful, watch, touch my heart, cry, God bless, tough time, ...

user keyword queries. VSeek first considers the *titles* and *tags* of all downloaded videos that partially match a user keyword query as a preprocessing filtering step. Hereafter, CombMNZ [13] is applied to compute the final ranking aggregation score on each filtered video by combining the ranking position of each feature of the video. Table 1 shows the metadata features of two religious videos used by VSeek to rank and recommend retrieved results to the user query "Trust and Mercy".

3.1 The Pre-selection Process

To enhance web search efficiency without affecting its effectiveness, relevant videos are pre-selected from among the downloaded religious videos if there is a match between any of the *non-stop, stemmed* keywords[2] in the *title* or *tags* of the videos with any of the keywords in a user query, which yield the *candidate videos* to be further evaluated.

3.2 Similarity of Keywords in Titles and a Query

The title of a video, which provides a general overview of the content of the video, captures a viewer's attention and is usually catchy and tends to be descriptive, enticing viewers to click and watch the video. VSeek performs *title match* using non-stop, stemmed words in a user's query Q against the non-stop, stemmed keywords in the title of a religious video V. VSeek examines each keyword q in

---

[2] *Stopwords* are words with little meaning, such as articles, prepositions, and conjunctions, which are insignificant in terms of capturing the *content* or *context* of a video and commonly occur in web documents and video titles, whereas *stemmed words* are words reduced to their grammatical roots. From now on, unless stated otherwise, whenever we mention *keywords* or *words*, we mean *non-stop, stemmed* words.

Q against each keyword in the title Tit in V by using the *word-correlation factor* (wcf) [11][3] as defined in Eq. 1.

$$wcf(w_i, w_j) = \sum_{x \in V(w_i)} \sum_{y \in V(w_j)} \frac{1}{d(x,y)} \tag{1}$$

where $d(x,y)$ denotes the *distance*, which is the number of words in between words x and y in a document D plus 1, and $V(w_i)$ $(V(w_j)$, respectively) is the set of words in D that include x (y, respectively) and its *stem* variations.

The *degree of similarity* among the keywords in the title Tit of a candidate video V and Q is computed in Eq. 2 based on the word-correlation factors, i.e., wcf, between a keyword in Tit and another keyword in Q, which captures the *content similarity* between V and Q.

$$Tit\_Match(Q, Tit) = \frac{\sum_{i=1}^{|Q|} \sum_{j=1}^{|Tit|} wcf(q_i, Tit_j)}{|Q| \times |Tit|} \tag{2}$$

where $q_i, 1 \leq i \leq |Q|$ $(Tit_j, 1 \leq j \leq |Tit|$, respectively), is a word in Q (Tit, respectively), and $|Q|$ ($|Tit|$, respectively) is the number of words in Q (Tit, respectively).

3.3   Similarity of Keywords in Tags and a Query

Tags are user-generated identifications, each of which is typically a word in length. Unlike video titles, tags provide the *context* of the videos created the users. By considering tags along with titles, VSeek analyzes not only the content of a video, but also its context as perceived by the users.

Tags are created by the end users of a video V, not the creator of V, and there can be many of them. In computing the similarity of tags, which are keywords describing the context of V, and words in a query Q, which specify the user's information need, VSeek determines their correlations differently than in computing the relevancy of V with respect to Q using the title keywords of V. The new relevance measure is desirable, since there are often more words in a set of tags than in a title, and adding many small wcf values does not accurately reflect their degree of relevance.

The correlation factor (wcf) of two words, w_1 and w_2, is assigned a value between 0 and 1 such that '1' denotes an *exact* match and '0' denotes *totally dissimilar*. Note that even for highly similar, non-identical words, their correlation factors are in the order of 5×10^{-4} or less. For example, the degree of similarity between "tire" and "wheel" is 3.1×10^{-6}, which can be treated as 0.00031% *similar* and 99.99% *dissimilar*. When the degree of similarity of the

---

[3] *A word-correlation factor* in the word-correlation matrix, which is a $54{,}625 \times 54{,}625$ symmetric matrix generated using a set of approximately 880,000 Wikipedia documents, indicates the *degree of similarity* of two words based on their (i) *frequency* of co-occurrence and (ii) relative *distance* in each Wikipedia document.

keywords in a query and tags of a video is computed using the correlation factors of their words, we prefer to ascertain how likely the words are on a scale of 0% to 100% in sharing the same semantic meaning. Hence, we assign a similarity value of 1, or rather 100%, to exact-word matches and comparable values (e.g., 0.7–0.9 or 70%–90%) for highly-similar, non-identical words. We accomplish this task by *scaling* the word-correlation factors in [11]. Since correlation factors of non-identical word pairs are less than 5×10^{-4} and word pairs with correlation factors below 1×10^{-7} do not carry much weight in the similarity measure, we use a logarithmic scale, i.e., *Scaled_Sim*, which assigns keywords w_1 and w_2 the similarity value SV of 1.0 if they are *identical*, 0 if $SV < 1 \times 10^{-7}$, and a value between 0 and 1 if $1 \times 10^{-7} \le SV \le 5 \times 10^{-4}$.

$$Scaled\_Sim(w_1, w_2) = \begin{cases} 1 & \text{if } w_1 = w_2 \\ Max(0, 1 - \frac{ln(5 \times 10^{-4}) - ln(wcf(w_1, w_2))}{ln(\frac{5 \times 10^{-4}}{1 \times 10^{-7}})}) & \text{Otherwise} \end{cases} \quad (3)$$

where $wcf(w_1, w_2)$ is as defined in Eq. 1.

We formulate Eq. 3 so that the proportion of the high/low word-correlation factors in the word-correlation matrix are adequately retained using their *scaled* values. Furthermore, using the natural logarithm, i.e., *ln*, in Eq. 3, we can represent a large range of data values, i.e., the word-correlation factors, which is in the order of 10^{-4} or less, in a more manageable, intuitive manner, i.e., values between 0% and 100%.

VSeek computes the degree of similarity of the set of tags T assigned to a candidate video and a query Q using

$$Tag\_Match(T, Q) = \frac{\sum_{i=1}^{m} Min(1, \sum_{j=1}^{n} Scaled\_Sim(i, j))}{m} \quad (4)$$

where m (n, respectively) denotes the number of tags assigned to a video V (keywords in a user query, respectively), i (j, respectively) is a keyword in T (Q, respectively), and $Scaled\_Sim(i, j)$ is as defined in Eq. 3.

Using the *Tag_Match* function, instead of simply adding the *Scaled_Sim* value of each tag in T with respect to each keyword in Q, we *restrict* the highest possible tag-query keyword value between T and Q to 1, which is the value for *exact* match. By imposing this constraint, we ensure that if T contains a tag k that is (i) an *exact* match of a keyword in Q, and (ii) similar to (some of) the other keywords in Q, then the degree of similarity of T with respect to Q cannot be significantly impacted/affected by k to ensure a balanced similarity measure of T with respect to Q.

3.4   Similarity of the Topic of a Video

To determine the topic covered in a candidate video, we employ the Latent Dirichlet Allocation (LDA) model [2], a powerful unsupervised learning algorithm.

Given a set of training articles S, LDA generates a number of latent topics (topics for short), each of which is a *list* of words, ranked according to their probability of co-occurrence in S. Using the created latent topics, LDA can be employed as a tool to determine the probability of a topic given a video V. Intuitively, LDA determines the *topic* covered in V based on the (distribution of) words in the brief description of V.

Training an LDA Model. To train an LDA model, the inputs to the model include (i) a set of training instances S, each of which is represented as a *sequence* of words, and (ii) the number of latent topics N to produce, which is 60 in our case.[4]

To construct the training set for LDA, we randomly selected 100 articles for each of the 60 pre-defined topics extracted from LDS.org, which is one of the church religious websites where religious articles are organized into their corresponding categories that are closely related to the categories of religious videos. The hundred articles for each topic are chosen, since an analysis conducted using 50, 200, 500, and 1,000 articles indicates that based on the selected number of 100 articles per topic, the trained LDA yields the most closely-related latent topics of the articles.

During the training process, LDA estimates the *probability* of a word w given a (latent) topic z, i.e., $P(w|z)$, and the *probability* of a topic z given the article D, i.e., $P(z|D)$. A number of algorithms have been proposed for estimating $P(w|z)$ and $P(z|D)$, such as variational Bayes [2], expectation propagation [12], and Gibbs sampling [7]. We have chosen Gibbs sampling, since it is easier to implement, more efficient, faster to obtain good approximations, and easily extended than others [16].

The Gibbs sampling algorithm first assigns each distinct word w in the set of training articles S to a separate cluster, i.e., w by itself. Hereafter, each article D in S is assigned to M (≥ 1) clusters that have been established earlier such that each cluster includes a word in D and M is the number of distinct words in D. Eventually, various clusters are merged, using the co-occurrence probabilities of words in S that exceed the predefined threshold [7], into a single cluster, which in turn reduces the number of clusters assigned to D. Intuitively, during the merging process, Gibbs sampling estimates $P(w_i|z_i)$ and $P(z_i|D_k)$ by iterating multiple times over each word w_i in each article D_k in S and samples a cluster (which eventually yields a *topic*) j for w_i based on the probability $P(z_i = j|w_i, D_k, z_{-i})$, in which z_i is the topic assigned to w_i and z_{-i} denotes all topic-and-word and article-and-topic assignments excluding the current assignment z_i for word w_i. This process is repeated until the LDA model parameters converge to N, the predefined number of topics to produce, which is 60 in our case, and no re-assignments for words and topics exist.

$$P(z_i = j|w_i, D_k, z_{-i}) \propto \frac{C_{w_i,j}^{WZ} + \beta}{\sum_w C_{w,j}^{WZ} + W\beta} \times \frac{C_{D_k,j}^{DZ} + \alpha}{\sum_z C_{D_k,z}^{DZ} + Z\alpha} \quad (5)$$

where the first multiplication factor computes $P(w_i|z_i = j)$, whereas the second calculates $P(z_i = j|D_k)$. C^{WZ} (C^{DZ}, respectively) is a count of the topic-and-

---

[4] We have chosen 60 as the number of latent topics, since it is the number of topics commonly found among the published religious articles posted under LDS.org.

Table 2. Some of the topics created by using LDA and Gibbs sampling and some of their corresponding keywords

Topics	Keywords
Help thy neighbor	Care, Community, Contribution, Grant, Labor, Lift, Needy, Neighbor, Poor, Praise, Service, Temporarily, Unity, Welfare, ...
Charity	Cherish, Comfort, Compassion, Embrace, Endure, Forever, Heavenly, Love, Neighbor, Perfect, Purity, Warm, Welcome, ...
Enduring hardships	Adversity, Afflict, Challenge, Comfort, Difficulty, Encounter, Endure, Mortal, Overcome, Pain, Peace, Persecute, Struggle, Suffer, Tragedy, Trial, Tribulation, Trouble, ...

word (topic-and-article, respectively) assignments, which are determined from the training dataset based on word co-occurrences such that $C_{w_i,j}^{WZ}$ is the number of times the ith distinct word, denoted w_i, in the kth article, D_k, in S assigned to topic j, $C_{w,j}^{WZ}$ is the total number of distinct words assigned to topic j. $C_{D_k,j}^{DZ}$ is the number of distinct words in the kth article, D_k, assigned to topic j, and $C_{D_k,z}^{DZ}$ is the total number of topics covered in D_k. Z is the total number of topics, W is the total number of distinct words in S, and α and β are the symmetric hyper-parameters, which serve as the *smoothing* parameters for the counts and are set to 0.23 and 0.1 in [7], respectively.

Table 2 shows some of the topics used by VSeek and a subset of their corresponding keywords in each topic created by using LDA.

Video Classification Using LDA. The classification process of LDA on a given video V can be described as finding the probabilities of a number of topics covered in the description D of V and selecting the *topic* with the *highest probability* as the topic covered in D. After creating the latent topics based on Eqs. 5 and 6 is employed to determine the topic z of D based on the distribution of words in D and their probabilities in each topic z_j, i.e., $P(w_i|z_j)$, such that the topic z_j that has the *highest probability*, i.e., $P(z_j|D)$, is selected as the topic of D, i.e., topic of V.

$$Topic\_Match(V,D) = P(z_j|D) = \max_{j=1}^{N} \sum_{i=1}^{M} P(w_i|z_j) \qquad (6)$$

where w_i is the ith distinct word in D, z_j is the jth latent topic among the N latent topics, which is 60, and is an input to LDA. $P(w_i|z_j)$ is the *probability* of w_i in z_j, and M is the total number of distinct words in D.

3.5 Sentiment of Videos' Comments

Viewers' comments on a video can be used for measuring the overall sentiment [17] towards the video. VSeek utilizes both like and dislike counts, as well as viewers' comments on a video V to rank V, since viewers who has clicked on the (dis)like button might opt out of comments and vice versa.

VSeek first determines the polarity of each word w in each comment C of a candidate video V such that w is positive (negative, respectively) if its positive (negative, respectively) SentiWordNet[5] (sentiwordnet.isti.cnr.it) score is higher than its negative (positive, respectively) counterpart. VSeek calculates the overall sentiment score of the comments made on V, denoted $StiS(V)$, by subtracting the sum of its negative words' scores from the sum of its positive words' scores, which reflects the sentiment orientation, i.e., positive, negative, or neutral, of the comments on V. As the length of the comments on V can significantly affect the overall sentiment on V, i.e., the longer each comment is, the more sentiment words are in the comment, and thus the higher its sentiment score is, VSeek normalizes the sentiment score of V by dividing the sum of the SentiWordNet scores of the words in the comments with the number of sentiment words in the comments on V, which yields $StiS(V)$.

$$StiS(V) = \sum_{i=1}^{n} \frac{\sum_{j=1}^{m} SentiWordNet(Word_{i,j})}{|Com_i|} \tag{7}$$

where n is the number of comments on V, m is the number of words in the kth ($1 \leq k \leq n$) comment on V, $Word_{i,j}$ ($1 \leq i \leq n$, $1 \leq j \leq m$) is the jth word in the ith comment, and $|Com_i|$ is the number of words in the ith comment.

As the highest (lowest, respectively) SentiWordNet score of any word is 1 (-1, respectively), $LS < StiS(V) \leq HS$, where $-0.9 \leq HS \leq 1$, $-1 \leq LS \leq 0.9$, and $HS - LS = 0.1$. $StiS(V)$ is further scaled so that its value, denoted $StiS_{Scaled}(V)$, is bounded between 0 and 1, since a negative $StiS(V)$ value can be returned if the overall sentiment of V leans towards the negative region.

$$StiS_{Scaled}(V) = CL(StiS(V)) + \frac{0.9 - FL(StiS(V))}{2},$$

$$CL(StiS(V)) = \frac{\lceil StiS(V) \times 10 \rceil}{10}, \quad FL(StiS(V)) = \frac{\lfloor StiS(V) \times 10 \rfloor}{10} \tag{8}$$

3.6 View Count of a Video

Community feedback provides invaluable resources to both the video's owner as well as the users. The view count of a video allows its owner and viewers to find out the popularity of the video [5,18] while enticing new users to click on the watch button, since a video is supposed to be popular based on its high view count.

VSeek ranks each candidate video V of a user query Q partially based on the view count score of V, denoted $VCR(V)$. $VCR(V)$ is computed using today's date and the publication date of V, along with the *view count* of V, denoted VC_V, to calculate a ranking score on view count of V. We anticipate that the

---

[5] SentiWordNet, a lexical resource for opinion mining, assigns to each word in WordNet three sentiment scores: positivity, objectivity (i.e., neutral), and negativity. A SentiWordNet score is bounded between -1 and 1, inclusively.

longer V has been posted, the more users would have viewed the video. For this reason, VC_V is normalized by the number of days for which V has become available to its viewers.

$$VCR(V) = \frac{VC_V}{Today\_Date - Publication\_Date} \tag{9}$$

3.7 Like and Dislike Count

Like/dislike count, a quantifiable alternative to express users' support/disapproval towards a video as opposed to making written comments, captures the favorite level of a video through the like and dislike votes. VSeek computes the likability, LDC, of candidate video V by utilizing the like count, LC_V, and dislike count, DC_V, of V.

$$LDC(LC_V, DC_V) = LC_V - DC_V \tag{10}$$

3.8 Rank Aggregation

With different feature scores of each candidate video V, which include the scores for Title Match (Tit_Match), Tag Match (Tag_Match), Topic Match ($Topic\_Match$), Sentiment Analysis ($StiS_{Scaled}$), View Count (VCR), and Like and Dislike Count (LDC), VSeek computes the ranking score of V by applying CombMNZ, a popular linear combination measure, based on the feature ranking positions determined by the feature scores of V, from the highest to the lowest.[6] CombMNZ, which is frequently used in fusion experiments, considers multiple existing lists of feature ranked scores on an item I to determine a joint ranking of I, a task known as rank aggregation.

$$CombMNZ_V = \sum_{f=1}^{N} V^f \times |V^f > 0| \tag{11}$$

where N is the number of ranked features to be fused, which is *six* in our case, V^f is the ranked score (position) of V on the feature f, and $|V^f > 0|$ is the number of non-zero, ranked scores (positions) of V in the feature ranked lists.

3.9 Snippet Generation

Useful search engine interface relies on its users' understanding the content of query results. To convey the content of a result R with respect to a query Q, existing search engines create a simple text summarization, called *snippet*, for

---

[6] For each feature, VSeek considers the top-10 candidate videos ranked according to the computed feature scores for fusion and assign the ranked position, i.e., between 10 and 1, as the corresponding fusion score of each top-10 ranked video. Top-10 ranked videos are chosen, since considering the top-10 ranked results is a reliable evaluation strategy [3].

R. VSeek relies on the *description* D of each candidate video V to generate the snippet, which is a sentence-based summary, for V. *Features* considered by VSeek in choosing a sentence S to be included in the snippet for V are (i) the *total number* of query terms of Q in S, (ii) the number of *unique* query terms of Q in S, (iii) whether S is the *first* or *second* sentence in D, and (iv) the number of *significant words* in S.[7] VSeek selects the top-2 ranked sentences in D based on the features to generate the snippet for V.

To compare the performance of VSeek with YouTube and MormonChannel (see details in Sect. 4), we include the individual snippet generated by each of these video search engines so that appraisers can quickly scan through the snippet, along with the title, of each retrieved video, to determine whether the video is relevant to the corresponding query.

4 Experimental Results

In this section, we discuss the results of the empirical studies conducted to assess the design of VSeek and compare its performance with YouTube and MormonChannel video search engines. The former is the well-known social video website, whereas the latter archives a significant number of religious videos to be searched by its users.

4.1 Datasets and the Performance Metric

To the best of our knowledge, there is no benchmark dataset that can be used to evaluate the performance of recommendation modules for religious videos. For this reason, we created our own dataset, called *RV_Set*, which includes religious videos available at YouTube. During the first three months of 2016, the metadata of over 8,000 online religious videos in RV_Set with diverse topics, publication date, and view counts archived at YouTube were randomly chosen and downloaded. The breakdown on the sources and number of religious videos are LDS General Conference (4303), MormonChannel (2,138), Mormon Tabernacle Choir (850), Mormon Newsroom (460), Mormon.org (225), and FamilySearch (133). Videos in RV_Set are either sermons or dramas presented by religious leaders, preachers, clergies, or institutions that cover various kinds of biblical, theological, and moral topics, usually expounding on different types of beliefs, behaviors, or laws, which yield a representative set.

In addition to RV_Set, we have randomly created 30 test queries, out of which eight are unigrams, seven bigrams, eight trigrams, and seven 4-grams, 5-grams and 6-grams,[8] to evaluate the performance of VSeek and other search engines on retrieving relevant religious videos. These test queries (as shown in Table 3) cover a wide range of religious beliefs commonly delivered at different forums.

---

[7] A *significant word* is a non-stop, high-frequency word W such that $frequency(W) \geq 7 - 0.1 \times (25 - S_D)$, where S_D is the number of sentences in D, which is widely-used in text summarization techniques [14].

[8] According to [9], keyword queries created by web search engine users are on the average 2.8 words in length.

Table 3. Test queries (sorted by alphabetical order) used for assessing the performance of YouTube, MormonChannel.org, and VSeek

---

Agency | Charity | Christ's Resurrection | Drug Addictions | Easter | Expressing Gratitude | Forgiveness through repentance | Happiness | Have I Done any Good | Having Courage | Healing | Hope | How to be a Parent | How to Prepare for a Mission | Jesus's Mary | Listen to the Prophet | Mercy and Compassion | Modesty in Dress | Opportunities to do good and serve | Our Home, Earth | Patience | Responsibility and Consequences | Prophet's Faith | Saving your Marriage | Selflessness | Steadfast in what we do | The Iron Rod | The Restoration | Trials | What to do with Pornography

---

To determine the relevance of videos recommended by VSeek, YouTube, and MormonChannel on each one of the thirty test queries, we applied a simple *counting* scheme on the videos retrieved by each of these search engines that were marked as *relevance* by Mechanical Turk appraisers (see detailed discussion on these appraisers in Sect. 4.2) such that a *point* is rewarded for each relevant suggestion. Using this counting strategy, we determined the top-3 counts of relevant suggestions made by the search engines for each test query, which yields the *gold standard* for our evaluation.[9] Table 4 shows the top-3 recommendations (identified by their titles) of a sample (out of the 30) test query made by VSeek, YouTube, and MormonChannel, respectively.

The degree of effectiveness of VSeek and others considered for comparison purpose in making useful suggestions is measured by using the *Normalized Discounted Cumulative Gain (nDCG)* [10] on their corresponding top-3 suggestions for each test query. nDCG *penalizes* relevant suggestions ranked *lower* in the list of suggested videos.

$$nDCG_3 = \frac{DCG_3}{IDCG_3}, DCG_3 = \sum_{i=1}^{3} \frac{2^{rel_i} - 1}{log_2(i+1)} \qquad (12)$$

Table 4. Top-3 recommendations (Identified by titles) of the test query "Happiness" suggested by YouTube, MormonChannel, and VSeek, respectively, where relevant videos are *italicized*

Search Engine	1st Recommendation	2nd Recommendation	3rd Recommendation
YouTube	What Makes a Good Life? ...	*The Surprising Science of Happiness* ...	Red Velvet (Happiness) - Music Video
MormonChannel	We Can Find Happiness	*We are the Architects of our Own Happiness*	To Have Peace and Happiness
VSeek	*Make It a Good Day - Happy* ...	What Family Means - Happy Families	*We are the Architects of our Own Happiness*

---

[9] Top-3 recommended videos are considered, since majority of search engine users view only the top few retrieved results.

where rel_i is the *graded relevance* (either 1 or 0) of the retrieved video at rank position i, $log_2 i$ is the discount/reduction factor applied to the *gain*, and $ICDG$ is the ideal (i.e., perfect) Discounted Cumulative Gain.

4.2   Mechanical Turk's Appraisers

We turned to Amazon's Mechanical Turk[10] to conduct our empirical studies, since it is a "marketplace for work that requires human intelligence" which allows individuals or businesses to programmatically access thousands of diverse, on-demand workers and has been used in the past to collect user feedback on various information retrieval tasks. The performance evaluation of VSeek based on independent appraisers are presented in the following sections.

4.3   Performance Evaluation of VSeek

The quality of religious videos recommended by VSeek is dictated by its relevant suggestions which were evaluated by the Mechanical Turk (MT) appraisers. Over 1,000 MT appraisers were involved in the evaluation of the (religious) videos retrieved by VSeek, YouTube, and MormonChannel.org on the 30 test queries[11] during the month of June 2016. Based on the feedback collected through the MT appraisers, we analyzed the performance of VSeek and compared its performance with the other two according to their respective nDCG values on videos retrieved and ranked by the corresponding search engine.

Evaluations on VSeek and Other Search Engines. Using the unigram, bigram, trigram, and other higher n-gram test queries, we analyzed the performance of VSeek in handling different types of queries using its computed nDCG values. Among all the test queries, VSeek provides suggestions ranked at the *first* (*second* and *third* position, respectively) in the gold standard 23 out of 30 (14 and 17 out of 30, respectively) times, i.e., on the average, 2 out of the three top-ranked videos retrieved by VSeek are relevant.

Compared with the performance of YouTube and MormonChannel, VSeek outperforms both of them in terms of the overall nDCG measure on the n-gram ($1 \leq n \leq 6$) test queries. Based on the overall nDCG values as shown in Fig. 1, we claim that suggestions made by VSeek are more appealing to the MT appraisers than the ones offered by YouTube and MormonChannel, respectively. These results are statistically significant in comparing VSeek with YouTube and MormonChannel based on the Wilcoxon signed-ranked test, with ($p \leq 0.005$) and ($p \leq 0.00001$), respectively. Even though YouTube has performed better than VSeek in suggesting relevant religious videos for higher n-gram ($n \geq 4$) queries, VSeek has done better on unigram and bigram queries and is comparable in answering trigram queries (as the results are *not* statistically significant).

---

[10] https://www.mturk.com/mturk/welcome.
[11] Each test query was evaluated by thirty-five MT appraisers.

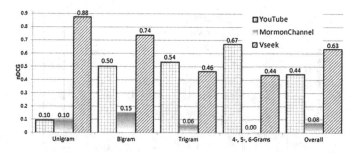

Fig. 1. nDCG scores on *n*-gram test queries achieved by YouTube, MormonChannel, and VSeek

Moreover, as mentioned earlier, since search queries are on the average 2.8 words in length, higher *n*-gram search queries are not as common as unigram, bigram, and trigram queries, and thus the lower nDCG value on higher *n*-gram queries does not significantly impact the performance of VSeek.

Top-Ranking Evaluations on VSeek, YouTube, and MormonChannel. As discussed earlier, since web search engine users tend to look at only the top part of a ranked list to find relevant results, users who perform a particular search task, such as searching for an answer to a question and navigation search, often have only one relevant result in mind and they expect the top-ranked results to be relevant. This scenario applies to searching for a religious video that preaches a particular principle that a user is interested in. To further evaluate the performance of VSeek, YouTube, and MormonChannel on retrieving top-ranked, relevant videos, we computed the average *Precision*@1 (*P*@1), which measures the relevance of the top-one results, average *Precision*@3 (*P*@3), which computes the ratio of the top-3 ranked relevant results, and *Mean Reciprocal Rank* (MRR), which calculates the *average* of the reciprocal ranks at which the *first* relevant result is retrieved. Figure 2(a) clearly shows that VSeek retrieved more top-3 ranked, relevant videos than YouTube and MormonChannel combined.

Individual Feature Evaluation. To justify the necessity of using all the features proposed in Sect. 3 to achieve the best performance of VSeek on retrieving and ranking religious videos, we computed the nDCG score of each feature employed by VSeek using the test queries and dataset discussed in Sect. 4.1, in addition to the overall nDCG score of VSeek achieved by invoking all the features combined using the CombMNZ strategy (as discussed in Sect. 3.8). As reflected by the nDCG scores in Fig. 2(b), the combined features used by VSeek outperforms each individual feature. By combining all of the features, VSeek takes the advantage of their individual strengths and greatly improves the degree of relevance and ranking of its retrieved videos. The overall nDCG of VSeek (as shown in Fig. 2(b)), which is 0.63, is a statistically significant improvement

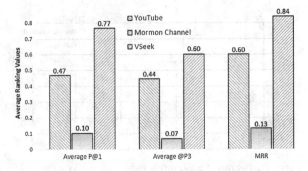

(a) The average P@1, P@3, and MRR scores achieved by YouTube, MormonChannel.org, and VSeek on the n-gram ($1 \leq n \leq 6$) test queries

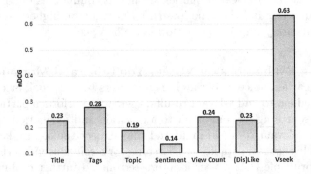

(b) Performance evaluation of VSeek using each individual feature as well as all the features

Fig. 2. Empirical study conducted for VSeek

($p < 0.0001$) over the nDCG score achieved by any individual feature based on the Wilcoxon signed-ranked test.

5   Conclusions

We have proposed a new video search engine, VSeek, which outperforms YouTube, a popular online video search engine, and MormonChannel, a media channel of the LDS Church, in terms of retrieving relevant religious videos. VSeek is unique, since it simply relies on online metadata, which includes titles, tags, topics, sentiment, view counts, and (dis)like counts of online videos that are widely accessible online, to determine relevant religious videos with respect to a user query. VSeek is novel, since it does not require user access history, i.e., user query logs, nor web search results, which are not widely available, to make recommendations. Moreover, results retrieved by VSeek are transparent, i.e., easy to explain why a video is suggested, to its users and the design of VSeek is straightforward.

References

1. Bian, J., Agichtein, E., Liu, Y., Zha, H.: A few bad votes too many? Towards robust ranking in social media. In: AIRWeb, pp. 53–60 (2008)
2. Blei, D., Ng, A., Jordan, M.: Latent dirichlet allocation. Mach. Learn. Res. **3**, 993–1022 (2003)
3. Bogers, T., van den Bosch, A.: Recommending scientific articles using CiteULike. In: RecSys, pp. 287–290 (2008)
4. Chen, B., Wang, J., Huang, Q., Mei, T.: Personalized video recommendation through tripartite graph propagation. In: ACM Multimedia, pp. 1133–1136 (2012)
5. Cheng, X., Dale, C., Liu, J.: Statistics and social network of YouTube videos. In: IEEE IWQoS, pp. 229–238 (2008)
6. Dobrian, F., Awan, A., Joseph, D., Ganjam, A., Zhan, J., Sekar, V., Stocia, I., Zhang, H.: Understanding the impact of video quality on user engagement. In: ACM SIGCOMM, pp. 362–373 (2011)
7. Griffiths, T., Steyvers, M.: Finding scientific topics. In: PNAS, pp. 5228–5235 (2004)
8. Hackett, C., Grim, B.: The global religious landscape. Technical report. Pew Forum on Religion & Public Life. Pew Research Center (2012)
9. Jansen, B., Spink, A., Saracevic, T.: Real life, real users, and real needs: a study and analysis of user queries on the web. IPM **36**(2), 207–227 (2000)
10. Järvelin, K., Kekäläinen, J.: Cumulated gain-based evaluation of IR techniques. ACM TOIS **20**(4), 422–446 (2002)
11. Koberstein, J., Ng, Y.-K.: Using word clusters to detect similar web documents. In: Lang, J., Lin, F., Wang, J. (eds.) KSEM 2006. LNCS (LNAI), vol. 4092, pp. 215–228. Springer, Heidelberg (2006). https://doi.org/10.1007/11811220_19
12. Lafferty, J., Minka, T.: Expectation-propagation for the generative aspect model. In: UAI, pp. 352–359 (2002)
13. Lee, J.: Analyses of multiple evidence combination. In: ACM SIGIR, pp. 267–276 (1997)
14. Luhn, H.: The automatic creation of literature abstracts. IBM J. Res. Dev. **2**(2), 159–165 (1958)
15. Mislove, A., Gummadi, K., Druschel, P.: Exploiting social networks for internet search. In: HotNets-V, p. 79 (2006)
16. Porteous, I., Newman, D., Ihler, A., Asuncion, A., Smyth, P., Welling, M.: Fast collapsed gibbs sampling for latent dirichlet allocation. In: ACM SIGKDD, pp. 569–577 (2008)
17. Siersdorfer, S., Chelaru, S., Nejdl, W., Pedro, J.: How useful are your comments: analyzing and predicting YouTube comments and comment ratings. In: WWW, pp. 891–990 (2010)
18. Zhou, R., Khemmarat, S., Gao, L.: The impact of YouTube recommendation system on video views. In: IMC, pp. 404–410 (2010)

Author Index

Printed in the United States
By Bookmasters